THE

50 GREATEST PLAYERS

IN

HOUSTON ASTROS

HISTORY

ALSO AVAILABLE IN THE 50 GREATEST PLAYERS SERIES

THE 50 GREATEST PLAYERS

IN

HOUSTON ASTROS HISTORY

ROBERT W. COHEN

LYONS
PRESS

ESSEX, CONNECTICUT

An imprint of Globe Pequot, the trade division of
The Rowman & Littlefield Publishing Group, Inc.
4501 Forbes Blvd., Ste. 200
Lanham, MD 20706
www.rowman.com

Distributed by NATIONAL BOOK NETWORK

Copyright © 2024 by Robert W. Cohen

British Library Cataloguing in Publication Information available

Library of Congress Cataloging-in-Publication Data

Names: Cohen, Robert W., author.
Title: The 50 greatest players in Houston Astros history / Robert W. Cohen.
Other titles: Fifty greatest players in Houston Astros history
Description: Essex, Connecticut : Lyons Press, [2024] | Series: 50 greatest players series |
    Includes bibliographical references.
Summary: "An examination of the careers of the 50 Houston Astros players who have made the
    greatest impact on one of Major League Baseball's most iconic franchises. Quotes from the
    subjects themselves and former teammates are provided along the way, as are recaps of each
    player's greatest season, most memorable performances, and most notable achievements"—
    Provided by publisher.
Identifiers: LCCN 2023031590 (print) | LCCN 2023031591 (ebook) | ISBN 9781493078608
    (hardback) | ISBN 9781493078615 (epub)
Subjects: LCSH: Houston Astros (Baseball team)—Biography. | Houston Astros (Baseball
    team)—History. | Baseball players—United States—Biography.
Classification: LCC GV875.H64 C65 2024 (print) | LCC GV875.H64 (ebook) | DDC
    796.357/64097641411—dc23/eng/20230721
LC record available at https://lccn.loc.gov/2023031590
LC ebook record available at https://lccn.loc.gov/2023031591

♾️™ The paper used in this publication meets the minimum requirements of American
National Standard for Information Sciences—Permanence of Paper for Printed Library
Materials, ANSI/NISO Z39.48-1992.

CONTENTS

ACKNOWLEDGMENTS

I would like to thank Kate Yeakley of RMYAuctions.com, Keith Allison, Christopher Ebdon, Ken Lund, Kenji Takabayashi, Eric Enfermero, Bryce Edwards, John Steelman, and Adam Baker, each of whom generously contributed to the photographic content of this work.

INTRODUCTION

THE ASTROS LEGACY

Originally founded as the Houston Colt .45s in 1962, the Houston Astros came into being primarily through the efforts of four men—public relations executive George Kirksey, wealthy businessman Craig F. Cullinan Jr., prominent oilman and real estate magnate R. E. Smith, and former Houston mayor Judge Roy Hofheinz—who formed the Houston Sports Association (HSA) in 1957 with the intent of bringing major-league baseball to the city of Houston. Finally granted an expansion franchise from the National League on October 17, 1960, the members of the HSA set about obtaining the territorial rights from the minor-league Houston Buffaloes, who had served as the city's only professional baseball club since 1888. Eventually forced to purchase the Buffaloes on January 17, 1961, the Houston Sports Association named its new team the Colt .45s, in honor of "the gun that won the west." After stocking their roster with players obtained mostly through an expansion draft held after the 1961 season, the Colt .45s began play the following year, combining with the newly formed New York Mets to increase the number of NL ballclubs to ten.

Managed by former Cincinnati Reds outfielder and Kansas City Athletics skipper Harry Craft, the Colt .45s spent their first three seasons playing at Colt Stadium, a 33,000-seat ballpark built just north of the construction site of their permanent home, the Astrodome. Experiencing very little success from 1962 to 1964, the Colt .45s failed to win more than 66 games in any of those seasons, finishing eighth in the league once and ninth in the circuit twice.

With Judge Roy Hofheinz having bought out his partners, appointed Spec Richardson GM, and replaced Craft as manager with former Baltimore Orioles skipper Lum Harris prior to the start of the 1965 campaign, the renamed Astros (so named because of Houston's new position as the center of the nation's space program) moved into the Astrodome, which would serve as their home ballpark for the next 35 years. The world's first multipurpose, domed sports stadium, which seated close to 50,000 patrons for baseball, would prove to be a torturous place for hitters through the years, with its distant fences and air-conditioned environment making it extraordinarily difficult to reach the seats. Nicknamed the "Eighth Wonder of the World," the Astrodome also served as home to the NFL's Houston Oilers from 1968 to 1996 and hosted many other notable sporting events, including the 1968 college basketball "Game of the Century" between the University of Houston Cougars and the UCLA Bruins, the 1973 "Battle of the Sexes" tennis match between Billie Jean King and Bobby Riggs, and Muhammad Ali's 1966 defense of his heavyweight championship against Cleveland Williams.

Continuing to struggle in their new venue from 1965 to 1968, the Astros failed to win more than 72 games and finished no higher than eighth in the NL standings under managers Harris (1965), Grady Hatton (1966–1968), and Harry Walker (1968). However, they began to show some improvement after each league expanded to 12 teams and adopted a new two-division setup in 1969. Placed in the NL West, which they shared with the Atlanta Braves, San Francisco Giants, Los Angeles Dodgers, Cincinnati Reds, and expansion San Diego Padres, the Astros reached the .500-mark for the first time in their brief history under Walker in 1969, finishing the regular season with a record of 81-81. But with the Astros posting identical 79-83 records the next two seasons, Walker received his walking papers during the latter stages of the 1972 campaign, with former Dodgers, Giants, and Cubs skipper Leo Durocher assuming the managerial reins of a team that ended up finishing third in the division with a record of 84-69. Durocher lasted just one more season in Houston, being dismissed following the conclusion of the 1973 campaign after guiding the Astros to a record of 82-80. Faring no better under former Padres manager Preston Gómez in 1974, the Astros compiled a regular-season mark of 81-81 that earned them a fourth-place finish in the division, before going just 64-97 in 1975 under Gómez and former Pirates and Yankees skipper Bill Virdon, who replaced Gómez at the helm late in the year.

Failing to seriously contend for a postseason berth at any point during the first 14 years of their existence, the Astros posted a winning record just twice and finished no higher than third in their division. Nevertheless, several extremely talented players graced the Astros roster at different times, with slugging first baseman Lee May serving as the team's primary power threat from 1972 to 1974, first baseman/outfielder Bob Watson developing into one of the league's most complete hitters, Joe Morgan establishing himself as arguably the league's finest all-around second baseman, Doug Rader winning five consecutive Gold Gloves for his outstanding defensive work at third base, Jim Wynn and César Cedeño both starring in center field, and Larry Dierker and Don Wilson excelling on the mound.

Continuing to play uninspired ball after General Electric and Ford Motor Company purchased them from Roy Hofheinz in 1975 and subsequently replaced Spec Richardson as GM with longtime baseball executive Tal Smith, the Astros finished fifth once and third twice under Bill Virdon from 1976 to 1978. However, with J. R. Richard and Joe Niekro developing into top-flight starters, outfielder José Cruz excelling at the bat, in the field, and on the basepaths, and New Jersey shipping tycoon John McMullen displaying a willingness to spend money in free agency following his purchase of the team in May 1979, the Astros emerged as one of the NL's top ballclubs.

After posting a regular-season record of 89-73 in 1979 that left them just 1.5 games behind the first-place Cincinnati Reds in the NL West, the Astros captured their first division title the following year by defeating the Dodgers in a one-game playoff (after losing the final three games of the regular season to them). The Astros subsequently suffered a heartbreaking five-game defeat at the hands of the eventual world champion Philadelphia Phillies in the NLCS, losing the series finale in 10 innings by a score of 8–7, after earlier taking a two-games-to-one lead. Returning to the playoffs the following year after compiling an overall record of 61-49 during the strike-interrupted 1981 campaign, the Astros failed to advance beyond the opening round of the postseason tournament, losing to the Dodgers in five games in the NLDS after winning the first two contests.

With the Astros finishing well out of contention in 1982, ownership replaced Bill Virdon at the helm with Bob Lillis, an original member of the Colt .45s who had spent the previous 10 years serving the team as a coach. Although the Astros posted a winning record under Lillis in two of the next three seasons, their inability to make the playoffs cost him and general manager Al Rosen their jobs, with Dick Wagner replacing Rosen as GM and former big-league infielder and St. Louis Cardinals coach Hal Lanier taking over for Lillis prior to the start of the 1986 campaign.

Led by slugging first baseman Glenn Davis, hard-hitting outfielder Kevin Bass, the ageless José Cruz, and an excellent pitching staff that included Cy Young Award winner Mike Scott, future Hall of Fame right-hander Nolan Ryan, southpaw Bob Knepper, and ace reliever Dave Smith, the Astros put together their finest season to date in 1986, finishing 10 games ahead of the runner-up Cincinnati Reds in the NL West, with a record of 96-66. They then battled the heavily favored New York Mets to the very end in the NLCS, losing to the eventual world champions in six games, with their 16-inning, 7–6 loss in the series finale going down as one of the most memorable contests in postseason history.

Failing to perform at the same lofty level in any of the next seven seasons, the Astros posted a winning record just three times from 1987 to 1993, as control of the team passed from Lanier (1987–1988) to former Astros third baseman Art Howe (1989–1993). And with the Astros failing to distinguish themselves on the playing field and conditions in the Astrodome growing increasingly worse, home attendance began to wane, prompting ownership to announce its intention to sell the ballclub and move it to the Washington, DC area. However, Texas businessman Drayton McLane ultimately came to the rescue, purchasing the Astros from John McMullen in 1993 and subsequently promising to keep the team in Houston.

With the NL adding the Florida Marlins and Colorado Rockies to its fraternity of ballclubs in 1993, the Astros underwent additional changes, moving to the league's newly formed Central Division in 1994, which they shared with the Cincinnati Reds, Chicago Cubs, St. Louis Cardinals, and Pittsburgh Pirates. Meanwhile, Drayton McLane named Bob Watson the team's new general manager, making the former Astros star one of the first African-American GMs in the history of professional sports. Although Watson left Houston two years later to assume the same position with the New York Yankees, he helped bring stability to the organization by hiring as manager former Pittsburgh Pirates coach Terry Collins, who led the Astros to three straight second-place finishes, before being replaced by former Astros pitcher and longtime announcer Larry Dierker following the conclusion of the 1996 campaign. And Watson left the team in good hands when he departed for New York, passing the torch to former New York Mets front office executive Gerry Hunsicker, who spent the next nine seasons helping to build the Astros into one of MLB's most successful franchises.

Beginning their return to prominence under Collins in 1994, the Astros, led by NL MVP Jeff Bagwell and perennial All-Star second baseman Craig Biggio, finished just one-half game behind the first-place Cincinnati Reds in the Central Division by compiling a record of 66-49 before the players went on strike. With Bagwell, Biggio, and fellow "Killer Bs" Derek Bell and Sean Berry leading the way, the Astros finished second in the division in each of the next two seasons as well, before laying claim to the division title three straight times from 1997 to 1999 after Dierker replaced Collins at the helm. Still, the Astros failed to advance beyond the divisional round of the postseason tournament, suffering a three-game sweep at the hands of the Atlanta Braves in the 1997 NLDS, before being eliminated in the opening round in four games by the Padres and Braves the next two seasons.

Despite being one of the NL's more successful teams, the Astros again came close to leaving Houston in 1996, when the city's failure to respond to Drayton McLane's request for a new stadium prompted him to put his team up for sale. McLane subsequently had a deal in place with businessman William Collins, who planned to move the Astros to Northern Virginia. But, with Collins having difficulty finding a site for a stadium himself, the other MLB owners stepped in and forced McLane to give Houston another chance to grant his stadium wish. Only after Houston voters responded favorably via a stadium referendum did the Astros decide to stay put.

Some four years later, the Astros christened their new home when the stadium now known as Minute Maid Park opened its doors to the public for the first time on April 7, 2000. Initially called Enron Field in deference to the energy corporation that purchased its naming rights, the 41,000-seat stadium, which was built on the grounds of the old Union Station, featured a retractable roof and a locomotive train that moved across the outfield and whistled every time an Astros player hit a home run. Renamed Minute Maid Park after the Houston-based company purchased the naming rights when Enron went bankrupt in 2002, the cozy ballpark has now served as home to the Astros for nearly a quarter of a century.

Following a poor showing in 2000, the Astros captured their fourth division title in five years by posting a regular-season record of 93-69 in 2001. However, they again exited the postseason tournament quickly, losing to the Braves in three straight games in the NLDS. With Larry Dierker handing in his resignation at the end of the year, former Toronto Blue Jays and Boston Red Sox skipper Jimy Williams assumed managerial duties, guiding the Astros to consecutive second-place finishes in 2002 and 2003, before being replaced by Phil Garner just past the midway point of the 2004 campaign after directing the team to a disappointing mark of 44-44. Performing well the rest of the year under Garner, the Astros earned a wild-card playoff berth by winning 48 of their final 74 games. However, after gaining a measure of revenge against the Braves by defeating them in five games in the NLDS, they lost a hard-fought seven-game NLCS to the St. Louis Cardinals. After making the playoffs as a wild card again in 2005, the Astros captured their first pennant by defeating the Braves and Cardinals, respectively, in the NLDS and NLCS. But they came up short in the World Series, losing to the Chicago White Sox in four straight games.

The 2005 campaign marked the end of one of the most successful periods in franchise history—one that saw the Astros make six playoff appearances, win four division titles, and capture their first pennant. Jeff Bagwell and Craig Biggio proved to be the team's most outstanding performers for much of the period, with both men earning several All-Star nominations and top-10 finishes in the NL MVP voting. But Bagwell and Biggio received a considerable amount of help along the way, with slugging outfielder Moisés Alou performing brilliantly his three years in Houston, Lance Berkman establishing himself as one of the finest hitters in team annals, and Mike Hampton, Shane Reynolds, Roger Clemens, Roy Oswalt, and closer Billy Wagner all excelling on the mound at different times.

Unfortunately, the Astros subsequently entered into arguably the darkest period in team annals due to a series of events that transpired over the course of the next few seasons. With former assistant GM Tim Purpura running the organization after Gerry Hunsicker handed in his resignation at the end of 2004, the Astros finished second in the division under Phil Garner in 2006. But after they compiled a record of just 73-89 the following year, ownership replaced Purpura with former Phillies GM Ed Wade and Garner with Cecil Cooper, who, despite the recent retirements of Bagwell and Biggio, guided the team to a winning mark in 2008. However, Wade handed Cooper his walking papers during the latter stages of the ensuing campaign after the Astros failed to win as many games as they lost for just the second time in nine seasons. After replacing Cooper with former Red Sox bench coach Brad Mills, Wade suddenly found himself in the middle of a rebuild that led to him parting ways with longtime fan favorites Lance Berkman and Roy Oswalt. Performing miserably under Mills the next three seasons, the Astros posted an overall record of just 187-299 from 2010 to 2012, losing more than 100 games twice.

Choosing to desert a sinking ship, Drayton McLane officially put the Astros up for sale on November 21, 2010. Almost exactly one year later, on November 17, 2011, MLB approved the sale of the Astros to Houston businessman Jim Crane, the founder of Crane Capital Group and an air freight business that later merged with CECA Logistics, for a reported $680 million. As part of the deal, Crane received $35 million in compensation from MLB for agreeing to move the Astros from the NL to the AL in 2013 to help facilitate a new five-team, three-division alignment in each league.

With Jeff Luhnow serving as GM and Bo Porter managing the team from the dugout, the Astros officially became members of the AL West in

2013, finding themselves in direct competition within the division with the Oakland Athletics, Seattle Mariners, Texas Rangers, and Los Angeles Angels of Anaheim. Continuing to struggle terribly their first two seasons in the junior circuit, the Astros finished well out of contention both years, winning just 51 games in 2013, before posting 70 victories the following year. But following the hiring of A. J. Hinch as manager, the front office additions of Nolan Ryan, his son, Reid, and former Cleveland Indians director of baseball operations, David Stearns, and the promotion to the parent club of top prospects José Altuve, George Springer, Carlos Correa, Alex Bregman, and Yuli Gurriel, the Astros began to establish themselves as a force to be reckoned with.

After earning a spot in the playoffs as a wild card in 2015 by compiling a regular-season record of 86-76, the Astros won another 84 games the following year. They subsequently laid claim to their first AL West title in 2017 by posting a mark of 101-61 that left them 21 games ahead of the second-place Angels. Continuing their outstanding play in the postseason, the Astros needed only four games to dispose of the Red Sox in the ALDS, before edging out the Yankees four games to three in the ALCS. The Astros then culminated their dream season with a seven-game victory over the Dodgers in the World Series, winning their first world championship.

Two more division titles followed, with the Astros finishing well ahead of every other team in the AL West in both 2018 and 2019 with win totals of 103 and 107. But after sweeping the Cleveland Indians in three straight games in the 2018 ALDS, the Astros fell to the Red Sox in five games in the ALCS. Then, after outscoring their opponents by a combined margin of 280 runs during the 2019 regular season and posting victories over the Tampa Bay Rays and New York Yankees in the ALDS and ALCS, the Astros failed to capture their second world championship, falling to the Washington Nationals in seven games in the World Series.

Shortly after losing the Fall Classic to Washington, the Astros became the villains of the baseball world when it surfaced that they had employed illegal tactics during their championship campaign of 2017. Relying on allegations made by former Astros pitcher Mike Fiers and other unnamed sources, Ken Rosenthal and Evan Drellich wrote an article in *The Athletic* that accused the Astros of using cameras and video monitors at Minute Maid Park to steal the signs of their opponents, which they then passed onto their hitters by banging on trash cans. Further allegations regarding other means of relaying signs, such as whistling, surfaced in subsequent weeks, prompting MLB commissioner Rob Manfred to conduct a sweeping investigation. Later finding the accusations to be true, Manfred suspended manager A. J. Hinch and general manager Jeff Luhnow for one year, levied a $5 million fine on the organization, and announced that the team would forfeit its top two draft picks in each of the next two seasons. Astros owner Jim Crane subsequently fired both Hinch and Luhnow, saying that he was unaware of the scheme and "extraordinarily troubled and upset," while adding, "We need to move forward with a clean slate. We will not have this happen again on my watch."

While Luhnow denied knowledge of the scheme, Hinch issued a statement that read: "While the evidence consistently showed I didn't endorse or participate in the sign stealing practices, I failed to stop them, and I am deeply sorry."

Some of the Astros players issued apologies as well, while others either feigned ignorance or refused to accept culpability. Meanwhile, the two men who helped devise the scheme, Carlos Beltrán and former Astros bench coach Alex Cora, both paid heavy prices. Beltrán, who had been named manager of the Mets shortly before the story broke, received his discharge immediately, as did Cora, who had spent the 2018 campaign managing the Red Sox to the world championship.

Seeking to move on from these troubling events, Jim Crane hired former Tampa Bay Rays vice president of baseball operations James Click to replace Luhnow as general manager and assigned managerial duties to former player and longtime big-league skipper Dusty Baker. Proving to be the perfect man for the job, Baker used his calm demeanor and affable personality to improve the organization's image in the eyes of the public. Meanwhile, with Baker leading the way in 2020, the Astros advanced to the ALCS, where they ended up losing to the Tampa Bay Rays in seven games.

Continuing to perform well under Baker in 2021, the Astros won 95 games during the regular season, before advancing to the World Series by defeating the White Sox in the ALDS and the Red Sox in the ALCS. However, they subsequently suffered a six-game defeat at the hands of the Braves in the Fall Classic. Still hurting from their World Series loss, the Astros entered the 2022 campaign on a mission. After posting a regular-season record of 106-56, the Astros swept the Mariners in the ALDS and the Yankees in the ALCS, before winning their second world championship by defeating the Phillies in six games in the World Series. Despite suffering injuries to several key players that caused them to get off to a slow start in 2023, the Astros rallied to edge out the Texas Rangers for their sixth division title in seven seasons. However, after defeating the Minnesota Twins three games to one in the ALDS, they lost to the Rangers in seven games in the ALCS, denying them their third consecutive trip to the World Series.

Although the Astros failed to reach their ultimate goal this past season, with standout performers such as José Altuve, Yordan Álvarez, Alex Bregman, Kyle Tucker, and Framber Valdez, it appears to be only a matter of time before they again hoist the World Series trophy. Their next world championship will be their third. Meanwhile, the Astros have won five pennants and 12 division titles.

In addition to the level of success the Astros have reached as a team over the years, a significant number of players have attained notable individual honors while playing in Houston. Aside from their two league MVP winners, the Astros boast five Cy Young Award winners and four batting champions. Meanwhile, six members of the Baseball Hall of Fame spent at least one full season playing for the Astros, three of whom had many of their finest seasons in Houston. The Astros have also inducted 21 players into their Hall of Fame, nine of whom have had their numbers retired by the team.

FACTORS USED TO DETERMINE RANKINGS

With the Astros having been in existence for more than six decades, it should come as no surprise that selecting the 50 greatest players in franchise history presented a difficult and daunting task. Even after narrowing the field down to 50 men, I found myself faced with the challenge of ranking the elite players that remained. Certainly, the names of Jeff Bagwell, Craig Biggio, José Altuve, Lance Berkman, and Roy Oswalt would appear at, or near, the top of virtually everyone's list, although the order might vary somewhat from one person to the next. Several other outstanding performers have gained general recognition as being among the greatest players ever to don the team's colors, with César Cedeño, Jim Wynn, José Cruz, Larry Dierker, and Nolan Ryan heading the list of other Astros icons. But how does one differentiate between the all-around excellence of Cedeño and the offensive dominance of Bagwell, or the superior pitching of Oswalt and the exceptional hitting ability of Berkman? After initially deciding whom to include on my list, I then needed to determine what criteria I should use to formulate my final rankings.

The first thing I decided to examine was the level of dominance a player attained during his time in Houston. How often did he lead the league in a major offensive or pitching statistical category? How did he fare in the annual MVP and/or Cy Young voting? How many times did he make the All-Star team?

I also needed to weigh the level of statistical compilation a player achieved while wearing an Astros uniform. Where does a batter rank in team annals in the major offensive categories? How high on the all-time list of Astros hurlers does a pitcher rank in wins, ERA, complete games, innings pitched, shutouts, and saves? Of course, I also needed to consider the era in which the player performed when evaluating his overall numbers. For example, starting pitchers such as Roy Oswalt and Dallas Keuchel who toed the rubber during the last 25 or 30 years are not likely to throw nearly as many complete games or shutouts as Larry Dierker, who anchored Houston's starting rotation during the late 1960s and early 1970s. And current sluggers Alex Bregman and Yordan Álvarez, who have spent their entire careers playing in hitter-friendly Minute Maid Park, have a distinct advantage over Jim Wynn and Glenn Davis, who had the misfortune of trying to reach the seats at the cavernous Astrodome.

Other important factors I needed to consider were the overall contributions a player made to the success of the team, the degree to which he improved the fortunes of the ballclub during his time in Houston, and the manner in which he impacted the team, both on and off the field. While the number of pennants or division titles the Astros won during a particular player's years with the ballclub certainly entered into the equation, I chose not to deny a top performer his rightful place on the list if his years in Houston happened to coincide with a lack of overall success by the team. As a result, the names of players such as Bob Aspromonte and Bob Watson will appear in these rankings.

One other thing I should mention is that I considered a player's performance only while they played for the Astros when formulating my rankings. That being the case, the names of great players such as Joe Morgan and Roger Clemens, both of whom had most of their best years while playing for other teams, may appear lower on this list than one might expect.

Having established the guidelines to be used throughout this book, we are ready to take a look at the 50 greatest players in Astros history, starting with number 1 and working our way to number 50.

1
JEFF BAGWELL

The choice for the top spot on this list ultimately came down to Jeff Bagwell and Craig Biggio—the central figures in the Astros' rise to prominence during the 1990s, and the two most decorated players in team annals. Both men boast an extremely impressive list of credentials that includes several All-Star nominations and team MVPs. In the end, though, Bagwell's prodigious slugging, 1994 NL MVP award, and five other top-10 finishes in the balloting persuaded me to place him just ahead of his longtime teammate.

Acquired from the Boston Red Sox in one of the most lopsided trades in sports history, Jeff Bagwell went on to establish himself as a tremendous offensive force in Houston, surpassing 30 home runs nine times, 100 RBIs eight times, and 100 runs scored nine times, while also batting over .300 six times and posting an OPS over 1.000 on five separate occasions. The Astros career leader in home runs, RBIs, and bases on balls, Bagwell ranks extremely high in team annals in virtually every major offensive category. A solid defender as well, Bagwell led all NL first basemen in assists five times, with his superior all-around play making him a huge contributor to Astros teams that won four division titles and one NL pennant. A four-time NL All-Star who also earned four *Sporting News* All-Star nominations, Bagwell later received the additional honors of having his #5 retired by the Astros, being inducted into the team's Hall of Fame, and gaining admission to Cooperstown.

Born in Boston, Massachusetts, on May 27, 1968, Jeffrey Robert Bagwell moved with his family at the age of one to Killingworth, Connecticut, where he grew up rooting for the Boston Red Sox and his favorite player, Carl Yastrzemski. The son of a former semiprofessional baseball player, Bagwell displayed an affinity for the sport at an early age, with his mother, Janice, recalling, "Jeff could throw a ball before he could walk. When he was six months old, we'd throw a ball to him, and he would throw it back."

Jeff Bagwell hit more homers, knocked in more runs, and drew more bases on balls than anyone else in team annals.
Courtesy of RMYAuctions.com

Developing into an outstanding all-around athlete during his teenage years, Bagwell excelled in baseball, basketball, and soccer at Xavier High School, a private all-male Catholic school located in nearby Middletown. Offered a baseball scholarship to the University of Hartford (Connecticut), Bagwell spent three seasons starring at third base for the Hawks, earning Eastern College Athletic Conference Player of the Year honors twice by setting school records for most home runs (31) and runs batted in (126).

Impressed with Bagwell's excellent play at Hartford, the Red Sox selected him in the fourth round of the 1989 MLB Amateur Draft, after which they sent him to their minor-league affiliate in Winter Haven, Florida. However, a little over one year later, the Red Sox traded the 22-year-old Bagwell to the Astros for 37-year-old right-handed reliever Larry Andersen.

Recalling his feelings at the time, Bagwell said, "I was one of the saddest guys you'll ever see. All my life, everything had been in Boston. I was born in Boston. My father was from Watertown; my mother was from Newton, both outside Boston. . . . our house was one of those places where you couldn't mention the word Yankees. . . . Every weekend the television would be tuned to the Red Sox. No other games. My grandmother, Alice Hare, she's 81 years old, she still lives in Newton, and she can tell you anything about the Red Sox. I called her to tell her the news. She started crying."

Making the jump from Double-A ball directly to the majors following his acquisition by the Astros, Bagwell joined his new team at the beginning of the 1991 campaign. With Ken Caminiti firmly entrenched at third base in Houston, Bagwell moved across the diamond to first, where he performed extremely well for the Astros in his first big-league season, earning NL Rookie of the Year honors by hitting 15 homers, driving in 82 runs, scoring 79 times, batting .294, and compiling an OPS of .824. Bagwell followed that up with two more solid seasons, totaling 38 homers, 184 RBIs, and 163 runs scored from 1992 to 1993, while compiling batting averages of .273 and .320, before beginning an extraordinarily productive eight-year run during which he posted the following numbers:

YEAR	HR	RBI	RUNS	AVG	OBP	SLG	OPS
1994	39	**116**	**104**	.368	.451	**.750**	**1.201**
1995	21	87	88	.290	.399	.496	.894
1996	31	120	111	.315	.451	.570	1.021
1997	43	135	109	.286	.425	.592	1.017
1998	34	111	124	.304	.424	.557	.981
1999	42	126	**143**	.304	.454	.591	1.045
2000	47	132	**152**	.310	.424	.615	1.039
2001	39	130	126	.288	.397	.568	.966

* Numbers printed in bold throughout this book indicate that the player led the league in that statistical category that year.

In addition to leading the NL in runs scored three times, Bagwell topped the circuit in doubles, total bases, RBIs, bases on balls, slugging percentage, and OPS once each, consistently ranking among the league leaders in each of the last five categories. Bagwell also finished second in the league in hits once and home runs twice, with his 47 round-trippers in 2000 setting a single-season franchise record that still stands. Bagwell also set single-season franchise marks in several other categories, including most runs scored (152 in 2000), highest batting average (.368 in 1994), and highest OPS (1.201 in 1994). Failing to reach the century-mark in RBIs and runs scored only in 1995, Bagwell came up a bit short in each category because he missed a month of action after having the same bone in his left hand broken for the third straight season. Named NL MVP and *Sporting News* MLB Player of the Year in 1994, Bagwell also earned four All-Star selections and won three Silver Sluggers, in helping the Astros win four division titles.

Generously listed at 6 feet, Bagwell weighed only 185 pounds when he first arrived in Houston. But, through a rigorous training program that included concentrated weightlifting, a change of diet, and the use of creatine and androstenedione, Bagwell gradually added some 35 pounds of muscle onto his frame, leaving him with massive forearms and large biceps that helped make him one of the game's great sluggers.

Hitting from an exaggerated crouch that shrunk his strike zone considerably, Bagwell spread his legs far apart as he awaited the pitcher's offering, appearing as if he was sitting on an invisible bench. He then stepped back with his front foot as he began his swing, before rising from his stance and addressing the ball in an uppercut fashion. In discussing Bagwell's style of hitting, Joe Torre said, "That wide stance keeps him from over striding, which can be your biggest problem when you're trying to hit for power."

In addition to generating a tremendous amount of power with his swing, Bagwell exhibited a keen batting eye, drawing more than 100 bases on balls in seven straight seasons at one point. Strong in the field and on the basepaths as well, Bagwell won one Gold Glove and, despite possessing only slightly-above-average speed, stole at least 30 bases twice.

Praising Bagwell for the totality of his game, former Astros manager Phil Garner said, "A Hall of Fame player has to have overall greatness. Some players had excellent defensive skills and might have gotten into the Hall of Fame, some have excellent offensive skills and might have gotten into the Hall of Fame, and here's a player that's a complete package."

The *Sporting News* said of Bagwell, "He's an extraordinary fielder who excels at charging bunts and throwing runners out at second and third. Although he has average speed, he's one of the game's smartest baserunners."

Extremely popular with his teammates, Bagwell drew praise from Lance Berkman, who said, "Baggy was just a great teammate, first and foremost. Everybody that played with him loved playing with him. He wasn't really a rah-rah guy but a quiet presence and was very professional."

Meanwhile, Bagwell stated, "It's all about my teammates. If they think I was a good teammate and enjoyed playing with me, then that's all that matters to me."

Bagwell remained a productive offensive player for three more years, averaging 32 homers, 96 RBIs, and 102 runs scored from 2002 to 2004, before appearing in only 39 games in 2005 due to an arthritic condition in

Bagwell captured NL MVP honors in 1994.
Courtesy of Christopher Ebdon

his right shoulder that left him virtually unable to throw a baseball. Despite being declared "completely disabled" by noted orthopedic surgeon Dr. James Andrews the following offseason, Bagwell reported to spring training in 2006. But, troubled by constant pain in his shoulder, Bagwell announced his retirement, saying at the time, "It's been a great ride. I wish I could still play and try to win a World Series here in Houston, but I'm not physically able to do that anymore. I'm OK with that."

Bagwell, who ended his playing career with 449 homers, 1,529 RBIs, 1,517 runs scored, 2,314 hits, 488 doubles, 32 triples, 202 stolen bases, a .297 batting average, a .408 on-base percentage, and a .540 slugging percentage, had his jersey #5 officially retired by the Astros during a special ceremony held on August 26, 2007, with Brad Ausmus saying of his close friend and former teammate during the festivities, "He was the quintessential teammate. He was a superstar who always put the team before himself. And between him and Bidge [Craig Biggio], they always shouldered the blame when we struggled and tried to deflect the credit when we won."

Since retiring as an active player, Bagwell, who is a recovering alcoholic, has spent much of his time with his family, although he has also served the Astros at various times as hitting coach, a guest instructor at spring training, and a special advisor to team owner Jim Crane. Currently employed by the Astros as a community outreach executive, Bagwell makes public appearances for the team as an ambassador and frequently appears in the broadcast booth for select home games.

Despite his many accomplishments on the playing field, Bagwell had to wait until his seventh year of eligibility to gain induction into the Baseball Hall of Fame, most likely because of widespread conjecture that he used steroids to enhance his performance. Bagwell, who once informed a *Houston Chronicle* reporter that he was taking androstenedione, a then commonly used androgen steroid hormone which, at the time, the US Food and Drug Administration classified as a nutritional dietary supplement, never tested positive for steroids. Nor was he mentioned in the Mitchell Report or José Canseco's book. And he publicly denied using any kind of performance-enhancing drug. But the development of Bagwell's physique, and its subsequent loss of mass as his career waned, mirrored that of a typical steroid user. And Bagwell did not seem particularly averse to the idea of using steroids when he offered this quote in 2001: "In my case, the temptation is always there. One thing I know is I can go home after my career is over and say, 'I did it myself.' . . . Now, let me tell you, if I'm on the bubble, the amount of money that's in the game, I probably would already have a needle in my butt. There's too much money out there. If it does make you better, why wouldn't you at least give it a shot to hang on? All you have to do is have one big year. Next thing you know, you're around for five or six more."

And, as for players who used PEDs, Bagwell said, "Sometimes I don't blame them. Yeah, it might be kind of risky, but they still have a family to feed. That's the big question. You have to go with yourself and determine what's more important to you."

CAREER HIGHLIGHTS

Best Season

Although Bagwell hit more homers, knocked in more runs, and scored more times in a few other seasons, he posted his most impressive stat-line in his MVP campaign of 1994, when, despite appearing in only 110 games due to a players' strike, he hit 39 homers, drove in 116 runs, scored 104 others, amassed 300 total bases, and compiled career-high marks in batting average (.368), slugging percentage (.750), and OPS (1.201), leading the league in five different offensive categories. Recalling his magical season, Bagwell said, "Crazy stuff happened that year. Every pitch that I was looking for, I got. And when I got it, I didn't miss it."

Memorable Moments/Greatest Performances

After hitting safely in four of his five previous trips to the plate, Bagwell gave the Astros a 9–6 win over the Giants on September 15, 1992, when he homered with two men out and two men on base in the bottom of the 11th inning.

Bagwell drove in all three runs the Astros scored during a 3–2 win over the Giants on May 16, 1994, with a pair of homers.

Bagwell hit three home runs in one game for the first of three times during a 16–4 win over the Dodgers on June 24, 1994, concluding the contest with four hits and six RBIs.

Bagwell led the Astros to a 7–5 victory over the Phillies on May 7, 1996, by collecting four hits, homering twice, and driving in four runs.

Bagwell again hit safely four times and homered twice during a 7–4 win over the Pirates on May 29, 1996, this time knocking in five runs.

Bagwell accomplished the rare feat of amassing four doubles in one game during a 9–1 win over the Giants on June 14, 1996.

Bagwell led the Astros to a 10–3 win over the Cubs on April 21, 1999, by hitting three homers and driving in six runs.

Bagwell again homered three times and knocked in six runs during a 13–4 rout of the White Sox on June 9, 1999, reaching the seats off three different pitchers.

Exactly one year later, on June 9, 2000, Bagwell delivered the decisive blow of a 7–6 victory over the San Diego Padres when he homered off Hall of Fame reliever Trevor Hoffman with one man aboard in the top of the ninth inning.

Bagwell helped lead the Astros to a 14–7 win over the Phillies on August 13, 2000, by going 4-for-5, with two homers, seven RBIs, and three runs scored.

Bagwell tied his career-high for RBIs when he knocked in seven runs with a homer and a pair of doubles during a 10–8 win over the Royals on July 7, 2001.

Bagwell led the Astros to a 17–11 win over the Cardinals on July 18, 2001, by hitting for the cycle, going 4-for-5 at the plate, with five RBIs and four runs scored.

Notable Achievements

- Hit more than 30 home runs nine times, topping 40 homers on three occasions.
- Knocked in more than 100 runs eight times, topping 120 RBIs five times.
- Scored more than 100 runs nine times, surpassing 120 runs scored on four occasions.
- Batted over .300 six times, topping the .360-mark once.
- Surpassed 30 doubles 10 times, topping 40 two-baggers on three occasions.
- Stole more than 20 bases three times, swiping at least 30 bags twice.
- Drew more than 100 bases on balls seven times.
- Compiled on-base percentage over .400 seven times.
- Posted slugging percentage over .500 10 times, topping .600 twice and .700 once.
- Posted OPS over .900 nine times, surpassing 1.000 five times.
- Hit three home runs in one game three times (vs. Los Angeles Dodgers on June 24, 1994; vs. Chicago Cubs on April 21, 1999; and vs. Chicago White Sox on June 9, 1999).
- Hit for the cycle vs. St. Louis on July 18, 2001.

- Led NL in runs scored three times and RBIs, doubles, total bases, walks, slugging percentage, OPS, and sacrifice flies once each.
- Finished second in NL in home runs twice, RBIs once, batting average once, hits once, on-base percentage twice, and walks once.
- Led NL first basemen in assists five times and double plays turned once.
- Holds Astros single-season records for most home runs (47 in 2000), runs scored (152 in 2000), total bases (363 in 2000), and bases on balls (149 in 1999), and highest batting average (.368 in 1994), on-base percentage (.454 in 1999), slugging percentage (.750 in 1994), and OPS (1.201 in 1994).
- Holds Astros career records for most home runs (449), RBIs (1,529), bases on balls (1,401), and sacrifice flies (102).
- Ranks among Astros career leaders in runs scored (2nd), batting average (tied for 4th), hits (2nd), extra-base hits (2nd), doubles (2nd), total bases (2nd), stolen bases (7th), on-base percentage (2nd), slugging percentage (3rd), OPS (3rd), games played (2nd), plate appearances (2nd), and at-bats (2nd).
- Four-time division champion (1997, 1998, 1999, and 2001).
- 2005 NL champion.
- Six-time NL Player of the Week.
- Five-time NL Player of the Month.
- 1994 Gold Glove Award winner.
- Three-time Silver Slugger Award winner (1994, 1997, and 1999).
- 1991 NL Rookie of the Year.
- 1994 *Sporting News* MLB Player of the Year.
- Six-time Astros team MVP (1991, 1994, 1996, 1997, 1999, and 2000).
- 1994 NL MVP.
- Finished in top 10 of NL MVP voting five other times, placing second in 1999 and third in 1997.
- Four-time NL All-Star selection (1994, 1996, 1997, and 1999).
- Four-time *Sporting News* NL All-Star selection (1994, 1996, 1997, and 1999).
- #5 retired by Astros.
- Inducted into Astros Hall of Fame in 2019.
- Elected to Baseball Hall of Fame by members of BBWAA in 2017.

2

CRAIG BIGGIO

Having fallen just short of earning the top spot on this list, Craig Biggio lays claim to the number two position, in the process edging out fellow second sacker José Altuve. The first player to be enshrined in Cooperstown with an Astros cap on his plaque, Biggio spent his entire 20-year major-league career in Houston, scoring more runs and amassing more hits, extra-base hits, doubles, and total bases than any other player in franchise history, while also appearing in more games and garnering more at-bats than anyone else in team annals. A hard-nosed player who became known for his tremendous hustle and determination, Biggio served as the offensive catalyst for Astros teams that won four division titles and one NL pennant, hitting at least 20 homers and scoring more than 100 runs eight times each, batting over .300 and compiling an on-base percentage over .400 four times each, and stealing more than 30 bases five times. An outstanding fielder as well, Biggio did an excellent job for the Astros at three different positions, performing especially well at second base, where he earned four Gold Gloves by leading all players at his position in putouts five times and assists on six separate occasions. A seven-time NL All-Star, Biggio also earned five *Sporting News* NL All-Star nominations and three top-10 finishes in the league MVP voting, before being further honored following the conclusion of his playing career by having his #7 retired by the Astros and gaining induction into both the Astros and the Baseball Hall of Fame.

Born in Smithtown, New York, on December 14, 1965, Craig Alan Biggio grew up in nearby Kings Park, a middle-class commuter town on the north shore of Long Island. Looking back on his early years, Biggio recalled the sacrifices his father made for him, saying, "My father's an air-traffic controller. When we were growing up, he worked nights and weekends. Shift work. Long hours, trying to make ends meet, providing for his family. When I was a senior, the high school ran out of money for sports. To play baseball, you had to pay, like, $200. That was a lot of money for us. My father didn't bat an eye. You don't forget that."

Craig Biggio scored more runs and collected more hits, extra-base hits, doubles, and total bases than anyone else in franchise history.
Courtesy of RMYAuctions.com

Adding that his father helped instill in him the values he has carried with him throughout his life, Biggio stated, "I'm who I am today because of the respect and values he made sure I had."

An outstanding all-around athlete, Biggio starred in multiple sports at Kings Park High School, earning a runner-up finish in the voting for Suffolk County's best baseball player his senior year, while also being named the county's top football player for his superb work at running back. Revealing that his dad also helped him develop his skills on the diamond, Biggio said, "My father was a catcher in high school, and he got me started in baseball. I liked catching because I wanted to control the game. I wasn't a Mets fan or a Yankees fan—I just liked to play—but the one guy I loved was Thurman Munson."

Despite his love for baseball, Biggio initially hoped to play football in college, until his struggles in the classroom prevented him from receiving a scholarship from one of the nation's better programs. Recalling his situation, Biggio told the *Houston Chronicle*, "Truly, what I wanted to do was football. When it was taken away from me, being able to go to a big-time school, I just said, 'Get your act together.'"

Offered a partial baseball scholarship to Seton Hall University in New Jersey, Biggio spent three years playing for head coach Mike Sheppard, starting out as an infielder before moving to catcher. Doing a remarkable job of improving his defensive skills, Biggio, who Sheppard once called "the worst defensive catcher I had ever seen," went on to earn All–Big East honors as a sophomore and gain All-America recognition his senior year, prompting the Astros to select him in the first round of the 1987 MLB Amateur Draft, with the 22nd overall pick.

Advancing rapidly through Houston's farm system, Biggio spent less than one full season in the minors, compiling a .344 batting average in 141 games, before joining the parent club in June 1988. Starting 40 games behind the plate for the Astros over the season's final three months, Biggio struggled somewhat offensively, hitting three homers, knocking in only five runs, and batting just .211 in 131 total plate appearances. Nevertheless, new Astros manager Art Howe named Biggio the team's starting catcher prior to the start of the ensuing campaign, after which he improved his performance dramatically, winning the first of his five Silver Sluggers by hitting 13 homers, driving in 60 runs, scoring 64 times, and batting .257, while also stealing 21 bases in 24 attempts and ranking among the NL's top receivers in putouts and fielding percentage.

Although Biggio also saw some action at other positions the next two seasons, he remained the Astros' primary catcher, earning his first All-Star nomination in 1991 by hitting four homers, knocking in 46 runs, scoring 79 times, stealing 19 bases, and batting .295, before moving to second base the following year at the suggestion of Howe.

Recalling the circumstances surrounding his change in positions, Biggio said, "He [Howe] said it would extend my career. He said it would help the team, let the team take more advantage of my speed, but he also said they weren't going to force me. I went home to Patty. We're a good team on making big decisions like this. She said to me, 'Do you think you can do it?' And I said, 'Yeah.' I wanted to do it because everybody said I couldn't. I'm stubborn."

Before moving to second base, Biggio excelled at catcher for the Astros.
Courtesy of Rick Dikeman via Wikipedia

Meanwhile, Howe remembered, "He had great speed, but catching wore him down. Bidge was maybe 165 pounds back then. I could picture Dave Parker (6'5" and 230 pounds) coming home and putting him in the nickel seats somewhere, and I knew how good he could be offensively."

Making a successful transition to second in 1992, Biggio started all but a handful of games at that post for the Astros, earning his second straight All-Star selection by hitting six homers, driving in 39 runs, scoring 96 times, stealing 38 bases, batting .277, ranking among the league leaders with 94 bases on balls, and leading all NL second sackers with 344 put-outs. Looking back on his switch in positions some years later, Biggio said, "Moving from catcher to second, I can't explain to you how hard that was.

That's like giving you a bat and telling you to get a hit off Randy Johnson. Not just stand in there, but get a hit off him."

Having gradually added some much-needed bulk onto his slender frame, Biggio increased his overall offensive production in 1993, concluding the campaign with 21 homers, 64 RBIs, 98 runs scored, a .287 batting average, and an OPS of .847, before beginning an outstanding six-year run during which he posted the following numbers:

YEAR	HR	RBI	RUNS	AVG	OBP	SLG	OPS
1994	6	56	88	.318	.411	.483	.893
1995	22	77	**123**	.302	.406	.483	.889
1996	15	75	113	.288	.386	.415	.801
1997	22	81	**146**	.309	.415	.501	.916
1998	20	88	123	.325	.403	.503	.906
1999	16	73	123	.294	.386	.457	.843

In addition to leading the NL in runs scored twice, Biggio topped the circuit in stolen bases once and doubles three times, amassing more than 50 two-baggers twice, with his 51 doubles and 50 steals in 1998 making him the first player since Tris Speaker in 1912 to surpass the 50-mark in both categories in the same season. A true ironman, Biggio also led the league in games played three times and total plate appearances on five separate occasions. Meanwhile, Biggio consistently ranked among the league leaders in hits and bases on balls, finished second in the circuit in on-base percentage once, and led all NL second sackers in putouts four times and assists five times over that six-year stretch. An All-Star in each of the first five seasons, Biggio also earned two top-five finishes in the NL MVP voting, four Silver Sluggers, and four Gold Gloves. More importantly, the Astros finished either first or second in the NL Central all six years, capturing the division title in each of the final three seasons.

Spending most of his time hitting out of either the first or second spot in the batting order, the right-handed-hitting Biggio, who stood 5'11" and weighed 190 pounds, did an excellent job of setting the table for middle-of-the-order sluggers Jeff Bagwell, Moisés Alou, Derek Bell, and Carl Everett, using his keen batting eye and ability to hit the ball hard to all fields to consistently get on base. A fearless batter who crowded the plate against opposing pitchers, Biggio added to his on-base percentage by getting hit by more pitches than anyone else in the league on five separate occasions.

In discussing his propensity for getting plunked, Biggio said, "I get in that box, and I'm not thinking about moving because, if I have to think about moving, I can't hit like I want to hit."

Blessed with unusual power for a second baseman and leadoff hitter, Biggio set an NL record by leading off 53 games with a home run. Meanwhile, Biggio's outstanding speed enabled him to go an entire season without grounding into a double play, making him just the fifth player ever to accomplish the feat.

Perhaps more than anything else, though, Biggio separated himself from others with his tremendous drive and determination, with Bill Doran, who helped him learn how to play second base, saying, "Craig's never going to talk that much about it, and you can talk about his athleticism and talk about his skills and all that stuff, but you don't become what Craig became if you're just not driven and you just don't have a lot more qualities about yourself that don't show up in the box score. He had all those intangibles."

Former Astros shortstop Adam Everett expressed similar sentiments when he stated, "It was an attitude of how to come to work every day and how to play the game. You can tell kids all the time, 'Hey, play the game hard,' but until you see a guy literally run until his last game he played, and he hits a pop up and runs it out under 4.5 seconds, and he tries to stretch a single into a double for his 3,000th hit, that was Biggio. That was the way he played."

Former Astros GM Gerry Hunsicker also praised Biggio for this hustle and resolve when he said, "Craig was a once-in-a-lifetime player. He was a manager's dream in the sense you could just pencil his name in the lineup every day. He brought his A game every day. He gave everything he had to win day in and day out."

After missing the final two months of the 2000 campaign with a torn ACL and MCL he sustained in a collision at second base, Biggio returned the following year to help lead the Astros to their fourth division title in five seasons by hitting 20 homers, driving in 70 runs, scoring 118 times, batting .292, and compiling an OPS of .838. Biggio followed that up by hitting 15 homers, knocking in 58 runs, scoring 96 others, and batting .253 in 2002, before moving to the outfield when Jeff Kent signed with the Astros at the end of the year. Splitting his time the next two seasons between center field and left, Biggio did a creditable job at both spots, while also contributing on offense by totaling 39 homers, 125 RBIs, and 202 runs scored, and compiling batting averages of .264 and .281.

Returning to his more familiar position of second base in 2005, Biggio spent the next three seasons there, experiencing a gradual decline in offensive production after hitting 26 homers, driving in 69 runs, scoring 94 times, and batting .264 in the first of those campaigns. Choosing to retire after he scored only 68 runs and batted just .251 in 2007, Biggio ended his career with 291 homers, 1,175 RBIs, 1,844 runs scored, 3,060 hits, 668 doubles, 55 triples, 414 stolen bases, a .281 batting average, a .363 on-base percentage, and a .433 slugging percentage, with his 668 two-baggers representing the sixth-highest total in MLB history.

Extremely proud of the fact that he never played for another team, Biggio, who twice rejected free agency, said, "Not a lot of guys get to play their whole careers with one team because of the economics of this game. I can't think of a better time to be wearing an Astros uniform."

Remaining with the Astros following his retirement as an active player, Biggio has served as an assistant to the general manager since 2008. In addition to participating in the club's community development program, Biggio works with the baseball operations staff in its major- and minor-league player development programs, the amateur draft and scouting, and major- and minor-league talent evaluation. Biggio also continues the work he began during his playing career by raising money for the Sunshine Kids organization that supports children with cancer.

Looking back on his playing career, Biggio, who gained induction into the Baseball Hall of Fame in his third year of eligibility, says, "I tried to play the game hard and play the game right every single day. I remembered where I came from. I remembered how hard it was to get to the big leagues. And I tried to go out there and play every game like it was going to be my last game."

CAREER HIGHLIGHTS

Best Season

Biggio performed brilliantly during the strike-shortened 1994 campaign, batting .318, compiling an OPS of .893, scoring 88 runs, and leading the NL with 44 doubles and 39 stolen bases. But, due to the brevity of the season, Biggio posted more impressive numbers in five or six other years, with the 1997 and 1998 campaigns standing out above all others. Although either season would make an excellent choice, we'll opt for 1998 since, in addition to hitting 20 homers, scoring 123 runs, compiling an OPS of .906, and leading the league with 51 doubles, Biggio established career-high marks with 88 RBIs, 210 hits, 50 steals, 325 total bases, and a .325 batting average, earning a fifth-place finish in the NL MVP voting and his fourth *Sporting News* NL All-Star nomination.

Memorable Moments/Greatest Performances

Biggio led the Astros to an 11–3 win over the Dodgers on September 14, 1989, driving in six runs with a pair of homers, reaching the seats once with the bases loaded and once with one man aboard.

Biggio helped lead the Astros to a 9–7 victory over the Padres on May 23, 1993, going 4-for-5, with two homers, a double, three RBIs, and three runs scored.

Biggio contributed to a 16–8 mauling of the Colorado Rockies on July 4, 1995, homering twice, knocking in three runs, and scoring five times.

Biggio recorded a career-high four stolen bases during a 7–4 win over the Montreal Expos on September 16, 1995.

Biggio knocked in all three runs the Astros scored during a 3–1 win over the Dodgers on April 20, 1997, with a pair of homers.

Biggio led the Astros to a lopsided 13–3 victory over the Cubs on August 23, 1998, by knocking in six runs with a pair of three-run homers.

Biggio scored three times and went a perfect 5-for-5 at the plate during an 11–3 win over the Milwaukee Brewers on April 3, 2001.

Biggio hit for the cycle during an 8–4 win over the Rockies on April 8, 2002, going 4-for-4, with four RBIs and two runs scored.

Biggio provided much of the offensive firepower when the Astros defeated the Phillies, 7–1, on July 25, 2005, homering twice, knocking in three runs, and scoring three times.

Biggio delivered the decisive blow of a 6–5 victory over the Brewers on April 20, 2007, when he homered off Greg Aquino with the bases loaded in the top of the ninth inning.

Biggio became a member of the 3,000-hit club on June 28, 2007, when he singled off Colorado's Aaron Cook in the bottom of the seventh inning of an 8–5 Astros win.

Notable Achievements

- Hit at least 20 home runs eight times.
- Scored more than 100 runs eight times, topping 120 runs scored on four occasions.
- Batted over .300 four times.
- Surpassed 200 hits once (210 in 1998).

- Surpassed 30 doubles 14 times, topping 40 two-baggers on seven occasions.
- Stole more than 30 bases five times, topping 40 thefts twice and 50 steals once.
- Compiled on-base percentage over .400 four times.
- Posted slugging percentage over .500 twice.
- Posted OPS over .900 twice.
- Hit for cycle vs. Colorado on April 8, 2002.
- Member of 3,000-hit club.
- Led NL in doubles three times, runs scored twice, and stolen bases once.
- Finished second in NL in hits once, stolen bases once, and on-base percentage once.
- Led NL in assists twice.
- Led NL second basemen in putouts five times, assists six times, and double plays turned once.
- Holds Astros single-season records for most doubles (56) and most plate appearances (749), both in 1999.
- Holds Astros career records for most runs scored (1,844), hits (3,060), extra-base hits (1,014), doubles (668), total bases (4,711), sacrifice hits (101), games played (2,850), plate appearances (12,504), and at-bats (10,876).
- Ranks among Astros career leaders in home runs (3rd), RBIs (2nd), triples (tied for 5th), stolen bases (2nd), bases on balls (2nd), and sacrifice flies (2nd).
- Ranks among MLB career leaders with 668 doubles (6th) and 285 hit-by-pitch (2nd).
- Four-time division champion (1997, 1998, 1999, and 2001).
- 2005 NL champion.
- Four-time NL Player of the Week.
- Four-time Gold Glove Award winner (1994, 1995, 1996, and 1997).
- Five-time Silver Slugger Award winner (1989, 1994, 1995, 1997, and 1998).
- 1997 Branch Rickey Award winner.
- 2005 Hutch Award winner.
- 2007 Roberto Clemente Award winner.
- Three-time Astros team MVP (1992, 1993, and 1995).
- Finished in top 10 of NL MVP voting three times, placing in top five twice.

- Seven-time NL All-Star selection (1991, 1992, 1994, 1995, 1996, 1997, and 1998).
- Five-time *Sporting News* NL All-Star selection (1994, 1995, 1997, 1998, and 2001).
- #7 retired by Astros.
- Inducted into Astros Hall of Fame in 2019.
- Elected to Baseball Hall of Fame by members of BBWAA in 2015.

3
JOSÉ ALTUVE

The spiritual leader of Astros teams that have won six division titles, four pennants, and two World Series, José Altuve has established himself as the face of the franchise over the last 13 seasons. Overcoming early doubts about his ability to succeed at the major-league level due to his diminutive stature, Altuve has excelled in every aspect of the game since laying claim to the starting second base job in 2012, winning six Silver Sluggers and one Gold Glove, while also stealing at least 30 bases six times. The first Astros player to win a batting title, Altuve has accomplished the feat three times, hitting .300 or better on seven separate occasions. Altuve has also hit more than 20 homers five times, scored more than 100 runs four times, and amassed more than 200 hits on four separate occasions, leading the AL in the last category four straight times. The 2017 AL MVP, Altuve has finished in the top five of the balloting two other times, while also earning eight All-Star selections and two *Sporting News* MLB Player of the Year nominations.

Born in Puerto Cabello, Venezuela, on May 6, 1990, José Carlos Altuve grew up some 33 miles southeast, in the town of Maracay, where he developed his baseball skills by competing against boys bigger and older than himself. Not allowed to participate in a Houston Astros tryout camp held in Maracay in 2006 because, after taking one look at him, team scouts believed that he had lied about his age, the 16-year-old Altuve returned to camp the following day with his birth certificate. Asked by Astros special assistant Al Pedrique, "Can you play?" Altuve responded, "I'll show you," after which he made such a strong impression on those in attendance that the Astros signed him as an undrafted free agent for $15,000.

Altuve subsequently spent the next five years advancing through Houston's farm system, posting excellent numbers at every stop. Yet even though Altuve compiled a batting average of .327 and an OPS of .867 in the minors from 2007 to 2011, his name never appeared on any top-100 prospects lists because of his diminutive 5'6" stature. Nevertheless, after Altuve

José Altuve has won three batting titles during his time in
Houston.
Courtesy of Eric Enfermerof

earned a spot on *Baseball America*'s 2011 Minor League All-Star Team by
posting a composite batting average of .389 in 87 games with Class A-
Advanced Lancaster and Double-A Corpus Christi, the Astros summoned
him to the big leagues in July 2011.

Despite bypassing Triple-A ball completely, the 21-year-old Altuve
acquitted himself extremely well over the final four months of the season.
Starting 51 games at second base for an Astros team that finished last in the
NL Central with a record of 56-106, Altuve batted .276, homered twice,
knocked in 12 runs, scored 26 times, and stole seven bases, while also committing only two errors in the field. Although the Astros fared no better in
2012, Altuve earned his first All-Star nomination after being named the

full-time starter at second by batting .290, scoring 80 runs, stealing 33 bases, hitting seven homers, and driving in 37 runs. Altuve followed that up by batting .283, hitting five homers, driving in 52 runs, scoring 64 times, stealing 35 bases, and leading all AL second sackers in putouts and double plays turned in 2013, before beginning an exceptional four-year run during which he posted the following numbers:

YEAR	HR	RBI	RUNS	AVG	OBP	SLG	OPS
2014	7	59	85	.341	.377	.453	.830
2015	15	66	86	.313	.353	.459	.812
2016	24	96	108	.338	.396	.531	.928
2017	24	81	112	.346	.410	.547	.957

In addition to leading the AL in batting average in three of those four seasons, Altuve finished first in stolen bases twice and topped the circuit in hits each year, becoming the first player in franchise history to collect at least 200 safeties four straight times. Altuve also consistently placed near the top of the league rankings in on-base percentage and doubles, amassing more than 40 two-baggers in each of the first three seasons. Outstanding in the field as well, Altuve led all players at his position in fielding percentage and double plays turned once each, with his exceptional all-around play earning him four straight All-Star selections, four consecutive Silver Sluggers, one Gold Glove, two MLB Player of the Year nominations, and three top-10 finishes in the voting for AL MVP, which he won in 2017, when he led the Astros to their first world championship.

Commenting on Altuve's emergence as one of the finest players in the game following the conclusion of the 2017 campaign, teammate Dallas Keuchel said, "I didn't know that he was going to actually be *this* good. I thought he was going to be an All-Star, but to win the MVP, which he should—and honestly, he should have been in the race the last three or four years—and I couldn't be happier for the guy, because he's an All-American dude. . . . The more you get to know him, the greater you think he is, because it's not just about his MVP-type talent. He's a leader in the clubhouse. He's a guy who can make you laugh at any point in time."

Craig Biggio also discussed Altuve's development into an elite player, stating, "It's really been fun to watch Altuve evolve from when they signed him, and he kept fighting his way to get here. Then, all of a sudden, year in and year out, it's batting title after batting title, and 200 hits after 200 hits, and winning Gold Gloves, and becoming the player that he is. José is a great player."

Meanwhile, Al Pedrique said of the man he first discovered as a 16-year-old in Venezuela, "He surpassed all our expectations. More than his hitting and speed, what I most liked about him was his intelligence and heart, and his drive and absolute faith in himself."

For his part, Altuve stated, "I never doubted myself because I already had too many other people doubting. I wanted to prove those people wrong. And not because one day I could tell them they were wrong. I wanted to prove them wrong for the guys behind me who are short, too. Guys who are not really strong, not really tall, guys who are 14 to 16 right now who are very small and want to get an opportunity."

Altuve amassed more than 200 hits in four straight seasons.
Courtesy of Keith Allison

After spending his first few seasons in Houston focusing on slapping the ball to all fields from either his first or second spot in the batting order, the right-handed-hitting Altuve, who is generously listed at 5'6" and 170 pounds, altered his swing somewhat to take better advantage of the inviting left field wall at Minute Maid Park. Although Altuve continued to drive outside pitches to the opposite field, he became more adept at lifting offerings on the inner half of the plate in the air to left field, making him more of a power threat. And with Altuve increasing his home run output, Astros manager A. J. Hinch eventually moved him into the number three spot in the lineup.

Expressing his admiration for Altuve's hitting ability, former Texas Rangers manager Ron Washington said, "He hits everything. You throw him a breaking ball and he stays inside and pulls it. Throw a fastball away and he goes away. He moves the ball around the ballpark. He doesn't try to do anything extra. He tries to make good contact and use the whole field. He's a pretty good hitter. That's why he leads the league."

Despite being an aggressive hitter who has never drawn more than 66 bases on balls in a season, Altuve does not strike out a great deal, fanning more than 90 times just once to this point in his career.

In discussing his approach at the plate, Altuve stated, "I don't think too much about mechanics. I just like to go up there and swing. It's more than my swing, though. It's my mindset. I always go to home plate with a plan."

Though limited by discomfort in his right knee to just 137 games in 2018, Altuve had another excellent year, earning All-Star and Silver Slugger honors for the fifth straight time by hitting 13 homers, driving in 61 runs, scoring 84 others, and finishing third in the league with a .316 batting average. Prior to the ensuing campaign, though, the reputation of Altuve and his teammates took a serious hit when the Astros sign-stealing scandal broke. Accused of using electronic equipment to steal the opposing team's signs during their championship season of 2017 and then communicating to the batter what pitch to look for by banging on trash cans, the Astros became villains in the eyes of the baseball world, with the validity of their World Series victory and the statistics compiled by Altuve during his MVP season both coming into question.

Asked by reporters to address the team's wrongdoings, Altuve, who is a very religious man and a born-again Christian, said, "I'm not going to say to you that it was good—it was wrong. We feel bad, we feel remorse, like I said, the impact on the fans, the impact on the game—we feel bad."

But while Altuve drew as much criticism as any other Astros player for his role in the shenanigans, his teammates tried to absolve him of any blame, with Carlos Correa stating during an interview with Ken Rosenthal after Dodgers outfielder Cody Bellinger accused the second baseman of stealing the MVP Award from runner-up Aaron Judge, "The few times that the trash can was banged was without his consent, and he would go inside the clubhouse and inside the dugout to whoever was banging the trash can and he would get pissed. He would get mad. He would say, 'I don't want this. I can't hit like this. Don't you do that to me.' He played the game clean."

Meanwhile, when noted columnist Peter Gammons approached Altuve in 2020 to discuss how players, coaches, and other members of the organization had stated that he had not participated in the sign-stealing, Altuve declined to broach the subject, saying that doing so would be a "betrayal of my teammates," and asking Gammons not to write about it.

Plagued by a left hamstring strain in 2019, Altuve missed more than a month of action. Nevertheless, he managed to hit 31 homers, knock in 74 runs, score 89 times, bat .298, and compile an OPS of .903. Altuve subsequently suffered through a dismal pandemic-shortened 2020 campaign, hitting just five homers, driving in only 18 runs, and batting just .219 in 48 games, before rebounding the following year to earn his seventh All-Star nomination by hitting 31 homers, knocking in 83 runs, batting .278, and finishing third in the league with 117 runs scored. After getting off to a slow start in 2022, Altuve went on to have another outstanding season, earning All-Star honors and a fifth-place finish in the AL MVP voting by hitting 28 homers, driving in 57 runs, scoring 103 times, batting an even .300, and compiling an OPS of .921.

Unfortunately, Altuve subsequently missed the first six weeks of the 2023 season after being hit on the thumb by a fastball thrown by USA pitcher Daniel Bard during the quarterfinals of the 2023 World Baseball Classic. But following his return to action on May 19, Altuve picked up right where he left off, finishing the season with 17 homers, 51 RBIs, 76 runs scored, a .311 batting average, and an OPS of .915. Heading into the 2024 campaign, Altuve boasts career totals of 209 homers, 747 RBIs, 1,062 runs scored, 2,047 hits, 400 doubles, 31 triples, and 293 stolen bases, a lifetime batting average of .307, a .364 on-base percentage, and a .471 slugging percentage. An outstanding postseason performer as well, Altuve has hit 27 homers, driven in 55 runs, scored 89 times, and batted .273 in 103 playoff and World Series games, with his 27 home runs placing him second all-time only to Manny Ramirez in postseason play.

In discussing what Altuve has meant to the Astros through the years, teammate Martin Maldonado stated, "The face of the franchise. I walked in today, and I said I couldn't believe that little guy is one of the best hitters in the game. If somebody's walking in the mall and sees Altuve walking, don't know anything about baseball, you wouldn't think that guy is the face of the franchise for the Houston Astros. Nobody would've thought that. That guy has a chance to get 3,000 hits. Like I told him today: I think you're gonna go back to hitting .320, .330. Now he's hitting for power. He's getting better every year."

CAREER HIGHLIGHTS

Best Season

Although Altuve also performed exceptionally well in 2019, 2021 and 2022, he played his best ball for the Astros from 2014 to 2017, with his MVP campaign of 2017 standing out as arguably his finest. In addition to winning his third batting title with a career-high mark of .346, Altuve hit 24 homers, knocked in 81 runs, led the AL with 204 hits, and placed near the top of the league rankings with 112 runs scored, 39 doubles, 323 total bases, 32 steals, a .410 on-base percentage, a .547 slugging percentage, and an OPS of .957, with his fabulous performance earning him *Sporting News* MLB Player of the Year honors for the second straight time.

Memorable Moments/Greatest Performances

Altuve punctuated a 4-for-5 performance by hitting a solo homer in the bottom of the ninth inning that gave the Astros a 5–4 victory over the Red Sox on July 23, 2015.

Altuve contributed to a lopsided 13–3 victory over the Anaheim Angels on July 24, 2016, by homering twice and driving in six runs.

Altuve helped lead the Astros to a 15–8 win over the Orioles on August 19, 2016, by knocking in five runs with a homer, double, and single.

Altuve starred during the Astros' four-game victory over Boston in the 2017 ALDS, going 8-for-15 (.533), with three home runs, four RBIs, and five runs scored, hitting all three homers during an 8–2 win in Game 1.

Altuve also came up big for the Astros in the 2019 postseason, homering three times, driving in five runs, and batting .350 against Tampa Bay in the ALDS, before earning ALCS MVP honors by hitting two homers, driving in three runs, scoring six times, and batting .348 against the Yankees, with his two-run homer off Aroldis Chapman in the bottom of the ninth inning of Game 6 giving the Astros a 6–4 win that sent them to the World Series.

Performing extremely well once again in the 2020 playoffs, Altuve led the Astros to a four-game victory over Oakland in the ALDS by batting .400, hitting two homers, knocking in five runs, and scoring five times. Although the Astros subsequently lost the ALCS to Tampa Bay in seven games, Altuve batted .462, hit three homers, knocked in five runs, and scored six times.

Altuve gave the Astros a 6–3 win over the Texas Rangers on June 15, 2021, when he homered with the bases loaded in the bottom of the 10th inning.

Altuve helped lead the Astros to a 9–6 victory over the Giants on July 30, 2021, by driving in five runs with a single and a pair of homers.

Altuve contributed to a 10–2 rout of the Arizona Diamondbacks on September 27, 2022, by going 3-for-4, with a pair of solo homers, a double, and four runs scored.

Altuve led the Astros to a 13–5 pasting of the Red Sox on August 28, 2023, by hitting for the cycle, going 4-for-6 at the plate, with four RBIs and four runs scored.

After collecting four hits and homering with no one aboard twice during a 13–6 win over Texas the previous afternoon Altuve led the Astros to a lopsided 14–1 victory over the Rangers on September 5, 2023, by hitting three solo home runs.

Although the Astros ended up losing the 2023 ALCS to Texas in seven games, Altuve finished the series with three homers, five RBIs, nine runs scored, a .313 batting average, and an OPS of 1.040, with his three-run homer in the top of the ninth inning of Game 5 proving to be the decisive blow of a 5–4 Astros win.

Notable Achievements

- Has hit more than 20 home runs five times, topping 30 homers twice.
- Has scored more than 100 runs four times.
- Has hit .300 or better seven times, topping the .330-mark on three occasions.
- Has surpassed 200 hits four times.
- Has surpassed 30 doubles eight times, topping 40 two-baggers on three occasions.
- Has stolen more than 30 bases six times, topping 50 thefts once (56 in 2014).

- Has compiled on-base percentage over .400 once (.410 in 2017).
- Has posted slugging percentage over .500 five times.
- Has posted OPS over .900 five times.
- Has led AL in batting average three times, hits four times, and stolen bases twice.
- Has finished second in AL in runs scored twice, doubles once, and stolen bases once.
- Has led AL second basemen in putouts once, fielding percentage once, and double plays turned three times.
- Holds Astros single-season record for most hits (225 in 2014).
- Ranks among Astros career leaders in home runs (5th), RBIs (7th), runs scored (3rd), batting average (2nd), doubles (3rd), hits (3rd), extra-base hits (4th), total bases (3rd), stolen bases (3rd), bases on balls (8th), OPS (11th), sacrifice flies (8th), games played (4th), plate appearances (4th), and at-bats (3rd).
- Six-time division champion (2017, 2018, 2019, 2021, 2022, and 2023).
- Four-time AL champion (2017, 2019, 2021, and 2022).
- Two-time world champion (2017 and 2022).
- Five-time AL Player of the Week.
- Two-time AL Player of the Month.
- 2015 Gold Glove Award winner.
- Six-time Silver Slugger Award winner (2014, 2015, 2016, 2017, 2018, and 2022).
- 2016 Lou Gehrig Memorial Award winner.
- 2017 Babe Ruth Award winner.
- 2017 AL Hank Aaron Award winner.
- 2017 Associated Press Male Athlete of the Year.
- 2017 AL MVP.
- Has finished in top 10 in AL MVP voting three other times, placing in top five twice.
- Two-time *Sporting News* MLB Player of the Year (2016 and 2017).
- 2019 ALCS MVP.
- Eight-time All-Star selection (2012, 2014, 2015, 2016, 2017, 2018, 2021, and 2022).
- 2022 All-MLB First Team selection.
- 2019 All-MLB Second Team selection.

4

LANCE BERKMAN

An outstanding switch-hitter who combined with fellow "Killer Bs" Jeff Bagwell and Craig Biggio to give the Astros a formidable threesome near the top of their batting order the first few years of this century, Lance Berkman spent parts of 12 seasons in Houston, establishing himself as one of the National League's finest batsmen. Berkman, who hit more than 30 homers five times, knocked in more than 100 runs six times, batted over .300 four times, and posted an OPS over .900 on nine separate occasions, helped lead the Astros to four playoff appearances, two division titles, and one pennant, earning five All-Star selections and four top-five finishes in the NL MVP voting. The franchise's all-time leader in on-base percentage, Berkman ranks extremely high in team annals in virtually every major offensive category, with his superior offensive production earning him a place in the Astros Hall of Fame.

Born in Waco, Texas, on February 10, 1976, William Lance Berkman grew up some 100 miles south, in Austin, Texas, where he developed an affinity for baseball at a very young age, recalling, "Ever since I could walk, I've had a bat in my hand."

A natural right-handed batter, Berkman learned how to switch-hit at the insistence of his father, remembering, "When things were tight and my team needed a run, my teammates used to beg me to hit right-handed. But my dad wouldn't allow it. He made sure I learned to switch-hit."

After getting his start in organized ball in the local youth leagues, Berkman spent two years excelling on the diamond at Austin High School, before moving with his family to New Braunfels, Texas, prior to the start of his junior year. Starring at first base for the Canyon High School baseball team the next two seasons, Berkman earned All-District First-Team honors as a senior by hitting eight homers, driving in 30 runs, batting .539, and posting a slugging percentage of .974, prompting Rice University to offer him an athletic scholarship. Continuing his exceptional play in college, Berkman ended up setting school records in several offensive categories, including highest career batting average (.385), most home runs (67), and most RBIs (272). Particularly outstanding his junior year, Berkman gained recognition from the National Collegiate Baseball Writers Association as the NCAA Player of the Year by hitting 41 homers, knocking in 134 runs, and batting .431.

While in college, Berkman also became more committed to Christianity, recalling, "I had a buddy who was a strong Christian and lived his life in accordance with that. This guy was different, and the more I was around him, I realized that I was a guy who claimed to be a Christian, yet my life didn't look any different from someone who didn't. That was my Damascus Road experience, where God said either you're in or you're out. If you're going to claim to be a Christian, you'd better demonstrate that. Otherwise, don't even bother."

Lance Berkman hit more than 30 home runs for the Astros five times.

Choosing to forgo his senior year at Rice after the Astros selected him with the 16th overall pick of the 1997 MLB Amateur Draft, Berkman received high praise at the time from Houston GM Gerry Hunsicker, who said, "He is the best hitting prospect we have drafted in some time. A switch-hitter with power is a rare commodity you just can't pass up."

Berkman spent the next two-and-a-half years in the minor leagues, during which time he transitioned from first base to the outfield due to the presence of Jeff Bagwell in Houston. Performing well at every stop, Berkman earned a callup to the parent club midway through the 1999 campaign, after which he went on to hit four homers, drive in 15 runs, and bat .237 in 34 games and 106 total plate appearances.

Although Berkman subsequently began the 2000 season in the minors, he returned to Houston in May. Spending the rest of the year starting for the Astros at both corner outfield positions, Berkman earned a sixth-place finish in the NL Rookie of the Year voting by hitting 21 homers, knocking in 67 runs, scoring 76 times, batting .297, and compiling an OPS of .949. Having established himself as a full-time starter, Berkman joined the NL's elite in 2001, when he began an outstanding eight-year run during which he posted the following numbers:

YEAR	HR	RBI	RUNS	AVG	OBP	SLG	OPS
2001	34	126	110	.331	.430	.620	1.051
2002	42	**128**	106	.292	.405	.578	.982
2003	25	93	110	.288	.412	.515	.927
2004	30	106	104	.316	.450	.566	1.016
2005	24	82	76	.293	.411	.524	.934
2006	45	136	95	.315	.420	.621	1.041
2007	34	102	95	.278	.386	.510	.896
2008	29	106	114	.312	.420	.567	.986

In addition to leading the NL with 128 RBIs in 2002, Berkman topped the senior circuit in doubles twice, with his 55 two-baggers in 2001 representing the second-highest single-season total in franchise history. Berkman also consistently placed near the top of the league rankings in on-base percentage, OPS, and walks, drawing more than 100 bases on balls on three separate occasions. An NL All-Star in five of those seasons, Berkman also earned four top-five finishes in the league MVP voting, one *Sporting News* All-Star nomination, and team MVP honors five times. Meanwhile, the

Astros advanced to the playoffs three times, the NLCS twice, and the World Series once, finishing either first or second in the NL Central Division in six of those eight seasons.

Blessed with good power, the ability to hit the ball hard to all fields, a keen batting eye, and outstanding patience at the plate, Berkman proved to be one of the NL's most complete hitters, with Astros manager Larry Dierker stating at one point during the 2001 season, "Maybe five times this year, Lance has had what you'd call a bad at-bat. Quite simply, he understands the art of hitting."

In discussing his role on the team, Berkman said, "The name of the game for a guy like me is scoring runs and driving guys in. Those are two stats that are very important for me personally. That's really my job. That's what I'm supposed to do to help this team win."

Berkman ranks among the most productive switch-hitters of all time.
Courtesy of Bryce Edwards

Despite being a natural right-handed batter, Berkman gradually developed into a better hitter from the left side of the plate, causing him to briefly consider abandoning switch-hitting. In fact, Berkman once claimed that he would bat left-handed only if he were to begin his major-league career again.

Nicknamed "Fat Elvis" and "Big Puma," the 6'1", 220-pound Berkman, who Gerry Hunsicker once described as "lumpy," did not have the body of a well-conditioned athlete. Because of Berkman's physique, others sometimes felt that he did not take the game seriously enough, with Astros manager Phil Garner saying, "Comparing him to some guys, he wasn't the hardest worker."

In his defense, though, Berkman stated, "I think that perception just comes from the fact that a lot of guys show up at two o'clock for a seven o'clock game. I don't feel the need to do that. I get dressed right before batting practice. To me, there's no sense in getting loose before batting practice, then sit around for an hour and then get ready for the game."

Berkman added, "I want to win as badly as anybody, and I want to do well to help this team win, and I care about it. I don't want people to think I don't care and have an 'Oh well, whatever' attitude. It can drive you crazy if you let it. You have to keep some perspective to stay sane."

Although Berkman developed a reputation as a clubhouse comedian who did not take himself too seriously, he remained dedicated to helping others during his time in Houston, establishing Berkman's Bunch, which provided a way for underprivileged children to attend Astros games. And after signing a lucrative long-term deal with the Astros in 2005, Berkman pledged $100,000 each season to the Astros in Action Foundation, which supports programs related to literacy, education, health issues, religious organizations, and reviving baseball in the inner city.

Berkman, who, after seeing extensive action at both corner outfield positions his first several years in Houston, moved to first base full-time in 2007, experienced a decline in offensive production in 2009, when, limited by injuries to 136 games, he hit 25 homers, knocked in 80 runs, scored 73 times, and batted .274. Off to a slow start the following year for an Astros team that ended up posting its third losing record in four seasons, the 34-year-old Berkman began to entertain thoughts of going elsewhere, stating, "This organization has been great to me. I love the Houston Astros. No matter what happens, I'm always going to be an Astro at heart. But as you get older, you definitely start to look at being on a losing team, and you say, 'How many sub-.500 seasons do you want to play?'"

Ultimately dealt to the Yankees just prior to the trade deadline for youngsters Mark Melancon and Jimmy Paredes, Berkman said at the time, "I'm excited for a new challenge. Coming to a first-place team and a team that's expected to go deep into the postseason is a great opportunity and one that I really felt like I couldn't pass up."

Berkman, who left Houston with career totals of 326 home runs, 1,090 RBIs, 1,008 runs scored, 1,648 hits, 375 doubles, 26 triples, and 82 stolen bases, a .296 batting average, a .410 on-base percentage, and a .549 slugging percentage, finished out the season in New York, before signing with the St. Louis Cardinals as a free agent at the end of the year. After hitting 31 homers, driving in 94 runs, and batting .301 for the world champion Cardinals in 2011, Berkman spent the next two seasons assuming a backup role in St. Louis and Texas, before retiring with career totals of 366 homers, 1,234 RBIs, 1,146 runs scored, 1,905 hits, 422 doubles, 30 triples, and 86 steals, a .293 batting average, a .406 on-base percentage, and a .537 slugging percentage. Second only to Mickey Mantle all-time among switch-hitters in on-base percentage, slugging percentage, and OPS, Berkman also became just the second switch-hitter in MLB history to surpass 40 home runs in multiple seasons.

After signing a one-day contract with the Astros on April 5, 2014, that allowed him to officially retire as a member of the team, Berkman became head baseball coach at Second Baptist High School in Houston, which he led to the state championship in 2016. Berkman remained in that post for two more years, before handing in his resignation after failing to get the head-coaching job at his alma mater, Rice University, saying at the time, "I was really coaching (at Second Baptist) to put myself in position to get the Rice job. When that didn't work out, it took the wind out of my sails a little bit. I never intended to be a high-school coach for the rest of my life."

Berkman subsequently spent one year serving as an assistant manager for the University of St. Thomas baseball team, before being named head coach of the Houston Baptist Huskies in 2021.

Looking back on his career after failing to receive the minimum number of votes needed to remain on the Hall of Fame ballot in his first year of eligibility, Berkman said, "Whether or not I'm a Hall of Fame-caliber player, I feel like in my decade-plus, from a percentage standpoint, I stack up against anybody. I may not have retired with what some people think are enough home runs and RBIs to merit induction, but, in my mind, I could hit with anybody in that building."

ASTROS CAREER HIGHLIGHTS

Best Season

Berkman had several outstanding years for the Astros, performing especially well in 2001, 2002, 2004, 2006, and 2008. While any of those seasons would make an excellent choice, Berkman posted his best overall numbers in 2001, when he earned his first All-Star selection and a fifth-place finish in the NL MVP voting by hitting 34 homers, driving in 126 runs, scoring 110 times, and establishing career-high marks with 191 hits, 55 doubles, 358 total bases, a .331 batting average, and an OPS of 1.051.

Memorable Moments/Greatest Performances

Berkman led the Astros to an 8–3 win over the Twins on June 14, 2001, by going 4-for-5, with two home runs and six RBIs, delivering the game's big blow in the top of the seventh inning when he homered with the bases loaded.

Berkman hit safely in 21 consecutive games from June 17 to July 8, 2001, going 40-for-85 (.471), with nine homers, one triple, 12 doubles, 10 walks, 30 RBIs, and 23 runs scored.

Berkman led the Astros to an 8–3 victory over the Reds on April 16, 2002, by hitting three homers and knocking in five runs.

Berkman starred in defeat on May 1, 2003, going 4-for-5, with a homer, double, and six RBIs during an 8–7 loss to the Braves.

In an 18-inning affair the Astros ended up winning by a score of 7–6, Berkman brought them to within one run of Atlanta in Game 4 of the 2005 NLDS when he homered with the bases loaded in the bottom of the eighth inning.

After homering earlier in the contest, Berkman delivered the decisive blow of a 6–5 win over the Cardinals on September 21, 2006, when he took Chris Carpenter deep with one man aboard in the bottom of the eighth inning.

Berkman knocked in all three runs the Astros scored during a 3–1 win over the Padres on August 17, 2007, with a pair of homers.

Berkman helped lead the Astros to a 6–5 win over the Washington Nationals on May 6, 2008, by going 5-for-5, with two doubles, two stolen bases, one RBI, and four runs scored.

Berkman accounted for both runs scored in a 2–0 win over the Pirates on July 8, 2010, with a pair of solo homers.

Notable Achievements

- Hit more than 20 home runs 10 times, topping 30 homers five times and 40 homers twice.
- Knocked in more than 100 runs six times, surpassing 120 RBIs on three occasions.
- Scored more than 100 runs five times.
- Batted over .300 four times.
- Surpassed 30 doubles seven times, topping 40 two-baggers on three occasions.
- Drew more than 100 bases on balls three times.
- Compiled on-base percentage over .400 seven times.
- Posted slugging percentage over .500 10 times, topping the .600-mark twice.
- Posted OPS over .900 nine times, topping 1.000 three times.
- Hit three home runs in one game vs. Cincinnati on April 16, 2002.
- Led NL in doubles twice and RBIs once.
- Finished second in NL in bases on balls once.
- Finished third in NL in home runs once, RBIs once, on-base percentage twice, slugging percentage once, OPS twice, and total bases once.
- Led NL first basemen in fielding percentage once.
- Holds Astros single-season records for most RBIs (136 in 2006) and extra-base hits (94 in 2001).
- Holds Astros career record for highest on-base percentage (.410).
- Ranks among Astros career leaders in home runs (2nd), RBIs (3rd), runs scored (4th), batting average (6th), slugging percentage (3rd), OPS (3rd), hits (6th), extra-base hits (3rd), doubles (4th), total bases (4th), bases on balls (3rd), sacrifice flies (6th), games played (5th), plate appearances (5th), and at-bats (6th).
- Two-time division champion (1999 and 2001).
- 2005 NL champion.
- Four-time NL Player of the Week.
- Two-time NL Player of the Month.
- Five-time Astros team MVP (2001, 2002, 2004, 2006, and 2008).
- Finished in top five of NL MVP voting four times, placing third twice.
- Five-time NL All-Star selection (2001, 2002, 2004, 2006, and 2008).
- 2006 *Sporting News* NL All-Star selection.
- Inducted into Astros Hall of Fame in 2020.

5

ROY OSWALT

Known for his fierce competitive spirit and ability to excel in big-game situations, Roy Oswalt established himself as one of baseball's premier pitchers during his 10 seasons in Houston. One of only two hurlers in team annals to win at least 20 games in consecutive seasons, Oswalt accomplished the feat in the middle of an exceptional eight-year run during which he earned five top-five finishes in the NL Cy Young voting and three All-Star selections by posting an overall record of 129-64. A member of Houston teams that made three playoff appearances and won one NL pennant, Oswalt ranks among the franchise's all-time leaders in virtually every major statistical category for pitchers, with his total body of work earning him a place in the Astros Hall of Fame.

Born in Kosciusko, Mississippi, on August 29, 1977, Roy Edward Oswalt grew up some 20 miles northeast, in the tiny town of Weir, where he spent his early years playing baseball with his brother and older sister, Tricia, who recalled, "We were in the yard every day throwing the baseball."

Remaining active in sports after his eldest sibling enrolled at Mississippi State University to pursue her undergraduate degree, Oswalt lettered in baseball and football at Weir High School, where he excelled as a pitcher on the diamond and a wide receiver and defensive back on the gridiron. Although Weir High became far more known for its football program, Oswalt helped put the school's baseball team on the map, stating, "I can't remember our record, but we made the playoffs all three years. Never could win the state [championship], though."

Even though Oswalt possessed excellent control and a mid-80s fastball by his senior year, he failed to garner much interest from college recruiters or major-league scouts due to his smallish 5'10", 150-pound frame, forcing him to attend Holmes Community College on a half scholarship. But, after Oswalt grew two inches, added some 20 pounds of muscle to his frame, and increased the velocity on his fastball by nearly 10 mph over the course of the next two seasons, the Astros selected him in the 23rd round of the 1996

Roy Oswalt ranks second in franchise history in wins and strikeouts.
Courtesy of Kenji Takabayashi

MLB Amateur Draft and Mississippi State University signed him to a letter of intent. Choosing to sign with the Astros after they offered him a $50,000 signing bonus, Oswalt later said, "I had always wanted to pitch for State, but it was just too much money to turn down. . . . Houston offered me something that was a great way to start out life. It came down to financial security more than anything."

Oswalt spent the next four years advancing through Houston's farm system, before finally being promoted to the parent club during the early stages of the 2001 campaign. Joining the Astros starting rotation shortly thereafter, Oswalt excelled in his first big-league season, earning a runner-up finish in the NL Rookie of the Year voting and a fifth-place finish in the Cy Young balloting by compiling a record of 14-3, a 2.73 ERA, and a 1.059 WHIP, while also registering 144 strikeouts in 141⅔ innings pitched for the NL Central Division champions.

Although the Astros failed to capture the division title again in 2002, Oswalt had a sensational season, earning another top-five finish in the Cy Young voting by ranking among the league leaders with 19 victories (against nine losses), a 3.01 ERA, a 1.189 WHIP, 208 strikeouts, and 233 innings pitched. Despite being limited by injuries to just 21 starts the following year, Oswalt pitched well whenever he found himself able to take the mound, going 10-5, with a 2.97 ERA, a 1.139 WHIP, and 108 strikeouts in 127⅓ innings of work. Meanwhile, the Houston chapter of the Baseball Writers Association of America voted Oswalt the winner of the Darryl Kile Award, which is presented annually to the individual "who reflects the qualities of decency and character represented by" the former Astros pitcher.

Fully healthy by the start of the 2004 campaign, Oswalt began an outstanding five-year run during which he posted the following numbers:

YEAR	W-L	ERA	SO	IP	WHIP
2004	**20**-10	3.49	206	237	1.245
2005	20-12	2.94	184	241.2	1.204
2006	15-8	**2.98**	166	220.2	1.169
2007	14-7	3.18	154	212	1.325
2008	17-10	3.54	165	208.2	1.179

Consistently ranking among the NL leaders in wins, ERA, and innings pitched, Oswalt earned three All-Star selections and another three top-five finishes in the Cy Young voting, placing as high as third in 2004, when his 20 victories led all NL hurlers. Meanwhile, the Astros advanced to the NLCS in 2004 and the World Series the following year, with Oswalt's superb pitching in the 2005 NLCS earning him series MVP honors.

A control pitcher who did an excellent job of spotting his pitches to the edges of the strike zone, the right-handed-throwing Oswalt, who stood 6 foot and weighed 190 pounds, possessed good velocity on his fastball, which he typically delivered to home plate at a speed that registered somewhere between 92 and 95 mph on the radar gun. Oswalt's repertoire of pitches also included a low-80s changeup, a mid-80s slider, a hard-snapping, low-80s curveball that he gripped with two forefingers over the seams, and a looping, low-70s curve that he threw with three fingers over the seams.

Inspiring tremendous confidence in his teammates, Oswalt drew praise from Jeff Bagwell, who said, "Roy Oswalt is one of the best I've seen. He's dominant. It's kind of like when Randy Johnson came over in 1998. It's been amazing to see. Every single time he goes out there, we're in the eighth inning, and the other team has no runs. That's nice because as a team you go out there feeling like you've won before you even go out there."

Although Oswalt went about his job in a somewhat understated manner, he proved to be an outstanding team leader as well, saying, "I've always believed in leading by doing it on the field and having others follow. I've never thought that you have to be too outspoken in the clubhouse, as long as you set an example for guys to follow. People watch that more than they listen to some guy talking, no matter who he is."

With the Astros finishing fifth in the division in 2009 with a record of just 74-88, Oswalt experienced a down-year, going 8-6, with a 4.12 ERA and a 1.241 WHIP. Although Oswalt pitched more effectively over the first four months of the ensuing campaign, posting an ERA of 3.42 and a WHIP of 1.109, poor run support from his teammates relegated him to a record of just 6-12. Not wanting to take part in a rebuilding program, the 32-year-old Oswalt requested a trade, after which the Astros dealt him to the Philadelphia Phillies for three young players and $11 million on July 29, 2010.

Oswalt, who left Houston with a career record of 143-82, an ERA of 3.24, a WHIP of 1.196, 19 complete games, seven shutouts, and 1,593 strikeouts in 1,932⅓ innings pitched, ended up performing extremely well for the Phillies the rest of the year, helping them advance to the playoffs by going 7-1 with a 1.74 ERA. His 2011 campaign interrupted by a one-month leave of absence he took to assist in the recovery efforts waged in Mississippi following the devastating tornadoes that struck his home state, Oswalt went just 9-10 with a 3.69 ERA, before signing with the Texas Rangers as a free agent in May 2012. Unable to regain his earlier form, Oswalt split the next two seasons between Texas and Colorado, going a combined 4-9, before retiring at the end of 2013 with a career record of 163-102, an ERA of 3.36, a WHIP of 1.211, and 1,852 strikeouts in 2,245⅓ total innings of work.

Although Oswalt made his decision much earlier, he signed a one-day personal services contract with the Astros on April 5, 2014, that enabled him to officially retire as a member of the team.

Oswalt posted 20 victories for the Astros two straight times.

Following his playing days, Oswalt returned to Mississippi, where he now spends most of his time working on his farm and hunting. A huge fan of Mississippi State sports, Oswalt also continues to follow baseball closely, saying, "Baseball's still a part of my life; it always will be."

ASTROS CAREER HIGHLIGHTS

Best Season

As well as Oswalt pitched when he won 20 games the previous season, he performed even better in 2005, earning his first All-Star selection and a fourth-place finish in the NL Cy Young voting by compiling a record of 20-12 and an ERA of 2.94, registering 184 strikeouts, and finishing second in the league with a career-high 241⅔ innings pitched.

Memorable Moments/Greatest Performances

Oswalt shut out the Milwaukee Brewers on just three hits on April 16, 2004, issuing no walks and recording 10 strikeouts during a 2–0 victory.

Oswalt tossed a two-hit shutout on June 12, 2005, yielding just a second-inning single by third baseman Shea Hillenbrand and a ninth-inning double by right fielder Alex Rios during a 3–0 win over the Toronto Blue Jays.

Oswalt earned 2005 NLCS MVP honors by winning both his starts against St. Louis, striking out 12 batters and allowing just eight hits and two runs in 14 total innings of work, en route to compiling an ERA of 1.29.

Oswalt hit the only home run of his career during a 14–1 rout of the Pirates on August 9, 2006, in which he allowed four hits and one run in six innings of work.

Oswalt struck out 10 batters and surrendered just one hit and two walks over the first eight innings of a 3–0 win over the Arizona Diamond-backs on August 17, 2008, yielding only a third-inning single by shortstop Stephen Drew.

Oswalt threw 33 consecutive scoreless innings from August 27 to September 11, 2008, tossing three straight shutouts during that time. Particularly outstanding in his last two starts, Oswalt allowed just one hit during a 2–0 win over the Colorado Rockies on September 6, yielding only a fifth-inning single by right fielder Brad Hawpe. Oswalt followed that up with a three-hit shutout of the Pirates on September 11.

Oswalt recorded eight strikeouts and allowed just two hits and two walks during a 3–1 complete-game victory over the Padres on June 29, 2009.

Oswalt tossed a one-hit shutout on July 8, 2010, yielding just two walks and a first-inning single by second baseman Neil Walker during a 2–0 win over the Pirates.

Notable Achievements

- Won at least 15 games five times, topping 20 victories twice.
- Posted a winning percentage of .824 in 2001.
- Compiled ERA under 3.00 four times.
- Struck out more than 200 batters twice.
- Threw more than 200 innings six times.
- Led NL with 20 sacrifice hits in 2006.
- Led NL pitchers in wins once, winning percentage once, ERA once, strikeouts-to-walks ratio once, putouts once, and starts twice.
- Finished second in NL in innings pitched once.
- Finished third in NL in wins three times, shutouts twice, complete games three times, and innings pitched twice.
- Ranks among Astros career leaders in wins (2nd), winning percentage (3rd), WHIP (11th), strikeouts (2nd), strikeouts-to-walks ratio (4th), innings pitched (3rd), games started (3rd), and pitching appearances (10th).
- 2001 division champion.
- 2005 NL champion.
- Two-time NL Player of the Week.
- Two-time NL Pitcher of the Month.
- 2001 *Sporting News* NL Rookie Pitcher of the Year.
- Finished in top five of NL Cy Young voting five times, placing as high as third in 2004.
- 2005 NLCS MVP.
- Three-time NL All-Star selection (2005, 2006, and 2007).
- Inducted into Astros Hall of Fame in 2020.

6

CÉSAR CEDEÑO

In discussing César Cedeño during the early stages of the 1973 campaign, Astros manager Leo Durocher said, "At 22, Cedeño is as good or better than Willie Mays at the same age. I don't know whether he can keep this up for 20 years, and I'm not saying he will be better than Mays. No way anybody can be better than Mays. But I will say this kid has a chance to be as good. And that's saying a lot."

Although Cedeño failed to attain the level of greatness Durocher and others predicted for him, he proved to be one of the finest all-around players in the game for much of the 1970s, surpassing 20 homers three times, batting over .300 four times, and stealing more than 40 bases on seven separate occasions, while also leading all NL outfielders in putouts and fielding percentage once each. A true five-tool player who served as the Astros' primary starter in center field from 1970 to 1980, Cedeño earned four NL All-Star nominations, one top-10 finish in the league MVP voting, and five Gold Gloves during his time in Houston, before splitting his final five big-league seasons between the Reds, Cardinals, and Dodgers. Nevertheless, Cedeño's career is generally considered to be something of a disappointment.

Born in Santo Domingo in the Dominican Republic on February 25, 1951, César Eugenio Cedeño knew at an early age that he wanted to pursue a career in baseball. Although his father, Diogene, wanted him to help out at the family grocery store and eventually become an engineer, César spent most of his free time on the local sandlots, developing into such an outstanding player by his early teens that he frequently competed against grown men.

Discovered in the fall of 1967 by Houston Astros scouts Pat Gillick and Tony Pacheco while playing for an amateur team sponsored by a local pharmacy, the 16-year-old Cedeño received an offer to attend a tryout, with Gillick recalling, "We noticed this kid and liked the way he moved, his actions and size. We saw him throw and then we saw him go up and get a

César Cedeño drew comparisons to the great
Willie Mays during the early stages of his career.

hit and go up and get another hit. We decided we wanted to look at him. After the game, we arranged for him to go with us and some more players to San Pedro, about 60 miles away, for a workout Monday morning."

Impressed with Cedeño's performance, Gillick and Pacheco went to his home later that afternoon to offer him a contract. But they had a difficult time convincing his father, who had earlier turned down a $1,000 offer from the St. Louis Cardinals, to grant his permission, with César remembering, "He did not want me to play baseball but to go to school." After dickering with the elder Cedeño for quite some time, Gillick finally reached a satisfactory figure when he offered his son a $3,000 signing bonus.

Beginning his professional career the following spring with Covington in the Appalachian League, Cedeño advanced rapidly through the Astros' farm system, excelling at Cocoa in the Florida State League and Peninsula in the Carolina League, before opening eyes at the Florida Instructional League in the fall of 1969. Subsequently sent to Triple-A Oklahoma City in 1970, Cedeño continued to flourish, hitting 14 homers, driving in 61 runs, and batting .373 in 54 games, with his brilliant play earning him a callup to the parent club in late June.

Inserted into the starting lineup immediately upon his arrival in Houston, Cedeño spent most of the season's final three months batting leadoff and patrolling center field for the Astros, although he also saw some action in right. Still only 19 years old, Cedeño acquitted himself extremely well as the youngest regular in the major leagues, earning a fourth-place finish in the NL Rookie of the Year voting by batting .310, hitting seven homers, driving in 42 runs, scoring 46 times, stealing 17 bases, and compiling an OPS of .790 in 90 games and 377 plate appearances. After slumping during the early stages of the ensuing campaign, Cedeño regained his stroke during the season's second half, enabling him to finish the year with respectable numbers. In addition to hitting 10 homers, knocking in 81 runs, scoring 85 others, leading the league with 40 doubles, and stealing 20 bases, Cedeño batted .264 and compiled an OPS of .690, doing most of his damage after being moved down to the middle of the batting order. Emerging as a true superstar in 1972, Cedeño began an outstanding three-year run during which he posted the following numbers:

YEAR	HR	RBI	RUNS	AVG	OBP	SLG	OPS
1972	22	82	103	.320	.385	.537	.921
1973	25	70	86	.320	.376	.537	.913
1974	26	102	95	.269	.338	.461	.799

An NL All-Star and Gold Glove winner all three years, Cedeño placed near the top of the league rankings in batting average in each of the first two seasons, finishing as high as second in 1973. Cedeño also led the NL with 39 doubles in 1972 and ranked among the league leaders in homers, runs scored, total bases, and OPS once each, slugging percentage twice, and stolen bases all three years, swiping more than 50 bags each season. By hitting more than 20 home runs and stealing more than 50 bases in the same season three straight times, Cedeño became the first player in MLB history to accomplish the feat multiple times (Lou Brock previously did it once, in 1967).

Blessed with a rare combination of power, speed, and exceptional defense, the right-handed-hitting Cedeño, who stood 6'2" and, after maturing somewhat physically, weighed close to 190 pounds, proved to be arguably the game's most complete player over the course of those three seasons. Capable of driving the ball into the seats, legging out a triple, stealing a base, or outrunning a long flyball, Cedeño had the ability to do anything on a baseball field, prompting Joe Torre to later say, "He was an electric player. He could do it all. He had all the tools of Mays—he could run, he could throw people out, he could hit a home run. . . . He didn't hit that many home runs, but the Astrodome was enormous."

Likening Cedeño to Roberto Clemente, Astros manager Harry Walker stated, "Clemente and Cedeño are the two most exciting players in baseball today. Whether they're catching the ball, or throwing it, or running the bases, or batting, they do it all-out, and with a flair. When they're involved, you're always on edge expecting something to happen. They make things happen."

Cedeño holds the franchise record for most career stolen bases.

In discussing Cedeño's tremendous speed and range in the outfield, Montreal Expos manager Gene Mauch commented, "The nice thing about Cedeño is that he can play all three outfield positions—at the same time."

Former Astros teammate Art Howe said, "He had every tool there was. He could beat you in any way—defense, speed, hitting, hitting with power. He had it all—as gifted a player as I ever played with. . . . And a great guy. I thought the world of CC. CC was kinda misunderstood by a lot of people, I think, but when he put the uniform on, he played hard."

Despite his outstanding performance in 1974, Cedeño was involved in an unfortunate incident in the Dominican Republic the previous offseason that ended up haunting him throughout the remainder of his career. With Cedeño and his 19-year-old mistress drinking and playing with a gun in a motel room, the firearm went off, killing the young woman. Initially charged with voluntary manslaughter, Cedeño spent 20 days in jail, before being released on bail and eventually fined just $100 after being found guilty of involuntary manslaughter.

Although Cedeño received a relatively light sentence in his homeland, the American public subsequently took a dim view of him, reminding him of his irresponsible and thoughtless act everywhere he went. Jeered in every ballpark he visited, Cedeño found it difficult to properly deal with the death and the abuse he received from fans, once even charging into the stands to confront a heckler. Even though Cedeño continued to put up good numbers the next few seasons, averaging 15 homers, 72 RBIs, 91 runs scored, and 56 stolen bases from 1975 to 1977, while also posting batting averages of .288, .297, and .279 and winning two more Gold Gloves, he never again performed at the same level he did from 1972 to 1974. Commenting on Cedeño's diminished play, a teammate told Peter Gammons in a 1977 *Sports Illustrated* profile, "He'll end up with decent statistics, but statistics are for people who don't know anything. He's never been the same hitter since that incident."

While Cedeño's involvement in his girlfriend's death likely impacted his on-field performance to some degree, other factors affected him as well, with longtime teammate Bob Watson suggesting, "He was so young, so proud, that I think he tried extra hard to prove to everyone that it never bothered him. He had a good season (in 1974), but he altered his swing trying to hit homers. After that, maybe pitchers adjusted, and he hasn't readjusted himself."

Cedeño was also plagued by sore knees and bad ankles, telling Peter Gammons in 1977, "It takes me 20 or 30 minutes to get loose every day." Making matters worse, Cedeño suffered a torn knee ligament in 1978 that forced him to miss more than half the season, lost 14 pounds the following year after contracting hepatitis, and, after batting .309 and stealing 48 bases during the 1980 regular season, broke his ankle in that year's NLCS.

Robbed of his once-blinding speed, Cedeño batted just .271 and stole only 12 bases during the strike-shortened 1981 campaign, while splitting his time between first base and the outfield. Dealt to the Cincinnati Reds for third baseman Ray Knight the following offseason, Cedeño left Houston with career totals of 163 homers, 778 RBIs, 890 runs scored, 1,659 hits, 343 doubles, 55 triples, and 487 stolen bases, a .289 batting average, a .351 on-base percentage, and a .454 slugging percentage. The franchise's all-time leader in games played, runs scored, hits, doubles, and stolen bases at the time of his departure, Cedeño continues to rank first in team annals in steals more than 40 years later.

After leaving Houston, Cedeño remained an everyday player for one more season, hitting eight homers, driving in 57 runs, stealing 16 bases, and batting .289 for the Reds in 1982, before assuming a part-time role the rest of his career, which he split between the Reds, Cardinals, and Dodgers. Released by Los Angeles midway through the 1986 campaign, Cedeño announced his retirement, ending his career with 199 homers, 976 RBIs, 1,084 runs scored, 2,087 hits, 436 doubles, 60 triples, 550 stolen bases, a .285 batting average, a .347 on-base percentage, and a .443 slugging percentage.

Commenting years later on Cedeño's inability to fulfill his enormous potential, Rusty Staub said, "You look at him, and you look at (Dave) Parker, and you look at (Darryl) Strawberry, Richie Allen—they just found the life a little too tough. Whether it was this temptation or that temptation, he did not end up as great a player as everyone thought he should have been."

Following the conclusion of his big-league career, Cedeño briefly competed in the Senior Professional Baseball Association, before becoming both a fielding and hitting coach in the Dominican and Venezuelan winter leagues. He also later served as a hitting coach in the minor-league systems of the Astros and Washington Nationals.

Unfortunately, Cedeño's troubles with the law did not end after he retired as an active player. After being charged with assault, causing bodily injury, and resisting arrest four years earlier, Cedeño was arrested on September 29, 1992, for attacking police and his pregnant girlfriend. Accused of struggling with officers after his girlfriend, Pamela Lamon, said he beat her for not cleaning their apartment, Cedeño spent several hours in jail, before being released on $2,500 bail. Elaborating somewhat on the events that transpired, Lamon, who was four months pregnant at the time, wrote on a crime victim's statement, "César has a serious drinking problem and only becomes abusive when he drinks. I have begged him to get help, but he won't."

ASTROS CAREER HIGHLIGHTS

Best Season

Although Cedeño stole 57 bases, scored 95 runs and established career-high marks with 26 homers and 102 RBIs in 1974, he posted better overall numbers in each of the previous two seasons, with the 1972 campaign standing out as his finest. En route to earning a sixth-place finish in the NL MVP voting and his first All-Star and *Sporting News* NL All-Star nominations, Cedeño hit 22 homers, knocked in 82 runs, led the league with 39 doubles, and ranked among the leaders with 103 runs scored, 179 hits, eight triples, 55 stolen bases, 300 total bases, a .320 batting average, a .385 on-base percentage, and a .537 slugging percentage.

Memorable Moments/Greatest Performances

Cedeño contributed to a 13–7 victory over the Giants on April 23, 1972, by going 5-for-6 at the plate, stealing two bases, driving in three runs, and scoring twice.

Cedeño helped lead the Astros to a 10–1 win over the Reds on August 2, 1972, by hitting for the cycle, going 4-for-5 with a homer, triple, double, and single, knocking in four runs, and scoring three times.

Cedeño led the Astros to a 7–1 win over the Pirates on June 10, 1973, by driving in five runs with a pair of homers.

Cedeño again homered twice and knocked in five runs during a 7–0 win over the Braves on April 22, 1974.

Cedeño proved to be a thorn in the side of Braves pitchers once again on September 8, 1975, hitting a pair of homers, driving in six runs, and scoring three times during a 9–6 Astros win.

Cedeño hit for the cycle for a second time on August 9, 1976, going 4-for-5, with five RBIs and four runs scored during a 13–4 rout of the Cardinals.

Cedeño knocked in all four runs the Astros scored during a 4–1 win over the Cardinals on August 6, 1977, with a pair of homers.

Cedeño hit safely in 22 consecutive games from August 25 to September 21, 1977, a period during which he went 37-for-93 (.398), with four homers, four triples, nine doubles, 12 stolen bases, 15 RBIs, and 21 runs scored.

Cedeño led the Astros to a 5–4 win over the Dodgers on June 24, 1980, by going a perfect 5-for-5 at the plate, with two doubles, two stolen bases, two RBIs, and two runs scored.

Notable Achievements

- Hit more than 20 home runs three times.
- Knocked in more than 100 runs once (102 in 1974).
- Scored more than 100 runs once (103 in 1972).
- Batted over .300 four times.
- Surpassed 30 doubles six times.
- Stole more than 40 bases seven times, topping 50 thefts on six occasions.
- Posted slugging percentage over .500 twice.
- Posted OPS over .900 twice.
- Hit for cycle twice (vs. Cincinnati on August 2, 1972, and vs. St. Louis on August 9, 1976).
- Led NL in doubles twice and sacrifice flies once.
- Finished second in NL in batting average, on-base percentage, stolen bases, extra-base hits, and total bases once each.
- Led NL outfielders in putouts once and fielding percentage once.
- Led NL center fielders in putouts once, assists once, fielding percentage twice, and double plays twice.
- Holds Astros career record for most stolen bases (487).
- Ranks among Astros career leaders in home runs (9th), RBIs (6th), runs scored (5th), batting average (11th), hits (5th), extra-base hits (5th), triples (tied for 5th), doubles (5th), total bases (6th), bases on balls (9th), sacrifice flies (4th), games played (7th), plate appearances (6th), and at-bats (5th).
- 1980 division champion.
- Two-time NL Player of the Week.
- Two-time NL Player of the Month.
- Five-time Gold Glove Award winner (1972, 1973, 1974, 1975, and 1976).
- Finished sixth in 1972 NL MVP voting.
- Four-time NL All-Star selection (1972, 1973, 1974, and 1976).

- Four-time *Sporting News* NL All-Star selection (1972, 1973, 1976, and 1980).
- Inducted into Astros Hall of Fame in 2020.

7

JOSÉ CRUZ

alled "one of the best and most underrated players I have ever seen" by Hall of Fame second baseman Joe Morgan, José Cruz spent 13 seasons in Houston serving as a regular member of the Astros' starting outfield. The team's primary starter in left field from 1979 to 1987, Cruz established himself as the finest player ever to man that post for the Astros by batting over .300 six times, stealing more than 30 bases five times, and leading all players at his position in putouts on five separate occasions. A two-time NL All-Star who also earned three top-10 finishes in the league MVP voting and one *Sporting News* All-Star nomination, Cruz ranks among the franchise's all-time leaders in virtually every offensive category, with his outstanding all-around play and tremendous popularity with the hometown fans, prompting the Astros to retire his #25 and induct him into their Hall of Fame. And, following the conclusion of his playing career, Cruz returned to Houston, where he has spent the last 27 years serving the organization in one capacity or another.

Born in Arroyo, Puerto Rico, on August 8, 1947, José Cruz first began to display his athletic prowess at Arroyo High School, where he excelled in baseball, softball, basketball, and track. Particularly proficient on the diamond, Cruz performed so well that the St. Louis Cardinals signed him right out of high school, after which he spent most of the next five seasons advancing through their farm system.

Finally arriving in the majors to stay in 1971 after appearing in six games with the Cardinals the previous season, Cruz acquitted himself extremely well in his first extended tour of duty at the big-league level, batting .274, hitting nine homers, driving in 27 runs, and scoring 46 times in 83 games and 292 official at-bats. However, after Cruz struggled somewhat in a part-time role the next three seasons, the Cardinals sold him to the Astros on October 24, 1974.

Cruz subsequently spent his first season in Houston sharing playing time with Greg Gross and Wilbur Howard, batting .257, hitting nine

José Cruz batted over .300 six times for the Astros.

homers, knocking in 49 runs, and scoring 44 others in 120 games and 377 total plate appearances, before becoming a regular member of the starting lineup in 1976, when he batted .303, hit four homers, knocked in 61 runs, scored 49 times, and stole 28 bases, while splitting his time between all three outfield positions. The Astros' full-time starter in right field in both 1977 and 1978, Cruz earned team MVP honors for the first of four times by hitting 17 homers, driving in 87 runs, scoring 87 times, batting .299, compiling an OPS of .843, and ranking among the NL leaders with 10 triples and 44 stolen bases in the first of those campaigns, before finishing third in the league with a .315 batting average, hitting 10 homers, knocking in 83 runs, scoring 79 times, and swiping 37 bags in the second.

An excellent line-drive hitter who drove the ball well to all fields, the left-handed-swinging Cruz, who stood 6 feet and weighed close to 180 pounds, employed a rather unusual batting stance in which he held his hands high and kicked his front leg high in the air before each swing. Specializing in hitting the ball to the opposite field, Cruz proved to be one of the league's more difficult men to strike out, fanning more than 70 times in a season just three times over the course of his career.

Recalling his former teammate's approach at the plate, Bob Watson said, "He had the knack for being able to put the bat on the ball. They would bring in side-arming left-handers and he'd go up there and stroke the ball the opposite way. If they would hang a breaking ball, he'd hit it out of the ballpark. He was one of the better hitters I've seen."

Although Cruz never hit more than 17 home runs in a season, he had the ability to deliver the long ball, with the cavernous Astrodome greatly impacting his power and run-production totals, as Larry Dierker suggested when he stated, "His offensive numbers are not even as good as they should be because of the Astrodome. He'd have more home runs, more RBIs, more runs scored—more everything—if he'd played in a more normal ballpark."

Admitting that his home ballpark forced him to alter his style of hitting, Cruz revealed that he rarely tried to pull the ball because the Dome "wasn't a place for home runs."

A consummate team player, Cruz also frequently sacrificed his personal statistics to advance runners on the basepaths, saying, "I always play for the team."

Cruz's talent, team-first mentality, and colorful personality, which earned him the nickname "Cheo," made him a fan favorite, with the patrons in attendance at the Astrodome chiming in every time he stepped to the plate to hear public-address announcer J. Fred Duckett introduce him thusly: "Now batting, the left fielder, number 25, Jose Cruuuuuuuuuuuuuuz."

Moved to left field permanently in 1979, Cruz began a nine-year stint during which he played some of the best ball of his career. Performing especially well in 1980, and from 1983 to 1985, Cruz posted the following numbers those four seasons:

YEAR	HR	RBI	RUNS	AVG	OBP	SLG	OPS
1980	11	91	79	.302	.360	.426	.787
1983	14	92	85	.318	.385	.463	.848
1984	12	95	96	.312	.381	.462	.842
1985	9	79	69	.300	.349	.426	.776

An NL All-Star in both 1980 and 1985, Cruz also earned three top-10 finishes in the league MVP voting, placing as high as third in 1980, when he helped lead the Astros to their first division title. A Silver Slugger award winner in both 1983 and 1984, Cruz led the league with 189 hits and finished third in the circuit in batting average in the first of those campaigns, before ranking among the NL leaders in batting average, on-base percentage, RBIs, runs scored, hits (187), triples (13), and total bases (277) in the second. Meanwhile, Cruz continued to excel in the field and on the basepaths, leading all NL left fielders in putouts five straight times, while also stealing more than 30 bases on three separate occasions.

Maintaining a high level of performance well into his 30s, Cruz managed to do so largely because he kept himself in tremendous physical condition. Blessed with the body of a much younger man according to Astros manager Bob Lillis, Cruz arrived at spring training each year in top shape after spending each offseason competing in the Puerto Rican winter league.

Cruz ranks among the Astros career leaders in virtually every major statistical category.
Courtesy of RMYAuctions.

In discussing his offseason regimen, Cruz said, "I've been playing winter ball for 15 years. Then I take two or three weeks off, and I don't even need spring training."

Cruz's age finally began to catch up with him, though, in 1987, when, garnering only 365 official at-bats in 126 games, he batted just .241, knocked in only 38 runs, and scored just 37 times. With the Astros choosing not to renew Cruz's contract at the end of the year, he signed with the Yankees as a free agent. Cruz, who left Houston as the franchise's all-time leader in games played (1,870), hits (1,937), RBIs (942), and triples (80), also hit 138 homers, scored 871 runs, collected 335 doubles, stole 288 bases, batted .292, compiled an on-base percentage of .359, and posted a slugging percentage of .429 as a member of the Astros.

Cruz ended up spending the first half of the 1988 campaign assuming a backup role in New York, batting just .200 in 80 official at-bats, before announcing his retirement when the Yankees released him on July 22.

In evaluating Cruz's impact on the game shortly thereafter, Puerto Rican baseball writer/historian Edwin Kako Vasquez called him a "great natural ballplayer" and stated that he had many fine attributes, the best of which were "his good character, his great friendship, and the fact that he was always ready, always prepared."

Following his retirement as an active player, Cruz spent nearly a decade managing in both the Texas-Louisiana League and the Puerto Rican Winter League, before returning to Houston as the Astros first base coach in 1997. After fulfilling that role for 13 seasons, Cruz moved into the front office as a special assistant to the general manager in 2010. Cruz remained in that post until 2014, when the Astros appointed him a community outreach executive—a position he currently holds.

ASTROS CAREER HIGHLIGHTS

Best Season

Cruz had some of his finest seasons for the Astros from 1977 to 1980, batting over .300 and posting an OPS over .800 twice each, while also stealing more than 35 bases each year. But Cruz earned *Sporting News* NL All-Star honors for the only time in 1984, when he hit 12 homers, stole 22 bases, batted .312, compiled an OPS of .842, and established career-high marks with 95 RBIs, 96 runs scored, 13 triples, 73 walks, and 277 total bases.

Memorable Moments/Greatest Performances

Cruz helped lead the Astros to a 14–12 win over the Cubs on August 23, 1975, by driving in five runs with a homer, double, and single, delivering the game's big blow in the top of the eighth inning when he homered with two men on base.

Cruz contributed to a lopsided 13–0 victory over the Braves on May 20, 1978, by going 4-for-5, with a homer, six RBIs, and three runs scored.

Cruz gave the Astros a 2–1 win over the Phillies on July 17, 1978, when he led off the bottom of the 11th inning with a home run off reliever Rawly Eastwick.

Cruz came up big in the clutch again on September 10, 1980, when his solo homer off Rick Sutcliffe in the bottom of the 12th inning gave the Astros a 6–5 win over the Dodgers.

Cruz led the Astros to a 9–1 mauling of the Reds on August 15, 1983, by homering twice and driving in five runs.

Cruz again homered twice and knocked in five runs during a 6–1 win over the Reds on September 17, 1986.

Cruz helped lead the Astros to a 7–3 victory over the Giants on August 11, 1987, by driving in four runs with a single and a pair of homers.

Notable Achievements

- Batted over .300 six times.
- Finished in double digits in triples twice.
- Surpassed 30 doubles four times.
- Stole more than 20 bases eight times, topping 30 thefts on five occasions.
- Led NL in hits once and sacrifice flies twice.
- Finished third in NL in batting average twice and triples once.
- Led NL left fielders in putouts five times and double plays three times.
- Holds Astros career record for most triples (80).
- Ranks among Astros career leaders in home runs (11th), RBIs (4th), runs scored (6th), batting average (9th), hits (4th), extra-base hits (6th), doubles (6th), total bases (5th), stolen bases (4th), bases on balls (5th), sacrifice flies (3rd), games played (3rd), plate appearances (3rd), and at-bats (3rd).
- Two-time division champion (1980 and 1986).
- Three-time NL Player of the Week.
- July 1984 NL Player of the Month.

- Four-time Astros team MVP (1977, 1980, 1983, and 1984).
- Two-time Silver Slugger Award winner (1983 and 1984).
- Finished in top 10 of NL MVP voting three times, placing as high as third in 1980.
- Two-time NL All-Star selection (1980 and 1985).
- 1984 *Sporting News* NL All-Star selection.
- #25 retired by Astros.
- Inducted into Astros Hall of Fame in 2019.

8

JIM WYNN

Although playing his home games in the cavernous Astrodome prevented him from compiling the power numbers he likely would have posted almost anywhere else, Jim Wynn proved to be one of the National League's top sluggers for much of his career. Nicknamed the "Toy Cannon" for his compact build and tremendous power at the plate, Wynn hit more than 30 homers twice and slugged more than 20 round-trippers five other times during his 11 seasons in Houston, while also driving in more than 100 runs once and surpassing 100 runs scored on three separate occasions. More than just a home-run hitter, Wynn also possessed superior running speed and a keen batting eye, stealing more than 20 bases and drawing more than 100 bases on balls three times each. A solid defender as well, Wynn led all NL outfielders in putouts, assists, and double plays turned twice each, with his strong all-around play earning him one trip to the All-Star Game and one *Sporting News* NL All-Star selection. Continuing to perform well after he left Houston, Wynn earned two more All-Star nominations and one top-five finish in the NL MVP voting, before being further honored following the conclusion of his playing career by having his #24 retired by the Astros and being inducted into the team's Hall of Fame.

Born in Hamilton, Ohio, on March 12, 1942, James Sherman Wynn grew up with his six younger siblings some 30 miles south, in a Cincinnati home located so close to Crosley Field that he remembered years later watching some of the Reds players walking past his house on their way to or from the ballpark. The son of a sanitation worker and a "stay-at-home mom," Wynn acquired his love of baseball from his father, Joseph Wynn, a former semipro player.

Recalling the influence that his dad had on him during his formative years, Wynn said, "My father made me the kind of hitter I am. I was a shortstop when I was a boy growing up in Cincinnati, and my father saw me as an Ernie Banks type—a good fielder who could hit home runs. He threw baseball after baseball at me, and when he got tired, he took me out

Jim Wynn's compact build and tremendous power at
the plate earned him the nickname "Toy Cannon."

to a place near the airport where they had pitching machines. I developed
the timing and the strong hands and wrists you need to hit homers."

Some years later, Wynn wrote in his autobiography, *Toy Cannon*, that
his father told him, "Jimmy, if you want to drive a Chevy someday, you will
need to become really good at hitting singles. If, on the other hand, you
hope to drive a Cadillac in the future, you will need to become very good
at hitting home runs."

An outstanding all-around athlete, Wynn starred in multiple sports at
Robert A. Taft High School, excelling in baseball, basketball, and football,
while also running cross-country. Offered a contract by the Reds shortly
after he graduated in 1960, Wynn, at his mother's insistence, instead
enrolled at Central State University in Wilberforce, Ohio, where he
remained for close to two years, before signing with the Reds early in 1962,
just before his 20th birthday. But when Cincinnati left Wynn unprotected

in that year's Winter Draft, the Houston Colt .45s swept in and plucked him from the Reds organization.

Called up to the major leagues just a few months later after hitting 16 home runs and batting .288 in 78 games with Double-A San Antonio in the Texas League, Wynn, who split his time in the minors between shortstop and third base, soon found himself starting in left field for the Colt .45s, although he also saw some action in center and at shortstop. Still only 21 years old, Wynn batted .244, hit four homers, and knocked in 27 runs, in 70 games and 286 plate appearances. Moved to the outfield full-time the following year, Wynn split the season between Houston and Triple-A Oklahoma City, for whom he hit 10 homers and batted .273. Far less successful in his 67 games with the parent club, Wynn batted just .224, hit only five homers, and knocked in just 18 runs, while also striking out 58 times in 248 total plate appearances.

Finally starting to fulfill his enormous potential after being named the Astros' starting center fielder in 1965, Wynn led the team with 22 homers and 73 RBIs, scored 90 runs, batted .275, compiled an OPS of .841, finished third in the league with 43 stolen bases (in 47 attempts), and led all players at his position with 384 putouts and 13 assists. With Wynn performing so well at the bat, in the field, and on the basepaths, he began to draw cautious, if somewhat unfavorable, comparisons to the NL's premier center fielder, Willie Mays, with one writer commenting, "Men will die waiting for another Willie Mays to come along, and Wynn isn't the one they're waiting for. But he's only 24, and he can do everything nicely. For a few years after Willie packs it in, Wynn may be the not-too-inferior substitute."

Wynn continued to establish himself as one of the NL's better all-around players over the first four months of the 1966 season, hitting 18 homers, driving in 62 runs, scoring 62 others, batting .256, and compiling an OPS of .761, before breaking his left wrist and elbow when he crashed into the center field wall at Philadelphia's Connie Mack Stadium on August 1 while trying to run down a drive hit by Dick Allen. Fully recovered by the start of the 1967 campaign, Wynn began an outstanding four-year run during which he posted the following numbers:

YEAR	HR	RBI	RUNS	AVG	OBP	SLG	OPS
1967	37	107	102	.249	.331	.495	.826
1968	26	67	85	.269	.376	.474	.850
1969	33	87	113	.269	.436	.507	.943
1970	27	88	82	.282	.394	.493	.886

After finishing second in the NL to Hank Aaron in homers in 1967, Wynn ranked among the league leaders in that category in each of the next two seasons as well. He also consistently placed near the top of the league rankings in runs scored, on-base percentage, slugging percentage, and walks, leading all NL batters with 148 bases on balls in 1969. An NL All-Star in 1967, Wynn also placed 11th in the league MVP voting, even though the Astros finished ninth in the standings, 32½ games behind the pennant-winning Cardinals.

With Wynn representing the Astros' only true power threat, teammate Joe Morgan commented at one point during the 1969 season, "Jim never sees a fastball anymore. They throw him breaking balls down and away all the time. If we had someone who could hit even 15 home runs batting fourth, the pitchers would have to give Jim at least one pitch to hit."

The right-handed-hitting Wynn, who stood just 5'9" and spent most of his career playing at about 170 pounds, possessed as much power as anyone in the game despite his rather smallish frame. Strengthened by offseason weightlifting sessions, Wynn used his muscular shoulders, arms, and legs to reach the seats by driving up and through the ball. Known for his tape-measure home runs, Wynn delivered a blast on June 10, 1967, at Crosley Field that cleared the 58-foot scoreboard in left-center field and landed on Interstate 75 outside the stadium. A month later, he hit a home run against the Pirates at Forbes Field that cleared that stadium's center field wall that stood 457 feet from home plate. And on April 12, 1970, Wynn became the first player to hit a home run into the upper deck of the Astrodome when he sent a pitch more than 500 feet down the left field line.

Marveling at his former teammate's prodigious power, Norm Miller said, "I'm a little bigger than him, and I had some strength, and I would have to stand on second base to hit a ball that far. Jimmy never hit a cheap home run. . . . He hit balls so far it was remarkable. He's the greatest guy in the world and pound-for-pound could hit the ball farther than anybody I've seen in my life."

Longtime Astros teammate Bob Aspromonte commented, "Jimmy had such power. He had that incredible upward swing. He brought the bat through with such speed and quickness. We used to laugh all the time about how his hits went into the stands and mine died at the warning track. He had such ability and such talent, and he handled himself so well off the field."

In discussing Wynn, former Astros pitcher Larry Dierker said, "He was a smaller version of Willie Mays. He had the same gait. He had the same uppercut swing and the same uniform number. He could run, and he could dunk a basketball. He could do extraordinary things on the field."

Yet, despite Wynn's outstanding offensive production, Astros manager Harry Walker, who some considered to be racist, objected to his style of hitting. A slap hitter during his playing days, Walker found fault with Wynn's approach at the plate, which typically resulted in rather mediocre batting averages and high strikeout totals. Choosing not to discuss Wynn's mammoth home runs with reporters, Walker said, "If he hits a home run that goes 450 feet and we all start to talk about it, then he'll start to think

Despite playing half his games in the Astrodome, Wynn hit more than 30 home runs twice.
Courtesy of RMYAuctions.com

that he should try to hit a 470-foot home run. When he tries to hit that 470-foot home run, he won't hit the ball 400 feet."

Recalling his differences with Walker, Wynn stated, "He kept telling me I'd hit .300 if I just choked up on the bat, went to the opposite field, and concentrated on average. No way. My swing was already grooved. I didn't get all those home runs being a Punch-and-Judy hitter. I guess when you're short, managers have a tendency to mess with you more."

Wynn continued, "Harry took things into his own hands, where he tried to change me from being what I was to what he wanted me to be. I couldn't do that. I rebelled; I rebelled a great deal. There was no name-calling or anything like that; it was just me doing what I wanted to do and not what he wanted me to do."

With Wynn already at odds with Walker, he found himself being further distracted in 1971 after he and his wife engaged in an offseason altercation that resulted in him being stabbed in the stomach with a kitchen knife. Although Wynn later downplayed the severity of his injury, he underwent abdominal surgery and divorced his wife shortly thereafter, causing him to stumble through the 1971 campaign. Spending much of his time thinking of his two children after moving to right field to make room for César Cedeño in center, Wynn hit just seven homers, knocked in only 45 runs, and batted just .203, later admitting, "I can honestly say that I never before felt less like playing ball or doing anything good for myself than I did that year."

Rebounding nicely in 1972, Wynn hit 24 homers, knocked in 90 runs, placed near the top of the league rankings with 117 runs scored, 103 walks, and a .389 on-base percentage, batted .273, and compiled an OPS of .860. But, after being moved up to the leadoff spot in the batting order by new Astros manager Leo Durocher in 1973, Wynn, who thought of himself as a middle-of-the-order hitter, slumped to 20 homers, 55 RBIs, 90 runs scored, and a .220 batting average.

Dealt to the Los Angeles Dodgers the following offseason for pitcher Claude Osteen and a minor leaguer, Wynn, who left Houston with career totals of 223 homers, 719 RBIs, 829 runs scored, 1,291 hits, 228 doubles, 32 triples, and 180 stolen bases, a .255 batting average, a .362 on-base percentage, and a .445 slugging percentage, helped his new team win the NL pennant in 1974 by batting .271 and ranking among the league leaders with 32 homers, 108 RBIs, 104 runs scored, and 108 walks, earning his second All-Star selection and a fifth-place finish in the NL MVP balloting. After one more year in Los Angeles, Wynn moved on to Atlanta, where he hit 17 homers, knocked in 66 runs, and batted .207 for the Braves in 1977, before splitting the ensuing campaign between the Yankees and Milwaukee Brewers. Released by the Brewers at the end of 1977, Wynn announced his retirement, ending his career with 291 homers, 964 RBIs, 1,105 runs scored, 1,665 hits, 285 doubles, 39 triples, 225 stolen bases, 1,224 walks, 1,427 strikeouts, a .250 batting average, a .366 on-base percentage, and a .436 slugging percentage.

After initially settling in Los Angeles following his playing days, Wynn eventually returned to Houston, where he first worked as a bartender in a Black social club, before becoming a member of the Astros community relations department in 1988. Retaining his position within the organization for more than two decades, Wynn spent most of his time speaking with children and adults throughout the city on the virtues of hard work, getting an education, and staying away from drugs.

After having his #24 retired by the Astros in 2005 and being inducted into the team's Hall of Fame 14 years later, Wynn died from unspecified causes at the age of 78 on March 26, 2020. Following his passing, the Astros issued a statement that read: "Jimmy's success on the field helped build our franchise from its beginnings. After his retirement, his tireless work in the community impacted thousands of young people in Houston. His legacy will live on at Minute Maid Park, at the Astros Youth Academy, and beyond."

Looking back on the career of his longtime Astros roommate some years earlier, Joe Morgan said, "He was a true five-tool player. He had the power to hit 37 home runs in a season while playing in the Astrodome, and one year he stole 43 bases and was caught four times. He could run the ball down in the outfield, he had a great arm, and if he could have gone to a winning team like I did, I think he could have made the Hall of Fame. There would have been nothing to stop him."

ASTROS CAREER HIGHLIGHTS

Best Season

Although Wynn hit more homers (37) and knocked in more runs (107) in 1967, compiled a higher batting average (.282) in 1970, and scored more runs (117) in 1972, he had his finest all-around season for the Astros in 1969, when he hit 33 homers, knocked in 87 runs, scored 113 times, stole 23 bases, batted .269, led the NL with 148 walks, and posted an OPS of .943 that represented the highest mark of his career.

Memorable Moments/Greatest Performances

Wynn gave the Astros a 6–3 victory over the Cardinals on June 26, 1966, when he homered off ace reliever Joe Hoerner with two men on base in the bottom of the ninth inning.

Wynn led the Astros to a 6–2 win over the Giants on June 15, 1967, by hitting three solo home runs, reaching the seats twice against right-hander Bob Bolin and once against lefty Bill Henry.

Wynn helped the Astros complete a doubleheader sweep of the Mets on July 30, 1967, by homering twice and driving in a career-high six runs during their 9–1 win in Game 2.

Wynn knocked in all three runs the Astros scored during their 3–1 win over the Giants on May 2, 1969, with a pair of homers off Gaylord Perry.

Wynn led the Astros to a 9–5 win over the Mets on August 30, 1970, by hitting two home runs off Nolan Ryan, singling twice, and driving in five runs.

Wynn contributed to a 15–11 victory over the Dodgers on September 17, 1972, by going 4-for-5, with a triple, double, three RBIs, and four runs scored.

After homering earlier in the contest, Wynn delivered the decisive blow of a 7–6 win over the Phillies on July 12, 1973, when he hit a solo home run off Barry Lersch in the top of the ninth inning.

Notable Achievements

- Hit at least 20 home runs seven times, topping 30 homers twice.
- Knocked in more than 100 runs once (107 in 1967).
- Scored more than 100 runs three times.
- Surpassed 30 doubles twice.
- Stole more than 20 bases three times, topping 40 thefts once (43 in 1965).
- Drew more than 100 bases on balls three times.
- Compiled on-base percentage over .400 once (.436 in 1969).
- Posted slugging percentage over .500 once (.507 in 1969).
- Posted OPS over .900 once (.943 in 1969).
- Hit three home runs in one game vs. San Francisco on June 15, 1967.
- Led NL with 148 walks in 1969.
- Finished second in NL in home runs once, walks twice, and on-base percentage once.

- Led NL outfielders in putouts twice, assists once, and double plays turned twice.
- Ranks among Astros career leaders in home runs (4th), RBIs (8th), runs scored (7th), hits (9th), extra-base hits (7th), doubles (9th), total bases (7th), bases on balls (4th), sacrifice flies (7th), games played (8th), plate appearances (7th), and at-bats (7th).
- 1967 NL All-Star selection.
- 1967 *Sporting News* NL All-Star selection.
- #24 retired by Astros.
- Inducted into Astros Hall of Fame in 2019.

9

JOE NIEKRO

One of the most durable and productive pitchers of his era, Joe Niekro spent 11 of his 22 big-league seasons in Houston, winning more games during that time than any other hurler in franchise history. The first Astros pitcher to win 20 games in a season twice, Niekro surpassed 15 victories on five separate occasions, while also compiling an ERA under 3.00 twice and throwing more than 250 innings four times. A key contributor to Houston's 1980 division-winning ballclub, Niekro earned one NL All-Star selection, one runner-up finish in the Cy Young voting, and one *Sporting News* NL Pitcher of the Year nomination, before being further honored following the conclusion of his playing career by being inducted into the Astros Hall of Fame. Yet, to this day, many people think of him as the little brother of Hall of Fame pitcher Phil Niekro, with whom he combined to win a total of 539 games that represents a major-league record for siblings that likely will never be broken.

Born in Martins Ferry, Ohio, on November 7, 1944, Joseph Franklin Niekro grew up in nearby Lansing, a small town located in the Upper Ohio Valley, where, as he recalled, "There wasn't that much to do. There was no TV, but we did have a radio. Of course, we played ball all the time."

The son of Polish immigrants who settled in the coal mining region along the Ohio River, young Joseph acquired his love of baseball from his father, a former semiprofessional pitcher who taught his two sons how to throw the knuckleball. After establishing himself as a star pitcher at Bridgeport High School, Niekro continued to excel on the mound at West Liberty University, in West Virginia, where he earned All-America honors.

Selected by the Cleveland Indians in the seventh round of the 1966 MLB January Draft, Niekro chose to remain in school until five months later, when the Chicago Cubs claimed him in the third round in the Secondary Phase of the draft. Niekro subsequently spent less than one full year in the minor leagues, before joining the Cubs early in 1967. Performing

Joe Niekro won more games than any other pitcher in team annals.

well in his first big-league season, Niekro compiled a record of 10-7 and an ERA of 3.34, before going 14-10 with an ERA of 4.31 the following year.

However, when Niekro got off to a slow start in 1969, the Cubs traded him to the San Diego Padres, for whom he posted a mark of 8-17 and an ERA of 3.70 in his lone season on the West Coast. Dealt to the Tigers at the end of the year, Niekro spent most of the next three seasons toiling in mediocrity in Detroit, while splitting his time between starting and reliev-ing. Released by the Tigers in August 1973, Niekro subsequently joined his brother Phil in Atlanta when the Braves claimed him off waivers.

Working almost exclusively out of the bullpen for the Braves in 1973 and 1974, Niekro compiled an overall record of 5-6 and saved just three games. While in Atlanta, though, Joe received advice from his brother, who, after working with him on the knuckleball, convinced him to make it his primary offering. Predominantly a fastball-curveball-slider pitcher up until that point, Joe threw much harder than his brother. But, since entering the majors several years earlier, he had lost some of the velocity on his fastball, making him much more hittable.

Taking his brother's advice, the right-handed-throwing Niekro, who stood 6'1" and weighed 190 pounds, altered his approach on the mound after the Astros purchased him from the Braves for $35,000 just prior to the start of the 1975 campaign. Working mostly out of the bullpen his first two seasons in Houston, Niekro compiled an overall record of 10-12, posted a composite ERA of 3.23, and saved four games for the Astros from 1975 to 1976. After gradually working his way into the starting rotation in 1977, Niekro finished the season with a record of 13-8, an ERA of 3.04, a WHIP of 1.212, 180⅔ innings pitched, nine complete games, and two shutouts.

A full-time starter in 1978, Niekro went 14-14, with a 3.86 ERA, a WHIP of 1.298, 10 complete games, one shutout, and 97 strikeouts in 202⅔ innings of work, before emerging as one of the NL's best pitchers the following year, when he earned All-Star honors and a runner-up finish to Chicago reliever Bruce Sutter in the Cy Young voting by compiling a record of 21-11, an ERA of 3.00, and a WHIP of 1.244, tossing 11 complete games, leading the league with five shutouts, and finishing third in the circuit with 263⅔ innings pitched.

Although Niekro continued to throw the fastball, slider, and changeup, Astros catcher Alan Ashby credited his improved pitching to his increased use of the knuckleball. But Ashby also suggested, "I think having been a fastball-slider pitcher worked to his advantage. It gave him something to fall back on when his knuckleball wasn't at its sharpest."

Meanwhile, former Astros GM Tal Smith later claimed that the organization's patience with Niekro allowed him to develop into a top pitcher, stating, "He was 30 when he came here, and this was his fifth club. He was, at best, a journeyman pitcher. We gave him the time it took to perfect the pitch. It's a great example of believing in people and giving them time to get better. From that standpoint, the fact that we were not a club in contention in 1975 or '76 or '77 gave us a chance to let guys develop."

Continuing to perform at an elite level in 1980, Niekro helped the Astros capture their first division title by going 20-12, with an ERA of 3.55, 11 complete games, two shutouts, and 127 strikeouts in 256 innings of work, earning a fourth-place finish in the NL Cy Young balloting. After subsequently compiling a record of 9-9 and an ERA of 2.82 during the strike-shortened 1981 campaign, Niekro had one of his finest statistical seasons in 1982, when he finished 17-12, with a 2.47 ERA, 16 complete games, five shutouts, and 130 strikeouts in 270 innings pitched.

Despite turning 38 years of age the following offseason, Niekro had two more good years for the Astros, going 15-14, with a 3.48 ERA and a career-high 152 strikeouts in 1983, before compiling a record of 16-12 and an ERA of 3.04 in 1984. But after Niekro won just nine of his 21 decisions and posted an ERA of 3.72 through the first few months of the 1985 campaign, the Astros traded him to the Yankees for three minor leaguers in mid-September. Niekro, who left Houston having compiled a record of 144-116, an ERA of 3.22, and a WHIP of 1.264, thrown 82 complete games and 21 shutouts, collected nine saves, and registered 1,178 strikeouts in 2,270 innings of work as a member of the Astros, subsequently split his final three big-league seasons between the Yankees and Minnesota Twins, before announcing his retirement at the end of 1988 with a career record of 221-204, an ERA of 3.59, a WHIP of 1.319, 107 complete games, 29 shutouts, 16 saves, 1,747 strikeouts, and 3,584⅓ innings pitched. Before

Niekro earned *Sporting News* NL Pitcher of the Year honors in 1979.

retiring, though, Niekro suffered the embarrassment of being suspended by the American League for 10 games in 1987 after umpires found a nail file in his back pocket that he claimed he put there by mistake.

Following his playing days, Niekro spent much of his time helping his son, Lance, who eventually spent parts of four seasons playing first base for the San Francisco Giants, develop his skills on the diamond, serving as pitching coach on many of his youth league teams, and even helping out on the coaching staff at Florida Southern during Lance's college days. Niekro also briefly coached for the Minnesota Twins and Colorado Rockies, before dying at the age of 61 on October 27, 2006, after suffering a brain aneurysm.

Upon learning of his former batterymate's passing, Alan Ashby stated, "In my opinion, he was the heart and soul of the pitching staffs of those teams in the 1970s and '80s. This was a complete shock to hear about Joe. He was way too young and way too full of life."

Former Astros teammate Larry Dierker said, "He was, really, in many ways the ultimate ballplayer. He seemed to fit into the baseball life better than just about anyone I knew. Plus, he was pretty darn good at it; a good athlete and a good pitcher."

Then-Astros president Tal Smith, who served as the team's general manager from 1975 to 1980, also had high praise for Niekro, saying, "Obviously, Knucksie was an accomplished pitcher, but he was a super guy, everybody loved him. He had a great sense of humor and was the life of the party. He always had a quip or a needle and had the talent of keeping people loose. I truly never heard anything disparaging about Joe. If you didn't like him, you didn't like people."

Smith then added, "And he was the consummate winner. . . . He played a very prominent role in our first trip to the playoffs. He was very popular with our fans, and he was truly one of our all-time greats."

ASTROS CAREER HIGHLIGHTS

Best Season

It could be argued that Niekro pitched his best ball for the Astros in 1982, when, en route to compiling a record of 17-12, he established career-best marks in ERA (2.47), WHIP (1.067), complete games (16), and innings pitched (270). Nevertheless, Niekro received far more acclaim in 1979, when he earned his lone All-Star nomination, a runner-up finish in the NL

Cy Young voting, and a sixth-place finish in the MVP balloting by leading the league with 21 wins and five shutouts, posting an ERA of 3.00 and a WHIP of 1.244, and throwing 11 complete games and 263⅔ innings.

Memorable Moments/Greatest Performances

Niekro earned a 4–3 victory over the Braves on May 29, 1976, by allowing just four hits and one earned run in eight innings of work, while also hitting the only home run of his career off brother Phil in the seventh inning.

Niekro worked all 11 innings of a 2–1 win over the Phillies on July 17, 1978, allowing five hits, issuing three walks, and recording eight strikeouts.

Niekro yielded just two hits and two walks in earning a complete-game 4–1 win over the Giants on July 31, 1978.

Niekro turned in arguably the most memorable performance of his career in the Astros' one-game playoff with the Dodgers to determine the NL West champion in 1980, earning his 20th victory of the year by allowing six hits and no earned runs during a complete-game 7–1 win.

Niekro followed that up with another brilliant outing, yielding six hits over the first 10 innings of a 1–0, 11-inning victory over the Phillies in Game 3 of the NLCS.

Niekro shut out the Dodgers on just two hits on September 18, 1982, surrendering just a pair of harmless singles by Derrel Thomas and Ron Cey during a 2–0 Astros win.

Niekro threw 28 consecutive scoreless innings from June 3 to June 18, 1983, a period during which he nevertheless posted just one victory due to poor run support from his teammates.

Niekro tossed a three-hit shutout on July 14, 1983, walking no one and recording three strikeouts during a 3–0 win over the Montreal Expos.

Niekro surrendered just two hits during a 5–0 shutout of the Giants on June 9, 1985, yielding only singles by shortstop José Uribe and third baseman Bob Brenly.

Notable Achievements

- Won at least 15 games five times, topping 20 victories twice.
- Compiled ERA under 3.00 twice.
- Threw more than 250 innings four times.
- Threw 16 complete games in 1982.
- Led NL pitchers in wins once, shutouts once, putouts once, and starts twice.

- Finished second in NL in wins, ERA, WHIP, and shutouts once each.
- Holds Astros career record for most wins (144).
- Ranks among Astros career leaders in shutouts (tied for 2nd), innings pitched (2nd), complete games (2nd), strikeouts (8th), pitching appearances (4th), and games started (2nd).
- 1980 division champion.
- May 1979 NL Pitcher of the Month.
- Finished in top five of NL Cy Young voting twice, placing second in 1979.
- 1979 Astros team MVP.
- Finished sixth in 1979 NL MVP voting.
- 1979 NL All-Star selection.
- 1979 *Sporting News* NL All-Star selection.
- 1979 *Sporting News* NL Pitcher of the Year.
- Inducted into Astros Hall of Fame in 2019.

10

BOB WATSON

One of the National League's most consistent hitters for nearly a decade, Bob Watson spent parts of 14 seasons in Houston, proving to be one of the few bright spots on mostly mediocre teams. An everyday member of the Astros' starting lineup from 1971 to 1978, Watson batted over .300 four times, knocked in more than 100 runs twice, and hit more than 20 homers once, while splitting his time between first base and the outfield. A two-time NL All-Star who later received the additional honor of gaining induction into the Astros Hall of Fame, Watson continued to add to his impressive resumé after his playing career ended, becoming in 1996 the first African-American general manager to win a World Series championship.

Born in Los Angeles, California, on April 10, 1946, Robert Jose Watson grew up on the city's lower east side, in a neighborhood now known as South Central LA. Raised by his maternal grandparents after his mother and father divorced shortly after his birth, Watson began playing Little League Baseball at the age of eight, spending his first several years in the game manning the catcher's position. Always big for his age, Watson stood 6 feet tall and weighed 195 pounds by the time he turned 13, making him one of the most powerful hitters in the three different youth leagues in which he competed.

Excelling on the diamond at Fremont High School as well, Watson earned All-City honors his senior year, when he led his team to the City Championship. Nicknamed "Bull" in high school, Watson acquired the moniker that stayed with him throughout his playing career when, after head coach Phil Pote learned that he admired slugging San Francisco Giants first baseman, Orlando "Baby Bull" Cepeda, he told his star catcher, "You're too big to be a baby anything. So, we'll just call you 'Bull.'"

Following his graduation from Fremont High, Watson enrolled at Harbor Junior College in nearby Wilmington, where he earned All-Conference honors as a freshman by batting .371. Subsequently signed by Astros scout

Bob Watson proved to be one of the NL's most consistent hitters for much of the 1970s.

Karl Kuehl for $2,000, the 19-year-old Watson left his family and familiar surroundings and flew to Melbourne, Florida, where he joined his new team for spring training.

Eventually assigned to Houston's Class A affiliate in Salisbury, North Carolina, Watson experienced blatant racism for the first time in his life. Not allowed to stay at the same hotel as his white teammates, Watson spent several nights sleeping on a wooden bench in a Black-owned funeral parlor, before the Astros finally located a room for him in the home of a Black man who lived in the area. Forced to eat alone each night, Watson spent his

evenings listening to Motown music on a portable record player and studying the Astros' team manual, Ted Williams's book on hitting, and the Bible.

Despite the shabby treatment he received from the city and his teammates, none of whom showed any empathy toward him, Watson managed
to hit 12 homers, drive in 55 runs, and bat .421 in 80 games at Salisbury,
before breaking his left wrist and injuring his right shoulder in a collision
with an outfield wall. Choosing to enlist in the US Marine Corps reserves
while recuperating from his injuries, Watson spent the next three years
serving part-time in the military, eventually earning the rank of sergeant.
Meanwhile, Watson continued to advance through the Astros' farm system,
spending time with three different teams from 1966 to 1967, while also
appearing in a handful of games with the parent club at the end of each
season.

Summoned to Houston in June 1968 after he compiled a batting average of .395 at Triple-A Oklahoma City the first two months of the season,
Watson struggled during his first period of extended action at the major-
league level, batting just .229 in 45 games with the Astros, before sustaining another serious injury when he blew out his ankle while running the
bases. Returned to the minor leagues during the early stages of the ensuing
campaign to hone his catching skills, Watson seriously considered quitting
the game altogether when the organization reneged on its promise to recall
him to the majors in two weeks. But after being assured by Astros GM Spec
Richardson that he still figured prominently in the team's plans, Watson
decided to stay the course and finish out the season at Oklahoma City.

Finally joining the Astros for good in 1970, Watson spent the early part
of the season assuming a backup role, before laying claim to the starting
first base job in mid-June. Performing well the rest of the year, Watson hit
11 homers, knocked in 61 runs, batted .272, and compiled an OPS of .768,
in 97 games and 327 official at-bats. Watson subsequently saw a significant
amount of action at both first base and left field in 1971, when, appearing
in a total of 129 games, he hit nine homers, knocked in 67 runs, batted
.288, and posted an OPS of .742.

With the Astros acquiring slugging first baseman Lee May in a huge
trade with the Cincinnati Reds prior to the start of the ensuing campaign,
Watson moved to left field full-time, beginning a three-year stint during
which he manned that position almost exclusively. And with more regular
playing time, Watson developed into one of the NL's finest hitters, posting
the following numbers from 1972 to 1978:

YEAR	HR	RBI	RUNS	AVG	OBP	SLG	OPS
1972	16	86	74	.312	.378	.464	.841
1973	16	94	97	.312	.403	.449	.852
1974	11	67	69	.298	.370	.412	.782
1975	18	85	67	.324	.375	.495	.870
1976	16	102	76	.313	.377	.458	.835
1977	22	110	77	.289	.360	.498	.858
1978	14	79	51	.289	.357	.451	.808

Extremely consistent, the right-handed-hitting Watson, who gained All-Star recognition in both 1973 and 1975, never batted any lower than .289 throughout the period, finishing as high as fifth in the NL batting race on three separate occasions. Watson also placed in the league's top five in RBIs twice and doubles once, with his 38 two-baggers in 1977 representing his highest single-season total.

Although the 6-foot, 205-pound Watson possessed good power at the plate, he never developed into a top home-run threat, primarily because he adopted a hitting style similar to that of two-time NL batting champion and former teammate, Tommy Davis, who served as his mentor during the early stages of his big-league career. Attempting to drive the ball hard to the outfield gaps rather than swinging for the fences, Watson made consistently hard contact with the baseball, striking out more than 70 times in a season just twice in his career.

Commenting on the similarities between Watson and Davis, Hall of Fame outfielder Billy Williams said, "He's kind of like Tommy with that sort of stiff-armed swing. He's also strong like him and can muscle the ball out there for hits when he gets jammed by a pitch."

Revealing that he tried to employ the same philosophy at the plate as his mentor, Watson said, "I've tried to pattern myself after Tommy in his theories toward hitting, and that basically is to try to hit the ball back through the middle. . . . If it's a hard pitch, I'll hit it to right field. If it's a slow pitch, I'll pull it. When Tommy was with the club, I talked with him every chance I got."

Praising Watson for his approach at the plate at one point during the 1973 season, Astros coach Grady Hatton stated, "I keep saying he is going to lead this league in hitting. He has a perfect stroke. He seldom overswings and is always hitting down through the ball. . . . Bob doesn't try to pull the ball. He does try to put the ball in play wherever he can. He swings down on even the high pitch. He never uppercuts the ball. This is rare. Listen, Bob just doesn't have too many bad days with the bat."

Hatton added, "Nothing he has done has forced me to change my opinion. If he could run, I know he'd lead this league. His are legitimate hits. He gets nothing on bunts or leggers. He just goes up there and pops the ball."

After being moved back to first base in 1975, Watson remained in serious contention for the batting title until a broken knuckle on his little finger that he sustained during a racially motivated off-field confrontation with two white men who objected to the idea of him driving an expensive car forced him to miss the final three weeks of the campaign. Discussing the altercation afterwards, Watson said, "I let a racial incident get the best of me, and it cost me. . . . How much restraint, how much can one person take, is really the question."

Despite his involvement in the brawl, Watson was, by nature, a mild-mannered man whose calm demeanor often prevented some of his more hot-tempered teammates from engaging in skirmishes. Held in particularly high regard by the team's other African-American players, Watson drew praise from Enos Cabell, who said of his former teammate, "He kept me out of trouble. He didn't fight that often, and I liked to fight. He'd say, 'You can't do that.' I'd say, 'Oh, OK, I can't? Why?' He was always the stable one. Me, J.R. [Richard], and a few other people, we'd want to jump up and down, and Bull would say sit down. He hardly ever cussed. You know me, I'll say it. But Bull would not say it. He would just grab you and tell you to sit down. What are you going to do? You're going to sit down."

Off to a slow start in 1979, Watson batted just .239 through the first third of the season, prompting the Astros to trade him to the Boston Red Sox on June 13 for minor-league pitcher Pete Ladd, cash, and a player to be named later. Watson, who left Houston with career totals of 139 homers, 782 RBIs, 640 runs scored, 1,448 hits, 241 doubles, 30 triples, a .297 batting average, a .364 on-base percentage, and a .444 slugging percentage, ended up recapturing his stroke in Boston, finishing the year with 16 homers, 71 RBIs, and a .303 batting average.

A free agent at season's end, Watson signed with the Yankees, for whom he batted .307 in 1980, before slumping to .212 the following year. Dealt to the Braves during the early stages of the 1982 campaign, Watson spent the next three seasons assuming a part-time role in Atlanta, before announcing his retirement at the end of 1984 with career totals of 184 homers, 989 RBIs, 802 runs scored, 1,826 hits, 307 doubles, 41 triples, a .295 batting average, a .364 on-base percentage, and a .447 slugging percentage.

Watson batted over .300 four times for the Astros.

Remaining in the game following his retirement as an active player, Watson spent four seasons serving as hitting coach of the Oakland Athletics, before accepting the position of assistant general manager of the Astros in 1989. Promoted to GM in 1994, Watson remained in that post until the end of 1995, when George Steinbrenner offered him more money to run the Yankees. Watson served as GM of the Yankees for the next two seasons, a period during which they won their first World Series in 18 years. Handing in his resignation after the 1997 season, Watson subsequently served as MLB's vice president in charge of discipline and vice president of rules and on-field operations for several years, before retiring from baseball altogether in 2010.

Diagnosed with Stage 4 kidney disease in 2016, Watson chose not to try to extend his life by accepting kidney donations from his two children, later saying, "I've had a good life, and I didn't want to take a kidney from young people who really need them and still have their whole lives ahead of them. That would be very selfish on my part." Watson lived another four years, ultimately dying of kidney failure at the age of 74, on May 14, 2020.

Upon learning of his passing, the Astros released a statement that read: "This is a very sad day for the Astros and for all of baseball. Bob Watson enjoyed a unique and remarkable career in Major League Baseball that spanned six decades, reaching success at many different levels, including as a player, coach, general manager, and MLB executive. He was an All-Star on the field and a true pioneer off of it, admired and respected by everyone he played with or worked alongside. Bob will be missed, but not forgotten. . . . We send our heartfelt condolences to his wife, Carol, his daughter, Kelley, his son, Keith, and to the rest of his family, friends, and many admirers."

Remembering his friend as both a player and a man, Enos Cabell stated, "He was a great hitter, a great hitter. He used to swing a 42-ounce bat. They couldn't spell 42-ounce bat nowadays. His defense was so-so, but hitting was his deal, and he could teach it. He was very calm, collected. I don't think he ever raised his voice. He was just a nice guy. . . . He was just a gentleman."

Meanwhile, Keith Watson said of his father, "I can't think of a better role model that I could've had as a man and as a father. He consistently showed and shared and gave of himself, of his time, and of his resources. . . . I know that he would want people to know how proud he was to be affiliated with the city, affiliated with the Astros, and that he could've been anywhere in the world and raised our family anywhere, but he did it here."

ASTROS CAREER HIGHLIGHTS

Best Season

Watson performed extremely well in both 1976 and 1977, earning an 11th-place finish in the NL MVP voting in the first of those campaigns by hitting 16 homers and ranking among the league leaders with 102 RBIs, 183 hits, a .313 batting average, and a .377 on-base percentage, before batting .289 and establishing career-high marks with 22 home runs and 110 RBIs in the second. But Watson had probably his finest all-around season in 1973, when, en route to earning the first of his two All-Star nominations, he hit 16 homers, knocked in 94 runs, collected 179 hits, finished fifth in the league with a .312 batting average, compiled an OPS of .852, and reached career-highs in runs scored (97), walks (85), and on-base percentage (.403).

Memorable Moments/Greatest Performances

Watson led the Astros to a 10–5 win over the Dodgers on June 29, 1970, by driving in five runs with a homer, double, and single.

Watson delivered the big blow of a 10–5 victory over the Padres on September 7, 1970, when he homered with the bases loaded in the top of the sixth inning.

Watson contributed to a 14–8 win over the Mets on May 6, 1973, by going 4-for-5, with a homer, four RBIs, and three runs scored.

Watson attained a degree of immortality on May 4, 1975, when, in the second inning of an 8–6 loss to the Giants, he scored baseball's one-millionth run when he crossed home plate following a three-run homer by Milt May.

Watson starred in defeat on May 22, 1976, driving in five runs with a single and a pair of homers during a 6–5, 13-inning loss to the Dodgers.

Watson drove in all four runs the Astros scored during a 4–1 win over the Padres on July 27, 1976, with a homer and two singles.

Watson led the Astros to a 6–5 victory over the Giants on June 24, 1977, by hitting for the cycle, going a perfect 4-for-5, with five RBIs.

Notable Achievements

- Hit more than 20 home runs once (22 in 1977).
- Knocked in more than 100 runs twice.
- Batted over .300 four times.
- Surpassed 30 doubles twice.
- Compiled on-base percentage over .400 once (.403 in 1973).
- Hit for cycle vs. San Francisco on June 24, 1977.
- Led NL first basemen in assists once.
- Ranks among Astros career leaders in home runs (10th), RBIs (5th), runs scored (9th), batting average (tied for 4th), on-base percentage (tied for 11th), hits (7th), extra-base hits (9th), doubles (7th), total bases (8th), bases on balls (11th), sacrifice flies (5th), games played (9th), plate appearances (8th), and at-bats (8th).
- August 1, 1976, NL Player of the Week.
- Two-time NL Player of the Month.
- Two-time NL All-Star selection (1973 and 1975).
- Inducted into Astros Hall of Fame in 2020.

11

MIKE SCOTT

A hard-throwing right-hander whose mastery of the split-finger fastball helped save his career, Mike Scott spent parts of nine seasons in Houston, establishing himself as one of the finest pitchers in team annals after failing in an earlier stint with the New York Mets. The winner of at least 18 games three times, Scott also compiled an ERA under 3.00 twice, struck out more than 300 batters once, and threw more than 200 innings six times, earning three All-Star selections, one *Sporting News* NL Pitcher of the Year nomination, and one Cy Young Award. Also named MVP of the 1986 NLCS after helping to lead the Astros to their second division title during the regular season, Scott later received the additional honors of having his #33 retired by the organization and being inducted into the team's Hall of Fame.

Born in Santa Monica, California, on April 26, 1955, Michael Warren Scott grew up in the nearby town of Hawthorne, where he excelled in multiple sports while attending Hawthorne High School, stating during a 2002 interview with the *Astros Daily* website, "I played basketball as well as baseball. I liked basketball better, but thought I had a better chance to go further in baseball."

A team captain and all-league selection in both sports, Scott performed especially well on the diamond his senior year, when he compiled a 9-1 record and a 0.67 ERA. Nevertheless, Scott went undrafted by all 24 major-league teams and received just one scholarship offer, which came from Wayne Wright, the head baseball coach at Pepperdine University in Malibu, just a little farther up the Pacific coast from his hometown. Starring on the mound for the Waves the next three seasons, Scott compiled an overall record of 26-14 and an ERA of 2.10, setting then school records for wins, strikeouts, and innings pitched.

Selected by the Mets in the second round of the 1976 MLB Amateur Draft after his junior year, Scott subsequently spent most of the next five seasons in the minor leagues, although he appeared briefly with the Mets in

Mike Scott earned NL Cy Young honors in 1986.

both 1979 and 1980, failing to make much of an impression either time. In trying to explain his inability to stick with the parent club, Scott recalled, "I threw a fastball, a curveball, and a slider. The higher the level I went, the more I realized I needed an off-speed pitch."

Arriving in the majors to stay in 1981, Scott assumed the role of a back-end starter/occasional reliever the next two seasons, going a combined 12-23 with ERAs of 3.90 and 5.14, before being traded to the Astros for outfielder Danny Heep following the conclusion of the 1982 campaign. Looking back on Scott's tenure in New York, former Mets general manager

Frank Cashen said, "Scott was a nice young man, and he always had a good arm, but he was just trying to be mediocre."

Meanwhile, Scott stated, "I really didn't have any mentors with the Mets. . . . I probably needed a change. I wasn't going anywhere with the Mets. The change of scenery was a good thing."

Despite missing the first month of the 1983 season with shoulder tendinitis, Scott performed somewhat better in his first year in Houston, compiling a record of 10-6 and an ERA of 3.72. But he reverted to his earlier form the following year, going just 5-11 with a 4.68 ERA, prompting him to later say, "I didn't know if my career was over, but I did know it wasn't moving very fast."

Scott, who threw a 95-mph fastball that lacked movement and a well-below average curveball and slider, added, "Batters just sat back on my fastball and ripped it."

Urged by Astros general manager Al Rosen to meet with Roger Craig the following offseason, Scott became a different pitcher after Craig taught him the split-finger fastball he had made famous while serving as pitching coach in Detroit.

Recalling his sudden transformation, Scott said, "I spent a week in San Diego with Roger Craig for about an hour a day. . . . I didn't have any idea at the time that it was going to be the pitch it turned out to be. Then, one day in spring training, I was throwing it, and guys were suddenly swinging at balls that were bouncing in the dirt. That's when I said to myself, 'This could work out.'"

Armed with his new weapon, Scott compiled a record of 18-8, an ERA of 3.29, and a WHIP of 1.236 in 1985, while also striking out 137 batters in 221⅔ innings of work. Improving upon those numbers the following year, Scott earned his first All-Star nomination, NL Cy Young honors, and a 10th-place finish in the league MVP voting by going 18-10, with a league-leading 2.22 ERA, 0.923 WHIP, five shutouts, 306 strikeouts, and 275⅓ innings pitched.

Scott, who stood 6'2" and weighed 210 pounds, possessed large hands that allowed him to get a comfortable grip on the ball for better control. Typically delivering his favorite offering to home plate at a speed that registered somewhere between 84 and 88 mph on the radar gun, Scott threw the split-finger fastball at least 35 percent of the time, discovering that, with greater usage, it became increasingly effective. Scott also added a cut fastball to his repertoire of pitches in 1986, making him even harder to hit.

Commenting on the level of excellence Scott attained at one point during the 1986 campaign, Scott Ostler wrote in the *Los Angeles Times*,

"Mike Scott is the best pitcher in baseball right now. . . . This season, he is a monster."

Scott's batterymate, Alan Ashby, stated, "When Mike has his good stuff, guys just really look helpless. If every pitcher in the league masters that thing, you'll have batting titles won by guys hitting .210."

Recalling the dominance that Scott displayed on the mound, former Astros first baseman Glenn Davis said, "Sometimes I felt like I could drop my glove by my side and watch him pitch. I didn't have to get ready because he was going to dominate. For the most part, it was art in motion. He was just brilliant."

Scott's superb pitching in 1986 helped lead the Astros to the NL West title and a date with the Mets in the NLCS. Although the Astros ultimately fell to the New Yorkers in six games, Scott did all he could to send them to the World Series, earning series MVP honors by recording 19 strikeouts and allowing just eight hits and one run over 18 innings, en route to posting a pair of complete-game victories.

Baffling New York's lineup with his signature pitch in both his starts, Scott drew praise from Mets center fielder Len Dykstra, who said, "I've never seen anything like it in my life. It's like a Wiffle ball moving in the wind."

Mets first baseman Keith Hernandez said of Scott, "He paints. He's a Rembrandt. If everybody threw like that all the time, this game would never make it because it would just be too bleeping boring."

Looking back on his stellar performance, Scott chose to put the team before himself, saying, "The loss was extremely tough for the team, and nothing good came out of it."

Then, when asked about the popular notion that he would have defeated the Mets in a decisive seventh game had the series gone that far, Scott stated, "I've been asked that a hundred times, and who knows? I could've been knocked out in the first inning. You never know what's going to happen. There's no guarantee."

Scott continued to perform at an elite level the next three seasons, earning two more All-Star selections by compiling an overall record of 50-31, posting a composite ERA of 3.10, and averaging just under 200 strikeouts per season. Particularly outstanding in 1989, Scott earned a runner-up finish in the Cy Young voting by leading all NL hurlers with 20 victories (against 10 losses), compiling an ERA of 3.10, finishing third in the circuit with nine complete games and a WHIP of 1.057, and striking out 172 batters in 229 innings pitched.

Posting those numbers despite tearing his rotator cuff at one point during the season, Scott recalled, "The second half of 1989, I was done. I had a real good start in 1989. I won a lot of games before the All-Star game and barely hung on. I had a real good chance to win a lot more than 20 that year, but I just barely got there. I remember the 20th game was against LA, and my arm was just done."

Pitching through pain in 1990, Scott compiled a record of 9-13 and an ERA of 3.81, before undergoing arthroscopic surgery on his labrum the following offseason. Although Scott attempted to return to the mound in 1992, he appeared in only two games before it became clear that his pitching days were over. Officially announcing his retirement at the end of the year, Scott said, "The timing on this is good. I got to throw my last pitch as an Astro, and that's good, too. I would need an operation on my shoulder and be out a year and a half with little guarantees."

Scott, who ended his career with an overall record of 124-108, an ERA of 3.54, a WHIP of 1.201, 45 complete games, 22 shutouts, and 1,469 strikeouts in 2,068⅔ innings pitched, compiled a record of 110-81, a 3.30 ERA, and a 1.144 WHIP, threw 42 complete games and 21 shutouts, and struck out 1,318 batters in 1,704 innings of work as a member of the Astros.

Returning to his home state of California following his retirement, Scott invested heavily in the stock market, saying, "I tell people I'm a broker with one client—myself." He also played a lot of golf and began helping out with the baseball team at Aliso Niguel High School.

In discussing his longtime friend in 2014, former college teammate Pat Murphy said of Scott, "He had a quiet confidence about him. He didn't say a lot but had a great arm. He went out there and just did it, didn't make a big deal of himself. He was a leader that way. And he's the exact same guy 40 years later as he was as a freshman. He's humble, a great family man, and a great person."

ASTROS CAREER HIGHLIGHTS

Best Season

Scott had a big year for the Astros in 1989, leading the league with 20 victories, while also ranking among the leaders with 172 strikeouts, nine complete games, and a WHIP of 1.057. Nevertheless, the 1986 campaign remains Scott's signature season. In addition to compiling a record of 18-10 that placed him third in the league in wins, Scott led all NL hurlers with a 2.22 ERA, a WHIP of 0.923, 306 strikeouts, five shutouts, and 275⅓ innings pitched, earning NL Cy Young and *Sporting News* NL Pitcher of the Year honors.

Memorable Moments/Greatest Performances

Although Scott allowed 10 hits over the first seven innings of a 9–2 win over the Reds on July 31, 1985, he hit one of his two career homers.

Scott shut out the Dodgers on just two hits on June 27, 1986, recording 11 strikeouts, issuing no walks, and yielding just a pair of harmless singles by Ken Landreaux during a 5–0 Astros win.

Scott no-hit the Giants on September 25, 1986, walking two batters and recording 13 strikeouts during a 2–0 Astros win that clinched the division title.

Although the Astros lost the 1986 NLCS to the Mets in six games, Scott earned series MVP honors by dominating New York's lineup in both his starts, compiling an ERA of 0.50, tossing two complete games, and recording 19 strikeouts in 18 innings of work. After earning a 1–0 victory in Game 1 by yielding just five hits, issuing one walk, and striking out 14 batters, Scott surrendered just three hits during his 3–1 win in Game 4 that tied the series at two games apiece.

Scott tossed a one-hit shutout on April 15, 1987, recording 10 strikeouts and yielding just a third-inning single by shortstop Mariano Duncan during a 4–0 victory over the Dodgers.

Scott registered 12 strikeouts and surrendered just two hits and two walks during a 3–0 shutout of the Expos on May 8, 1987, allowing just a sixth-inning triple by center fielder Casey Candaele and an eighth-inning single by catcher John Stefero.

Scott yielded just one hit during a 5–0 shutout of Atlanta on June 12, 1988, holding the Braves hitless until third baseman Ken Oberkfell singled to right field with two men out in the bottom of the ninth inning.

Scott hurled another gem on May 19, 1989, yielding just two walks and an eighth-inning single by right fielder Glenn Wilson during a 3–0 win over the Pirates.

In addition to surrendering just three hits during a 10-inning, 3–1 win over the Reds on June 8, 1990, Scott recorded a career-high 15 strikeouts.

Notable Achievements

- Won at least 18 games three times, posting 20 victories once.
- Compiled ERA under 3.00 twice.
- Posted WHIP under 1.000 twice.
- Struck out more than 200 batters twice, topping 300 strikeouts once (306 in 1986).
- Threw more than 200 innings six times.
- Threw no-hitter vs. San Francisco on September 25, 1986.
- Led NL pitchers in wins, ERA, WHIP, strikeouts, strikeouts-to-walks ratio, shutouts, and innings pitched once each.
- Finished second in NL in WHIP twice, strikeouts once, and strikeouts-to-walks ratio once.
- Ranks among Astros career leaders in wins (4th), WHIP (6th), strikeouts (5th), shutouts (tied for 2nd), innings pitched (7th), complete games (5th), and games started (6th).
- 1986 division champion.
- Three-time NL Player of the Week.
- June 1989 NL Pitcher of the Month.
- 1986 NLCS MVP.
- 1986 NL Cy Young Award winner.
- Finished second in 1989 NL Cy Young voting.
- 1986 *Sporting News* NL Pitcher of the Year.
- Three-time NL All-Star selection (1986, 1987, and 1989).
- Two-time *Sporting News* NL All-Star selection (1986 and 1989).
- #33 retired by Astros.
- Inducted into Astros Hall of Fame in 2019.

12

J. R. RICHARD

When asked by a sportswriter to identify the toughest pitcher he ever faced, two-time NL MVP Dale Murphy said, "Anybody that played in the late 70s or early 80s will probably give you the same answer: J.R. Richard."

Perhaps the most intimidating pitcher ever to toe the rubber, 6'8", 235-pound J. R. Richard gave opposing hitters nightmares with his size, blazing fastball, patented slider, and occasional wildness, all of which helped make him the most feared hurler in the game throughout his career, which he spent entirely in Houston. A member of the Astros for parts of 10 seasons, the right-handed-throwing Richard assumed a regular spot in the team's starting rotation from 1975 to 1980, a period during which he posted at least 18 victories, compiled an ERA under 3.00, recorded more than 200 strikeouts, and threw more than 250 innings four times each, en route to establishing himself as one of the franchise's all-time leaders in all four categories. A onetime NL All-Star who also finished in the top five of the NL Cy Young voting twice, Richard later received the additional honor of being inducted into the Astros Hall of Fame. Yet, had Richard not suffered a career-ending stroke while still in his prime, there is no telling how much more he would have accomplished.

Born in Vienna, Louisiana, on March 7, 1950, James Rodney Richard grew up in nearby Ruston, where he gained prominence at historically Black Lincoln High School by excelling in both baseball and basketball. Already standing 6'8" and weighing 220 pounds by the start of his senior year, Richard dominated the opposition in both sports, proving to be especially proficient on the diamond, where he never lost a game he pitched, did not surrender a single run in his final season, and once hit four home runs in one game.

Offered more than 200 basketball scholarships as graduation neared, Richard instead chose to sign with the Astros after they selected him with the second overall pick of the 1969 MLB Amateur Draft. Richard subsequently spent less than three full seasons in the minor leagues, before making a brief appearance with the parent club during the latter stages of the 1971 campaign. Displaying tremendous potential, Richard went 2-1 in his four starts, compiled an ERA of 3.43, and recorded 29 strikeouts in 21 innings of work. However, he also exhibited an inability to properly locate his pitches, issuing 16 bases on balls.

Richard's lack of control continued to haunt him the next few seasons, causing him to be shuttled back and forth between the Astros and their top minor-league affiliate. After appearing in just four games with the Astros in 1972, Richard started only 19 contests for them over the course of the next two seasons, compiling an overall record of 8-5, while posting ERAs of 4.00 and 4.18.

Joining the Astros for good in 1975, Richard performed somewhat erratically in his first full big-league season, going 12-10 with a 4.39 ERA,

J. R. Richard proved to be the most intimidating pitcher in the game throughout his career.

posting a WHIP of 1.557, completing seven of his 31 starts, and registering 176 strikeouts in 203 innings pitched, while also issuing a league-high 138 bases on balls. Although Richard continued to struggle with his control in 1976, he emerged as one of the NL's best pitchers, beginning an exceptional four-year run during which he posted the following numbers:

YEAR	W-L	ERA	SO	SHO	CG	IP	WHIP
1976	20-15	2.75	214	3	14	291	1.278
1977	18-12	2.97	214	3	13	267	1.184
1978	18-11	3.11	**303**	3	16	275.1	1.209
1979	18-13	**2.71**	**313**	4	19	292.1	1.088

By recording more than 300 strikeouts in both 1978 and 1979, Richard became just the third pitcher of the so-called modern era to surpass the 300-mark in consecutive seasons, joining Sandy Koufax and Nolan Ryan on an extremely exclusive list. In addition to leading the NL in strikeouts those two years, Richard finished second in that category two other times. Richard also ranked among the league leaders in wins, shutouts, complete games, and innings pitched all four years, earning a pair of top-five finishes in the NL Cy Young voting.

Capable of overpowering the opposition with a fastball that often reached 100 mph, Richard also possessed an even more devastating slider that registered in the low-to-mid 90s on the radar gun. And because of Richard's reputation for wildness, hitters rarely dug in against him, making him that much more difficult to face.

In describing the challenges that Richard presented to opposing batters, Mike Schmidt said, "He was unique in that he was so big, so tall, and his slider was so hard, like his fastball. From the right side of the batter's box, it was very, very intimidating. You almost had to go into a defensive hitting mode—do anything you could to just make contact. It was a very unusual night when he pitched."

Art Howe stated, "When I faced him, he was wild. You didn't dig in against him. It took him several years to corral all that. The last couple of years I played with him, he was the most dominant pitcher in our league. I was glad I was on his side."

Commenting on Richard's fastball, former Giants, Braves, Phillies, and Cubs outfielder Gary Matthews said, "I kid you not: If they took the radar gun that they're using right now and they put it on J.R., when the ball left his hand like that, it was probably going 110."

Choosing to focus on Richard's other signature offering, Larry Bowa commented, "I've seen Nolan [Ryan]. I've seen [Tom] Seaver. I've seen [Bob] Gibson. I've never seen a slider as hard as he threw. Pete Rose, who I admire a lot as a hitter, told me he was thinking of hitting right-handed against him because that slider just ate him up. [Mike] Schmidt and [Greg] Luzinski were power hitters who wanted no part of him. I mean, they played, but they said, 'This guy's unbelievable!'"

Joe Torre offered, "He was very intimidating as a pitcher. When you looked at the upcoming assignments, if you were going in there [Houston] to play, you wanted to see if you missed him or not."

Meanwhile, former Dodgers and Braves outfielder Tom Paciorek stated, "He had the ability to throw a no-hitter every time he walked out to the mound. You thought he would because you knew you weren't going to get a hit off him. You just maybe hoped he walked you or didn't hit you. The main thing you didn't want to get was hit by him. . . . He got great control as he got older. He became one of the really great pitchers in the game. It's just a shame he didn't last longer. He'd have had to win 30 games a couple of times with that kind of stuff. He was scary."

As Paciorek suggested, Richard improved his control dramatically as his career progressed, issuing only 98 bases on balls in almost 300 innings pitched in 1979, after walking more batters than any other NL pitcher in three of the previous four seasons, including a total of 151 in 1976. Continuing his brilliant mound work in 1980, Richard earned All-Star honors by compiling a record of 10-4, posting an ERA of 1.90 and a WHIP of 0.924, and registering 119 strikeouts through the first week of July, despite being plagued by various physical ailments that included stiffness in his shoulder, back, and forearm. Often forced to leave games earlier than usual, Richard complained of a "dead arm" for more than a month before the Astros finally placed him on the disabled list. After Richard underwent a battery of tests, doctors discovered some arterial blockage in his right shoulder. Nevertheless, they cleared him for workouts.

Things finally came to a head on July 30, when Richard collapsed on the field during pregame throwing drills. Rushed to the hospital, Richard was found to have suffered a major stroke that required emergency surgery to save his life. Diagnosed with a condition known as arterial thoracic outlet syndrome, Richard had to undergo surgery again in September to remove the arterial blockage in his right arm. Although Richard later attempted to mount a comeback, he found that the stroke had slowed his reaction time and weakened his depth perception, forcing him to eventually abandon his dream of pitching again in the major leagues.

Over parts of 10 seasons in Houston, Richard compiled a record of 107-71, an ERA of 3.15, and a WHIP of 1.243, threw 76 complete games and 19 shutouts, and struck out 1,493 batters in 1,606 innings pitched. In discussing the unfortunate circumstances surrounding the premature ending to his playing career years later, Richard said, "I don't think I was even in my prime when my baseball career ended. I kept getting better and better every year. I think I would have struck out 300 batters four or five more years."

Following his playing days, Richard experienced great hardship, losing all his money and his suburban home in an oil business scam and a pair of divorce settlements. Homeless and destitute by the winter of 1994, Richard found himself living under a highway overpass in Houston, later saying, "You get used to the sound of the cars going overhead, because you become so fatigued, so tired—when you lay your head, you be gone. . . . I had some people I knew when I was playing ball, and I would go to their house and wash my clothes and eat, maybe spend a night or two. But some of those people had families, and I did not feel right just coming in. So, I would go under the bridge."

Richard continued, "Everything at that point became a point of survival. You're trying to survive, you have no transportation, no food, no finances. You ask yourself a lot of times, 'Where do I go from here?'"

Finally finding solace in a local church, Richard eventually found his way, becoming a Christian minister, working in construction, and even marrying for a third time. Richard lived until August 4, 2021, when he died in a Houston hospital at the age of 71 due to complications from COVID-19.

Upon learning of his former teammate's passing, José Cruz said in a statement released by the Astros: "This is very sad to hear. I have great memories of J.R. He was one of the greatest Astros ever. When he was pitching, we knew that we were going to get a 'W.' I didn't get too many balls hit to me in the outfield when he pitched because he was so dominating. He was a great friend and a great teammate. I send my condolences to his wife and kids."

Enos Cabell expressed his feelings in another statement released by the team, saying, "He was one of the greatest pitchers we ever had and probably would have been in the Hall of Fame if his career was not cut short. On the mound, he was devastating and intimidating. Nobody wanted to face him. Guys on the other team would say that they were sick to avoid facing him. This is very sad news. He will be missed."

Gary Matthews said of his longtime friend, "If he doesn't have that stroke, he's in the Hall of Fame. He had Hall of Fame stuff, and he would have had Hall of Fame stats. J.R. Richard doesn't have to take a back seat to any pitcher that's ever pitched in the major leagues."

Matthews then added, "After the stroke, he was never, ever the same again, from the laughter, from the mannerisms, you could tell. He would be trying, but as far as I was concerned, from knowing him since we were in the minor leagues, he was a totally different person after the stroke—and who wouldn't be? He was almost lucky, through the grace of God, to be able to live."

CAREER HIGHLIGHTS

Best Season

Richard appeared to be on the verge of posting the best numbers of his career in 1980, before he suffered a stroke that brought his season and career to a premature end. That said, Richard had his greatest season in 1979, when, in addition to compiling a record of 18-13, he led all NL hurlers with a 2.71 ERA, 313 strikeouts, and a strikeouts-to-walks ratio of 3.194 and finished second in the circuit with a WHIP of 1.088, 19 complete games, and 292⅓ innings pitched.

Memorable Moments/Greatest Performances

Richard gave a hint of what lay ahead in his first big-league start on September 5, 1971, when he struck out 15 batters, issued three walks, and yielded seven hits and just two earned runs during a 5–3 complete-game win over the Giants.

Richard turned in a tremendous all-around effort on October 2, 1976, allowing just four hits and recording 13 strikeouts during a complete-game 10–1 win over the Giants, while also going 3-for-4 at the plate, with a homer and three RBIs.

Richard shut out the Montreal Expos on just three hits on August 27, 1977, also issuing no walks and recording seven strikeouts during a 4–0 Astros win.

Richard tossed another three-hit shutout on September 17, 1977, this time walking three batters and striking out 10 during an 11–0 win over the Padres.

Richard recorded eight strikeouts, issued four walks, and allowed just two hits during a 1–0 shutout of the Dodgers on April 11, 1978, yielding only a fourth-inning double by Steve Garvey and a sixth-inning single by Reggie Smith.

Richard again surrendered just two hits during a 5–0 shutout of the Phillies on May 15, 1978, allowing just a pair of harmless fifth-inning singles by third baseman Richie Hebner and center fielder Garry Maddox, while also issuing three walks and recording nine strikeouts.

Richard dominated Atlanta's lineup on August 3, 1979, allowing just six hits and registering 15 strikeouts during a 4–1 complete-game victory.

Richard shut out the Padres on just three hits on September 6, 1979, issuing no walks and striking out nine batters during a 2–0 Astros win.

Although Richard did not figure in the decision, he recorded 15 strikeouts and allowed just seven hits and two runs over the first 11 innings of a September 21, 1979, matchup with the Reds that the Astros eventually won in 13 innings.

Returning to the mound four days later, Richard recorded 13 strikeouts, issued two walks, and surrendered just four hits during an 8–0 shutout of the Braves on September 25, 1979.

In addition to recording 12 strikeouts during a 2–0 shutout of the Dodgers on April 19, 1980, Richard surrendered just one hit, yielding only a fourth-inning infield single by Reggie Smith.

Richard beat the Reds with both his arm and his bat on April 30, 1980, recording eight strikeouts and allowing just three hits and one run in 7⅓ innings of work during a 5–1 Astros win, while also hitting a solo home run off Tom Seaver.

Richard threw 32 consecutive scoreless innings from May 26 to June 17, 1980, proving to be particularly dominant on June 6, when he recorded 13 strikeouts and allowed just three hits during a 2–0 win over the Giants.

Notable Achievements

- Won at least 18 games four times, posting 20 victories once.
- Posted winning percentage over .700 twice.
- Compiled ERA under 3.00 four times, finishing with mark below 2.00 once (1.90 in 1980).
- Posted WHIP under 1.000 once (0.924 in 1980).
- Struck out more than 300 batters twice, surpassing 200 strikeouts two other times.
- Threw more than 250 innings four times.

- Threw more than 15 complete games twice.
- Led NL pitchers in ERA once, strikeouts twice, strikeouts-to-walks ratio once, and putouts once.
- Finished second in NL in WHIP once, strikeouts twice, shutouts once, complete games once, and innings pitched three times.
- Ranks among Astros career leaders in wins (5th), ERA (tied for 8th), strikeouts (3rd), shutouts (5th), innings pitched (9th), complete games (4th), and games started (9th).
- 1980 division champion.
- May 21, 1978, NL Player of the Week.
- Three-time NL Pitcher of the Month.
- 1976 Astros team MVP.
- Finished in top five of NL Cy Young voting twice.
- 1980 NL All-Star selection.
- Inducted into Astros Hall of Fame in 2019.

13

BILLY WAGNER

One of baseball's premier closers for more than a decade, Billy Wagner spent parts of nine seasons in Houston, amassing more saves than any other pitcher in franchise history. A hard-throwing left-hander who depended primarily on his blazing fastball to retire opposing batters, Wagner saved more than 30 games five times and compiled an ERA under 2.00 twice, helping the Astros win four division titles. A seven-time NL All-Star, Wagner earned three nominations during his time in Houston, before being traded to the Philadelphia Phillies following the conclusion of the 2003 campaign after expressing dissatisfaction with team management. Nevertheless, Wagner, who currently ranks sixth in MLB history in saves, eventually received the honor of gaining induction into the Astros Hall of Fame.

Born to teenage parents in Marion, Virginia, on July 25, 1971, William Edward Wagner grew up in poverty, later describing a typical breakfast as "a few crackers with peanut butter and a glass of water." Raised in a toxic environment characterized by frequent domestic squabbles between his mother and father, who divorced shortly after he turned five years of age, Billy and his younger sister, Chastity, ended up spending most of their youth being shuttled back and forth between their parents and grandparents. Finally gaining some sense of stability in his life after he moved in with his aunt, uncle, and cousins at the age of 14, Wagner spent the rest of his teenage years living some 30 miles northwest of Marion, in the Tannersville/Tazewell region of Virginia.

An outstanding all-around athlete, Wagner, a natural right-hander who, after breaking his right arm twice at the age of seven while playing football, learned to throw left-handed, starred in baseball and football at Tazewell High School. Especially proficient on the diamond, Wagner excelled as both a center fielder and pitcher, earning Virginia Region IV Player of the Year honors as a senior in 1990 by batting .451 and stealing 23 bases, while also posting a record of 7-1, compiling an ERA of 1.52, and striking out

Billy Wagner ranks first in franchise history in career saves.

116 batters in only 46 innings of work. But, with Wagner standing just 5'5" and weighing only 135 pounds at the time, he received very little attention from major-league scouts or Division I schools, prompting him to enroll at Ferrum College, a small Division III liberal arts college located in Ferrum, Virginia.

In explaining his decision years later, Wagner told FOX Sports, "The thing that sold me was that my cousin had been there. He'd played two years—football and baseball. I'd traveled there, seen the school. I knew what it was all about. . . . It was a perfect fit for me. It certainly wasn't appealing to everybody. It's off the beaten path, out in the boonies. All we had was a Dairy Queen and a pizza place. There wasn't a lot to do, so it gave you a chance to grow up. You could be with your teammates and just kind of figure out who you were."

After playing both baseball and football his freshman year, Wagner chose to focus exclusively on further developing his mound skills when Ferrum's defensive coordinator suggested he do so after watching him pitch in the spring. Embarking on a weightlifting program, Wagner added some 40 pounds onto his frame, allowing him to increase the velocity on his fastball from 84 to 98 mph. Developing into a dominant pitcher, Wagner struck out 327 batters in 182⅓ total innings of work and set an NCAA career record that still stands by allowing just 2.22 hits per nine innings pitched.

Creating quite a stir with his extraordinary mound work, Wagner made tiny Ferrum the place to be on days he pitched, with veteran MLB evaluator Roy Clark remembering, "Billy's junior year, you couldn't even get a seat in the stands when he started. Not only scouts, but word of mouth from all over the area. When Billy was on the mound, it was a show. . . . For all three years, he was appointment viewing. It was such an event in that little town."

Recalling the first time he saw Wagner pitch, Clark said, "I was scouting with Atlanta at the time, but I would go up to Ferrum and do the clinics. I go up there one time, and Coach Abe Naff says to me, 'Roy, I want you to see this left-hander I got.' So, the kid started throwing. I break out the radar gun—and at the time, I knew my gun was a couple ticks slow—but his first pitch was 95, which I think was the equivalent of 100 or 101."

Clark continued, "Someone said to me, 'I think your gun is broken.' Well, I got a couple more pitches, and it wasn't too broken. It was the hardest I've ever seen anybody throw."

Former North Carolina Wesleyan head coach Mike Fox also stood in awe of Wagner, remembering, "The first two years, he'd close Games 1 and 2 of a series and start Game 3. I vividly remember players coming back to the dugout with looks on their faces I'd never seen before. A left-hander throwing in the mid-90s? At that level, it seemed like 105. It was amazing. Certainly, the best I saw at my time at Wesleyan, for sure."

Unfortunately, Wagner's accuracy did not match his velocity, with Coach Naff stating, "He'd either strike 'em out or walk 'em early in his career. We always thought his wildness was a positive, instead of a negative."

Wagner himself admitted, "My mechanics at the beginning were . . . not good."

With Wagner having grown to 5'10" and 180 pounds by his junior year, the Astros selected him as the 12th overall pick of the 1993 MLB Amateur Draft. Wagner subsequently spent most of the next three seasons starting in the minor leagues, before making a brief appearance with the parent club toward the end of the 1995 campaign. Arriving in the big leagues to stay in 1996, Wagner worked exclusively out of the bullpen, going 2-2 with a 2.44 ERA, saving nine games, and recording 67 strikeouts and 30 walks in 51⅔ innings pitched.

Asked about his transition from starter to reliever, Wagner replied, "It's tough to blow three games in a row and have the courage to go back out there. But if you go through what I went through as a kid, not knowing if I was going to eat or who I was going to live with, this is nothing."

With Wagner displaying better command of his pitches early in 1997, manager Larry Dierker inserted him into the role of closer, where he experienced mixed results. Although Wagner compiled an ERA of 2.85, saved 23 games, and recorded 106 strikeouts in 66⅓ innings pitched, he also lost eight of his 15 decisions and blew several save opportunities, with opposing batters learning to sit back and wait on his fastball since he rarely threw anything else. Posting slightly better overall numbers in 1998 despite spending three weeks on the disabled list after being hit in the head by a line drive off the bat of Arizona Diamondbacks catcher Kelly Stinnett, Wagner helped lead the Astros to the second of their three straight NL Central Division titles by going 4-3, with a 2.70 ERA, 30 saves, and 97 strikeouts in 60 innings of work.

Joining baseball's elite in 1999 after adding a reliable curveball to his repertoire of pitches and further improving his control, Wagner earned his first All-Star selection, a fourth-place finish in the NL Cy Young voting, and Rolaids Relief Man of the Year honors by compiling a record of 4-1 and an ERA of 1.57, finishing third in the league with 39 saves, and striking out 124 batters in 74⅔ innings of work, while yielding only 36 hits to the opposition.

Plagued by elbow problems the following year, Wagner saved just six games and compiled an ERA of 6.18, before undergoing season-ending surgery in June. Healthy again by the start of the 2001 campaign, Wagner began an exceptional three-year run during which he saved a total of 118 games, earning a pair of All-Star selections. Particularly outstanding in 2003, Wagner finished third in the league with a career-high 44 saves, compiled an ERA of 1.78 and a WHIP of 0.872, and recorded 105 strikeouts in 86 innings pitched.

Commenting on his development into a more complete pitcher and one of the game's most reliable closers, Wagner said, "I hated when people called me a thrower. I didn't appreciate that . . . I put a lot of effort into my control and my thought process into each pitch."

Meanwhile, in addressing his ability to consistently reach 98 mph on the radar gun with his fastball, Wagner stated, "I threw 78 miles per hour in high school. I hit 92 miles per hour during my freshman year in college, and today I can throw 98. If I can name one thing that contributed most to my increase in velocity, it would be long toss."

Although the Astros remained extremely competitive in both 2002 and 2003, finishing second in the division both years, Wagner grew increasingly disenchanted with management's practice of trading away top talent to bring in less expensive players. Never one to hide his feelings, Wagner voiced his dissatisfaction to reporters more than once, prompting the Astros to trade him to the Phillies for three young pitchers on November 3, 2003, with Wagner later saying, "How can I say this politely? They had become tired of my bluntness."

Wagner, who left Houston with a career total of 225 saves, a record of 26-29, an ERA of 2.53, a WHIP of 1.039, and 694 strikeouts in 504⅓ innings pitched, ended up spending two seasons in Philadelphia, saving 38 games and compiling an ERA of 1.51 for the Phillies in 2005, before signing with the Mets for four years and $42 million when he became a free agent at the end of the year. Remaining one of the game's top closers the next three seasons, Wagner saved a total of 101 games for the Mets from 2006 to 2008, before developing arm problems early in 2009. Dealt to the Red Sox during the latter stages of the campaign, Wagner finished out the season in Boston, before signing with Atlanta as a free agent. After earning All-Star honors for the Braves in 2010 by amassing 37 saves, winning seven of his nine decisions, and compiling an ERA of 1.43, the 39-year-old Wagner announced his retirement, ending his career with 422 saves, an overall record of 47-40, an ERA of 2.31, a WHIP of 0.998, and 1,196 strikeouts in 903 innings pitched.

Following his playing days, Wagner returned home to Virginia, where he became a full-time dad to his four children, worked on the family farm, and eventually became the head baseball coach at The Miller School of Albemarle. Concerned greatly with the welfare of others, Wagner also remains heavily involved with the Second Chance Learning Center he established in 2005 to assist at-risk youth with counseling and other help.

ASTROS CAREER HIGHLIGHTS

Best Season

Wagner performed brilliantly in 2003, when en route to registering a franchise record 44 saves, he compiled an ERA of 1.78 and a WHIP of 0.872, struck out 105 batters in 86 innings of work, and allowed just 52 hits. But he proved to be even more dominant in 1999, when he went 4-1, with 39 saves, a 1.57 ERA, and a WHIP of 0.777, recorded 124 strikeouts in 74⅔ innings pitched, and yielded only 36 hits.

Memorable Moments/Greatest Performances

Wagner earned a save by allowing one hit and recording four strikeouts over three scoreless innings during a 9–1 win over the Giants on June 14, 1996.

Wagner contributed to a 4–2 victory over the Dodgers on June 20, 1996, by working 2⅔ scoreless innings, facing 11 batters, allowing one hit, issuing two walks, and striking out seven of the eight batters he retired.

Wagner helped the Astros earn a 4–3 win over the Florida Marlins on July 2, 1996, by throwing 3⅔ hitless innings during which he walked three batters and recorded three strikeouts.

Wagner saved a 5–4 win over the Mets on May 5, 1999, by striking out all four batters he faced.

Wagner worked two perfect innings during a 12-inning, 2–1 win over the Colorado Rockies on May 25, 1999, striking out five of the six batters he faced.

Notable Achievements

- Saved more than 30 games five times, topping 40 saves once (44 in 2003).
- Compiled ERA under 3.00 seven times, posting mark under 2.00 twice.
- Posted WHIP under 1.000 three times.
- Struck out more than 100 batters three times.
- Finished third in NL in saves twice.
- Holds Astros single-season record for most saves (44 in 2003).
- Holds Astros career records for most saves (225) and strikeouts per nine innings pitched (12.385).
- Ranks among Astros career leaders in ERA (tied for 4th), WHIP (2nd), strikeouts-to-walks ratio (3rd), and pitching appearances (2nd).
- Four-time division champion (1997, 1998, 1999, and 2001).
- Finished fourth in 1999 NL Cy Young voting.
- 1999 NL Rolaids Relief Man of the Year.
- Three-time NL All-Star selection (1999, 2001, and 2003).
- Inducted into Astros Hall of Fame in 2020.

14

ALEX BREGMAN

The greatest third baseman in franchise history, Alex Bregman has served as one of the key figures on Astros teams that have won six division titles, four AL pennants, and two World Series since he established himself as the starter at the hot corner in 2017. A productive hitter, Bregman has hit more than 20 homers four times and knocked in more than 100 runs twice, while also posting an OPS over .900 twice. A solid fielder as well, Bregman has led all players at his position in assists twice and fielding percentage once, with his excellent all-around play earning him two All-Star selections and two top-five finishes in the AL MVP voting.

Born in Albuquerque, New Mexico, on March 30, 1994, Alexander David Bregman grew up in the city's Northeast Heights section, where he began playing tee-ball at the age of four. The great-grandson of Russian-Jewish immigrants who came to the United States during the first few years of the 20th century to escape persecution in their homeland, Bregman acquired his love of baseball from his father, Samuel Bregman, who played the game his freshman year at the University of New Mexico. Knowing early on that he wanted to pursue a career in baseball, Bregman said during his bar mitzvah speech: "I want to be a professional athlete who plays for the love of the game, never quits trying to give my best, and is a good role model for all of the kids who look up to baseball players."

Primarily a shortstop at Albuquerque Academy, Bregman led his high school team to the state championship as a freshman in 2009 by compiling a batting average of .514 from his leadoff spot in the batting order. Bregman followed that by becoming the first high school player to win the USA Baseball Player of the Year Award in 2010, before earning First-Team All-State, All-Metro, and All-District honors his junior year by hitting 19 home runs and batting .678. Bregman subsequently missed most of his senior year after breaking the second knuckle on his right hand while attempting to field a hard-hit ball barehanded. As a result, he slid to the 29th round of the 2012 MLB Draft, where the Boston Red Sox ultimately selected him. But with Bregman having made it clear prior to the draft that he did not intend to sign with any team that did not pick him in the first round, he chose to attend Louisiana State University on a baseball scholarship.

Proving himself worthy of a higher selection while at LSU, Bregman hit 21 homers, knocked in 148 runs, stole 66 bases, and batted .338 in 196 games with the Tigers over the course of the next three seasons, earning two All-America selections, National Freshman of the Year honors from *Baseball America*, and the Brooks Wallace Award as the country's best college shortstop in 2013. Considered one of the top prospects heading into the June 2015 MLB Amateur Draft, Bregman received high grades for his knowledge of the strike zone, excellent bat speed, ability to make consistent contact at the plate, strong throwing arm, and outstanding range

Alex Bregman has placed in the top five of the AL MVP voting twice.
Courtesy of Keith Allison

at shortstop. Still, some scouts projected him more as a second baseman, prompting LSU head coach Paul Mainieri to proclaim, "If you don't think Alex Bregman can play shortstop at the Major League level, you don't know the first thing about baseball."

Agreeing with Mainieri's assessment, the Astros selected Bregman with the second overall pick of the draft, with GM Jeff Luhnow saying at the time that there was "no question" Bregman had the skills to play shortstop.

Bregman subsequently spent nearly two full seasons playing shortstop for four different teams in the minor leagues, gaining recognition as Minor League Player of the Year from *USA Today* in 2016, before joining the Astros in late July 2016. Moved to third base following his arrival in Houston, Bregman performed well the final two months of the season, hitting eight homers, driving in 34 runs, and batting .264, in 49 games and 217 total plate appearances.

Although Bregman also started 21 games at shortstop the following year, he spent most of his time at third, committing just 10 errors in 132 games at the hot corner, while also hitting 19 homers, knocking in 71 runs, scoring 88 times, stealing 17 bases, batting .284, and compiling an OPS of .827. Emerging as one of the game's top players at his position in 2018, Bregman earned All-Star honors and a fifth-place finish in the AL MVP voting by hitting 31 homers, batting .286, leading the league with 51 doubles, and ranking among the leaders with 103 RBIs, 105 runs scored, 96 walks, and an OPS of .926. Performing even better in 2019, Bregman earned his second consecutive All-Star nomination and a runner-up finish in the AL MVP balloting by batting .296, drawing a league-leading 119 bases on balls, and placing near the top of the league rankings with 41 homers, 112 RBIs, 122 runs scored, and an OPS of 1.015.

The right-handed-hitting Bregman, who, although officially listed at 6 foot and 192 pounds, stands closer to 5'10", possesses an extremely quick bat and outstanding power to all fields. Also blessed with a keen batting eye, Bregman rarely offers at bad pitches and generally makes good contact at the plate, striking out more than 90 times just once to this point in his career. A good baserunner as well, Bregman has stolen at least 10 bases twice and knows how to take full advantage of mistakes made by opposing fielders. Meanwhile, on defense, Bregman displays soft hands, excellent range to both sides, and a strong and accurate throwing arm.

Far less effective at the plate during the pandemic-shortened 2020 campaign, Bregman hit just six homers, knocked in only 22 runs, and batted just .242. Limited to just 91 games and 400 total plate appearances the following year by a strained left quadricep, Bregman finished the season with

12 homers, 55 RBIs, and a .270 batting average. However, he rebounded nicely in 2022, hitting 23 homers, driving in 93 runs, scoring 93 times, batting .259, and compiling an OPS of .820 for an Astros team that ended up winning the World Series. Bregman had another excellent year in 2023, finishing the season with 25 homers, 98 RBIs, 103 runs scored, a .262 batting average, and an OPS of .804, giving him career marks of 165 homers, 588 RBIs, 615 runs scored, 981 hits, 235 doubles, 16 triples, a .274 batting average, a .373 on-base percentage, and a .487 slugging percentage heading into 2024.

In addition to the contributions Bregman has made to the Astros on the playing field, he has proven to be one of the team's clubhouse leaders, helping to bridge the gap between the ballclub's American-born players and those of Latin descent by constantly striving to improve his Spanish, which he began studying as a child in school in his hometown of Albuquerque. A pillar of strength within the community as well, Bregman created the Bregman Cares Foundation, which is devoted to helping people and families dealing with autism. Bregman, who learned the importance of raising autism awareness through his godson, Brady Columbus, hopes to raise $10 million to build a school in Houston for students with autism. In discussing his dedication to his foundation, Bregman said, "It's super important. My godson, Brady, was diagnosed when he was three years old. He wasn't speaking, and now he is. He's gaining social skills by the day. . . . Just watching him grow up and the impact he's made on our lives, we want to do something to help. Brady's allowed us to do that."

CAREER HIGHLIGHTS

Best Season

Bregman had a big year for the Astros in 2018, earning his first All-Star selection and a fifth-place finish in the AL MVP voting by hitting 31 homers, batting .286, leading the league with 51 doubles, and ranking among the leaders with 103 RBIs, 105 runs scored, 170 hits, 96 walks, a .394 on-base percentage, a .532 slugging percentage, and an OPS of .926. But he posted slightly better overall numbers in 2019, earning a runner-up finish in the MVP balloting by batting .296 and placing in the league's top five in seven other offensive categories, including homers (41), RBIs (112), runs scored (122), bases on balls (119), and OPS (1.015), with his 119 walks topping the circuit.

Memorable Moments/Greatest Performances

Bregman gave the Astros a 13–12 victory over the Dodgers in Game 5 of the 2017 World Series when he drove home the winning run with an RBI single with two men out and two men on base in the bottom of the 10th inning.

Bregman helped lead the Astros to a 7–0 win over the Toronto Blue Jays on June 26, 2018, by going 4-for-5, with a homer, three doubles, two RBIs, and two runs scored.

Bregman followed that up by hitting a two-run homer in the bottom of the ninth inning that gave the Astros a 7–6 victory over the Blue Jays the very next day.

Bregman had a huge hand in the Astros' three-game sweep of Cleveland in the 2018 ALDS, going 5-for-9, with two homers, a double, four walks, four RBIs, and five runs scored.

Bregman contributed to a lopsided 15–5 victory over the Texas Rangers on May 12, 2019, by homering twice and driving in five runs.

Bregman supplied most of the offensive firepower during a 4–1 win over Oakland on August 18, 2019, going 4-for-4, with a homer, double, and three RBIs.

Bregman delivered the big blow in Game 4 of the 2019 World Series when he homered with the bases loaded in the top of the seventh inning of an 8–1 victory over the Washington Nationals.

Bregman contributed to a 21–5 pasting of the White Sox on August 18, 2022, by going 4-for-6 at the plate, with two homers, two doubles, six RBIs, and four runs scored.

Bregman delivered what proved to be the decisive blow of a 3–2 win over the Yankees in Game 2 of the 2022 ALCS when he homered off Luis Severino with two men out and two men on in the bottom of the third inning.

In addition to walking four times during a 9–6 win over the Los Angeles Angels on June 3, 2023, Bregman delivered the game's pivotal blow in the bottom of the fourth inning, when he homered with the bases loaded off right-handed reliever Jacob Webb.

Notable Achievements

- Has hit more than 20 home runs four times, topping 30 homers twice and 40 homers once.
- Has knocked in more than 100 runs twice.

- Has scored more than 100 runs three times.
- Has surpassed 30 doubles four times, topping 50 two-baggers once (51 in 2018).
- Has drawn more than 100 bases on balls once (119 in 2019).
- Has compiled on-base percentage over .400 once (.423 in 2019).
- Has posted slugging percentage over .500 twice.
- Has posted OPS over .900 twice, topping the 1.000-mark once (1.015 in 2019).
- Has led AL in doubles once, bases on balls once, and sacrifice flies once.
- Has finished second in AL in on-base percentage once and bases on ball once.
- Has led AL third basemen in assists twice and fielding percentage once.
- Ranks among Astros career leaders in home runs (8th), RBIs (10th), runs scored (10th), doubles (8th), extra-base hits (8th), total bases (10th), bases on balls (10th), on-base percentage (8th), slugging percentage (8th), and OPS (5th).
- Six-time division champion (2017, 2018, 2019, 2021, 2022, and 2023).
- Four-time AL champion (2017, 2019, 2021, and 2022).
- Two-time world champion (2017 and 2022).
- Two-time AL Player of the Week.
- Three-time AL Player of the Month.
- 2019 Silver Slugger Award winner.
- Two-time Astros team MVP (2018 and 2019).
- Finished in top five of AL MVP voting twice, placing second in 2019.
- Two-time AL All-Star selection (2018 and 2019).
- 2019 All-MLB Second Team.

15

LARRY DIERKER

The first Astros pitcher to win 20 games in a season, Larry Dierker spent 13 years in Houston, throwing more innings, complete games, and shutouts than anyone else in franchise history during that time. Also ranking extremely high in team annals in wins and strikeouts, Dierker posted at least 15 victories three times and fanned more than 200 batters once while pitching for mostly losing teams. A two-time NL All-Star, Dierker, who has spent nearly all his adult life serving the Astros in one capacity or another, later received the additional honors of having his #49 retired by the organization and being inducted into the team's Hall of Fame.

Born in Hollywood, California, on September 22, 1946, Lawrence Edward Dierker grew up in nearby Reseda, before moving with his family in his early teens to the Los Angeles neighborhood of Woodland Hills. After getting his start in baseball in the West Valley Little League at the age of seven, Dierker eventually emerged as a standout pitcher at William Howard Taft Charter High School, performing so well on the mound that 18 of the then-20 major-league teams pursued him as graduation neared. Offered contracts by both the Chicago Cubs and Houston Colt .45s, Dierker chose to sign with the latter because he knew that they represented his best chance to reach the majors quickly.

Proving that he made the right decision, Dierker started just nine games for Cocoa in the Florida Instructional League, before being promoted to the parent club in late September 1964. Making his first big-league start on his 18th birthday, Dierker surrendered five hits, three walks, and four runs (two earned) over the first three innings of a 7–1 loss to the San Francisco Giants, before working six scoreless innings in two subsequent relief appearances.

With the newly named Astros moving into the Astrodome the following year, Dierker gradually earned a regular spot in the starting rotation, finishing the season with a record of 7-8, an ERA of 3.50, and 109 strikeouts in 146.2 innings of work. A full-time starter by 1966, Dierker went

In 1969, Larry Dierker became the first Astros pitcher to win 20 games in a season.

10-8 with a 3.18 ERA, before missing much of the ensuing campaign while serving a six-month stint in the Army Reserves. Returning to the Astros in 1968, Dierker established himself as a rock upon which the team could build its pitching staff, compiling an ERA of 3.31, registering 161 strike-outs, and tossing 233⅔ innings and 10 complete games, although poor run support relegated him to a record of just 12-15.

Emerging as one of the NL's top starters in 1969, Dierker earned All-Star honors for the first time by ranking among the league leaders with 20 victories (against 13 losses), a 2.33 ERA, a WHIP of 1.022, 232 strikeouts, four shutouts, 20 complete games, and 305⅓ innings pitched. Although Dierker proved to be less dominant in 1970, he had another solid season, going 16-12, with a 3.87 ERA, 191 strikeouts, 17 complete games, and 269⅔ innings pitched. Off to a tremendous start in 1971, Dierker earned his second All-Star selection by winning 10 of his first 11 decisions. However, the heavy workload he assumed the previous few seasons caused him to develop a sore arm midway through the campaign that ended up limiting him to just 24 starts, a record of 12-6, and 91 strikeouts.

Despite his arm problems in 1971, the right-handed-throwing Dierker, who stood 6'4" and weighed 215 pounds, proved to be one of the NL's more durable pitchers for much of his career, starting more than 30 games and throwing well over 200 innings six times each between 1968 and 1975. A hard thrower who also possessed a good curveball, Dierker drew praise for his ability to navigate his way through opposing lineups from former Astros GM Tal Smith, who said, "Dierker was the consummate major-league pitcher. Larry was big, strong, durable, competitive, and obviously talented. He had the complete repertoire—a good fastball, a good breaking ball, and a good changeup. As such, he was able to keep batters off stride and to affect their timing—the essence of getting hitters out."

Healthy again by the start of the 1972 campaign, Dierker helped lead the Astros to the first winning record in their 11-year history by going 15-8, with a 3.40 ERA, five shutouts, 12 complete games, and 115 strikeouts in 214⅔ innings pitched. However, he subsequently suffered a hand injury early in 1973, which, coupled with shoulder problems he developed shortly thereafter, limited him to just three starts and 27 total innings. Although Dierker took his regular turn in the starting rotation in each of the next three seasons, compiling an ERA under 3.00 and tossing more than 10 complete games once each from 1974 to 1976, he failed to experience the same level of success, posting an overall mark of just 38-40.

Feeling that Dierker's best days were behind him, the Astros traded him to the St. Louis Cardinals for catcher Joe Ferguson following the conclusion of the 1976 campaign. Dierker, who left Houston with a career record of 137-117, an ERA of 3.28, a WHIP of 1.214, 25 shutouts, 106 complete games, and 1,487 strikeouts in 2,294⅓ innings of work, ended up starting just nine games and throwing only 39 innings for the Cardinals in 1977 after breaking his leg during spring training. Released by the Cards just prior to the start of the 1978 regular season, Dierker announced his retirement, after which he rejoined the Astros as a member of their promotions department. Shortly thereafter, Dierker began a 19-year stint as a color commentator on the team's radio and television broadcasts that lasted until 1996, when the Astros named him their new manager. Dierker remained in that post for the next five seasons, guiding the Astros to four NL Central Division titles and an overall record of 448–362, before handing in his resignation when the pressures of the job began to wear on him in 2001. Two years earlier,

Dierker nearly lost his life when he, after experiencing severe headaches for several days, had a grand mal seizure during a June game against San Diego that rendered him unconscious. Forced to undergo emergency brain surgery, Dierker spent four weeks in recovery, after which he returned to the dugout to lead the Astros to their third straight division title.

Honored by the Astros on May 19, 2002, by having his #49 jersey retired by the team, Dierker remained close to the organization for the next decade, before being named special assistant to the president on May 31, 2013. In announcing Dierker's appointment, team president Reid Ryan said, "Larry is a huge part of our history. He has a great deal of knowledge and years of experience that we will utilize. We're excited that he is back in the organization, and we know the fans will be as well."

Meanwhile, Dierker told the assembled media, "I'm extremely pleased to be working with the Astros organization. . . . I'm excited about interacting with the fans again and look forward to writing for the program. I take a great deal of pride in the organization and am anxious to be a part of it again."

Dierker, who is 77 years old as of this writing, has spent the last several years serving in an advisory role to the team president, handling speaking engagements, and interacting with fans during games at Minute Maid Park.

ASTROS CAREER HIGHLIGHTS

Best Season

Dierker had the finest season of his career in 1969, when he earned the first of his two All-Star nominations by compiling a record of 20-13, an ERA of 2.33 ERA, and a WHIP of 1.022, registering 232 strikeouts, and setting single-season franchise records that still stand by throwing 20 complete games and 305⅓ innings.

Memorable Moments/Greatest Performances

Dierker shut out the Reds on just two hits on April 30, 1968, surrendering just a pair of harmless singles to Pete Rose and Tony Pérez during a 3–0 Astros win.

Dierker tossed another two-hit shutout on April 23, 1969, yielding just two walks and singles by second baseman Roberto Peña and third baseman Ed Spiezio during a 4–0 win over the Padres.

Dierker allowed just five hits and recorded a career-high 14 strikeouts during a complete-game 6–1 victory over the Phillies on May 7, 1969.

Dierker turned in an outstanding all-around effort on June 8, 1969, recording seven strikeouts and yielding just five hits and two walks during a 2–1 victory over the Cardinals, while also driving in the winning run with an RBI single in the bottom of the 11th inning.

Although the Astros ultimately lost to the Braves in 13 innings by a score of 3–2 on September 13, 1969, Dierker worked 12 scoreless innings, allowing just four hits and four walks, before turning the game over to the bullpen.

Dierker shut out the Padres on just one hit on May 26, 1971, issuing three walks and yielding just a seventh-inning single by right fielder Ollie Brown during an 8–0 Astros win.

Dierker tossed another one-hit shutout on June 19, 1972, allowing just two walks and a third-inning single by catcher Duffy Dyer during a 3–0 win over the Mets.

Dierker no-hit the Montreal Expos on July 9, 1976, issuing four walks and recording eight strikeouts during a 6–0 Astros win. Looking back on his extraordinary effort years later, Dierker said, "I never expected to throw a no-hitter at that point in my career, especially after the injuries and arm problems. It really was a gift from God."

Dierker threw a two-hit shutout on July 26, 1976, issuing one walk and yielding just a fourth-inning single by shortstop Enzo Hernández and a fifth-inning double by left fielder Johnny Grubb during a 7–0 win over the Padres.

In addition to earning a complete-game 4–3 victory over the Cardinals on August 28, 1976, Dierker hit the last of his four career home runs.

Notable Achievements

- Won 20 games in 1969.
- Compiled ERA under 3.00 three times.
- Struck out more than 200 batters once (232 in 1969).
- Threw more than 250 innings twice, topping 300 innings once (305⅓ in 1969).
- Threw 20 complete games in 1969.
- Holds Astros single-season records for most innings pitched (305⅓) and most complete games (20), both in 1969.
- Holds Astros career records for most shutouts (25), innings pitched (2,294⅓), complete games (106), and starts (320).

- Ranks among Astros career leaders in wins (3rd), strikeouts (4th), and pitching appearances (8th).
- Two-time NL All-Star selection (1969 and 1971).
- #49 retired by Astros.
- Inducted into Astros Hall of Fame in 2019.

16

NOLAN RYAN

onsidered to be on the downside of his career by the time he arrived in Houston in 1980, 33-year-old Nolan Ryan had posted an overall record of just 26-27 for the California Angels over the course of the previous two seasons after earlier tossing four no-hitters, striking out more than 300 batters five times, and earning five All-Star nominations. Proving his doubters wrong, Ryan ended up pitching well into his 40s, setting MLB records for most strikeouts and no-hitters thrown that still stand. A member of the Astros from 1980 to 1988, Ryan made significant contributions to their first two division championship teams, tossing the fifth of his seven career no-hitters, and registering more strikeouts than any other hurler in franchise history, en route to earning two All-Star selections and a pair of top-five finishes in the NL Cy Young voting. Ryan, who later received the additional honors of having his number retired by the Astros and gaining induction into the team's Hall of Fame, continued to excel after he left Houston, tossing another two no-hitters and recording almost 1,000 more strikeouts for the Texas Rangers before finally announcing his retirement at the age of 46 following the conclusion of the 1993 campaign with a list of career accomplishments that prompted the *Sporting News* to accord him a No. 41 ranking on its 1999 list of Baseball's 100 Greatest Players, and the Baseball Hall of Fame to open its doors to him in his first year of eligibility.

Born in Refugio, Texas, on January 31, 1947, Lynn Nolan Ryan grew up some 145 miles northeast, in the city of Alvin, where he began playing baseball with his father in the family's front yard at the age of seven. After getting his start in organized ball in the local Little Leagues, Ryan first began to display his powerful throwing arm in junior high school, where he exhibited the ability to toss a softball the length of a football field—30 yards farther than any other boy in the area.

Eventually emerging as a standout pitcher at Alvin High School, Ryan drew the attention of big-league scouts by averaging two strikeouts per inning his junior year. Even better as a senior, Ryan pitched the Yellow

Jackets into the Texas high school state finals by compiling a record of 19-3, throwing 12 complete games, and striking out 211 batters.

Commenting on the velocity of Ryan's fastball years later, former New York Mets scout Red Murff remembered the first time he saw the young right-hander pitch: "The night before, I had seen the two fastest pitchers in the National League at that time, Jim Maloney and Turk Farrell. Nolan Ryan was already faster than both of them, by far."

On Murff's recommendation, the Mets selected Ryan in the 12th round of the 1965 MLB Amateur Draft, with the 295th overall pick. Ryan subsequently spent the next three years advancing through New York's farm system, dominating the hitters he faced at every level. After striking out 445 batters in a total of 291 innings pitched from 1965 to 1967 and making a brief appearance with the parent club in 1966, Ryan arrived in the major leagues to stay in 1968.

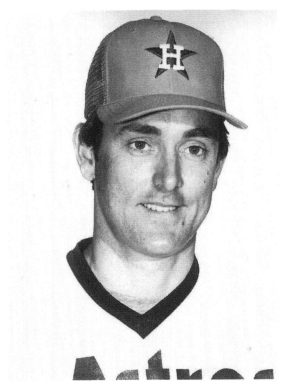

Nolan Ryan recorded more strikeouts than any other pitcher in team annals.

Although Ryan proved to be somewhat erratic during his first extended tour of duty at the big-league level, often failing to locate his pitches properly, he made an extremely favorable impression on St. Louis Cardinals slugging first baseman Orlando Cepeda, who said, "Nolan Ryan is the best young pitcher I've ever seen in the major leagues."

Over the course of the next three seasons, Ryan showed flashes of brilliance, displaying an ability to throw his fastball past even the league's best hitters and recording nearly a strikeout an inning. But irregular work due to injuries, finger blisters, and a continuing military obligation prevented Ryan from realizing his full potential, limiting him to an overall record of just 29-37 and a total of only 373 innings pitched.

Having finally lost patience with Ryan, the Mets made what has since gone down as one of the worst trades in baseball history when, on December 10, 1971, they dealt him and three lesser players to the California Angels for veteran shortstop Jim Fregosi. While Fregosi never panned out in New York after the Mets moved him to third base, Ryan went on to establish himself as one of the game's most dominant pitchers during his time in California, winning more than 20 games twice and leading the AL in strikeouts in seven of the next eight seasons. Particularly outstanding from 1972 to 1974, Ryan compiled a record of 19-16 and an ERA of 2.28 for the weak-hitting Angels in the first of those campaigns, while also throwing 20 complete games and 284 innings, leading the league with nine shutouts and 329 strikeouts. Ryan followed that by going 21-16, with a 2.87 ERA, 26 complete games, 326 innings pitched, and an AL record 383 strikeouts in 1973, earning a runner-up finish in the Cy Young voting. Ryan placed third in the balloting the following year after finishing the regular season with a record of 22-16, an ERA of 2.89, 26 complete games, and a league-leading 367 strikeouts in 332⅔ innings pitched.

More regular work, the elimination of his blister problem by using a surgeon's scalpel to remove scar tissue and calluses on his fingers before each start, and improved coaching, which helped him alter his delivery to home plate and develop a sharp-breaking curveball, all contributed greatly to the success Ryan experienced in California. So, too, did the weight-training program he employed, with Ryan later saying, "It's weight *conditioning*, not weightlifting. I was not trying to see how much weight I could lift. I was trying to lift the right weights in the right way."

Although the 6'2", 190-pound Ryan continued to struggle with his control, leading all AL hurlers in walks in six of his eight seasons in California, his outstanding curve and blazing fastball, which often approached the plate at more than 100 mph, made him the league's most feared and unhittable pitcher, with Reggie Jackson once admitting, "I've never been afraid at the plate, but Mr. Ryan makes me uncomfortable. He's the only pitcher who's ever made me consider wearing a helmet with an ear flap."

On another occasion, Jackson said, "You don't face Ryan without your rest. He's the only guy I go against that makes me go to bed before midnight."

Oakland catcher and future major-league pitching coach Dave Duncan commented, "A good night against Nolan Ryan is going 0-for-4 and you don't get hit in the head. Ryan doesn't just get you out. He embarrasses you."

Yet, despite the dominance that Ryan displayed on the mound, he regularly lost almost as many games as he won due to the poor run support he received from his teammates, prompting him to say, "I feel like I have to pitch a shutout every night or lose. If I throw one bad pitch, I'll be beaten."

After Ryan finished the 1979 season with a record of 16-14 and a rather mediocre 3.60 ERA, the Angels chose not to re-sign him when he became a free agent at the end of the year, with GM Buzzie Bavasi saying at the time, "Nolan Ryan can be replaced by two 8-7 pitchers." Feeling differently, new Astros owner John McMullen offered Ryan a four-year, $4.5 million contract that made him the first athlete in professional team sports to be paid $1 million per year.

Looking back on the signing, Ryan said, "Ever since the Colt .45s came in, I had hoped that someday I would be able to play with the Astros and be at home. It was a dream come true for me."

Ryan experienced a moderate amount of success his first year in Houston, going 11-10 with a 3.35 ERA, and striking out 200 batters in 233⅔ innings pitched for the NL Western Division champions in 1980. Improving upon his performance the following year, Ryan concluded the strike-shortened 1981 campaign with a record of 11-5, a league-leading 1.69 ERA, a WHIP of 1.121, and 140 strikeouts in 149 innings of work, earning All-Star honors and a fourth-place finish in the NL Cy Young voting. Remaining one of the senior circuit's better pitchers the next five seasons, Ryan compiled an overall record of 64-52 and ranked among the league leaders in strikeouts each year. Particularly effective in 1982, Ryan went 16-12 with a 3.16 ERA and placed near the top of the league rankings with 245 strikeouts, 250 innings pitched, and 10 complete games. Ryan had another excellent year in 1983, when he finished 14-9 with a 2.98 ERA and struck out 183 batters in 196 innings of work, breaking Walter Johnson's all-time strikeout record.

Although Ryan registered fewer strikeouts and threw fewer innings for the Astros than he did for the Angels, he proved to be just as effective, compiling an almost identical ERA (3.13 vs 3.07) and a significantly better WHIP (1.206 vs 1.294). Developing into a more complete pitcher during his time in Houston, Ryan retained the big breaking ball he had learned from pitching coach Tom Morgan in California, added a more effective changeup, and gained better command of his fastball, allowing him to significantly reduce his walk total. Meanwhile, Ryan amazingly lost very little, if any, velocity on his heater, with Pete Rose stating in 1988, "At the age of 41, Nolan Ryan is the top power pitcher in the league. You can talk about Dwight Gooden, you can talk about Mike Scott, you can talk about whoever you want, but none of them throw as consistently hard as Ryan does."

Owing his longevity to his tremendous physical condition, Ryan maintained the body of a much younger man by adhering to a grueling exercise program that Gene Coleman, Houston's strength and conditioning advisor, developed specifically for him. On nights he pitched, Ryan rode a stationary bicycle for at least 45 minutes after the game. In between starts, Ryan spent more than two hours every day lifting weights, running, and bicycling. And during the offseason, Ryan typically spent nearly five hours a day working out.

Due to poor run support in 1987, Ryan compiled the worst won-lost record of his career, finishing the season just 8-16. Nevertheless, he earned a fifth-place finish in the NL Cy Young voting by leading the league with a 2.76 ERA and 270 strikeouts. Ryan followed that by going 12-11 with a 3.52 ERA and a league-leading 228 strikeouts in 1988, before signing with the Texas Rangers as a free agent at the end of the year when Astros owner John McMullen attempted to reduce his salary by 20 percent.

Ryan, who, during his time in Houston, compiled an overall record of 106-94, an ERA of 3.13, and a WHIP of 1.206, threw 38 complete games and 13 shutouts, struck out 1,866 batters in 1,854⅔ innings pitched, and notched the 3,000th, 4,000th, and 4,500th strikeouts of his illustrious career, ended up spending five seasons with the Rangers, winning his 300th game, recording his 5,000th strikeout, and tossing two more no-hitters, before retiring at the end of 1993 after tearing the ulnar collateral ligament in his right elbow in a September start against Seattle. Discussing his injury after the game, Ryan told reporters, "I heard the ligament pop like a rubber band. There's no way I'll ever be able to throw again. My body is telling me it's time to move on and do something else."

Officially announcing his retirement shortly thereafter, Ryan ended his 27-year big-league career with a record of 324-292, an ERA of 3.19, a

WHIP of 1.247, 222 complete games, 61 shutouts, and 5,714 strikeouts in 5,386 total innings of work. In addition to holding the major-league record for most strikeouts, Ryan ranks first all-time in fewest hits allowed per nine innings pitched (6.555) and second in games started (773). He also walked more batters (2,795) than any other pitcher in baseball history.

Following his playing days, Ryan became a partner in a group that brought two of the Astros' minor-league affiliates to Texas. He also signed a personal services contract with the team that made him a de facto part-time minor-league pitching coach. Leaving the Astros in 2008 to become president of the Texas Rangers, Ryan continued to serve the organization in that capacity until 2010, when he became part of an ownership group that purchased the team from Tom Hicks. Choosing to step down as the Rangers CEO three years later, Ryan subsequently accepted a position as an executive advisor for the Astros under owner Jim Crane. Ryan remained in that post until the end of the 2019 season, when he handed in his resignation.

ASTROS CAREER HIGHLIGHTS

Best Season

Despite being limited by a players' strike to just 21 starts, 149 innings, and 140 strikeouts in 1981, Nolan pitched his best ball as a member of the Astros, earning All-Star honors and a fourth-place finish in the NL Cy Young voting by going 11-5 with a league-leading 1.69 ERA, which set a single-season franchise record that still stands.

Memorable Moments/Greatest Performances

Ryan threw the fifth of his record seven no-hitters on September 26, 1981, issuing three walks and registering 11 strikeouts during a 5–0 blanking of the Dodgers.

Ryan tossed a one-hit shutout on August 11, 1982, yielding just three walks and a fifth-inning single by catcher Terry Kennedy during a 3–0 win over the Padres.

Ryan again shut out the Padres on just one hit on August 3, 1983, recording 10 strikeouts, issuing six walks, and surrendering only a third-inning single by second baseman Tim Flannery during a 1–0 Astros win.

Ryan threw 27⅔ consecutive scoreless innings from May 11 to June 1, 1984, turning in his finest performance over that stretch on May 16, when he allowed just five hits and struck out 11 batters during a 1–0 shutout of the Pirates.

Although Ryan didn't figure in the decision, he hurled another gem on July 22, 1986, issuing four walks, recording 14 strikeouts, and yielding just a fifth-inning double by catcher Mike Fitzgerald in 9⅓ innings of work, before Glenn Davis gave the Astros a 1–0 victory over the Montreal Expos by hitting a walkoff homer in the bottom of the 10th inning.

In addition to allowing just three hits and one run over the first 6⅔ innings of a 12–3 win over the Braves on May 1, 1987, Ryan hit one of his two career homers, going deep with two men on base in the top of the seventh inning.

Ryan earned a 4–2 victory over the Giants on September 9, 1987, by recording 16 strikeouts and allowing just two runs on six hits in eight innings of work.

Notable Achievements

- Compiled ERA under 3.00 three times, posting mark under 2.00 once.
- Struck out more than 200 batters five times.
- Threw more than 200 innings five times.
- Threw no-hitter vs. Los Angeles Dodgers on September 26, 1981.
- Led NL pitchers in ERA twice, strikeouts twice, and strikeouts-to-walks ratio once.
- Finished second in NL in strikeouts once.
- Holds Astros single-season record for lowest ERA (1.69 in 1981).
- Holds Astros career record for most strikeouts (1,866).
- Ranks among Astros career leaders in wins (6th), ERA (7th), shutouts (tied for 7th), innings pitched (4th), complete games (tied for 8th), and starts (4th).
- Holds MLB career record for most strikeouts (5,714).
- Two-time division champion (1980 and 1986).
- Three-time NL Player of the Week.
- Two-time NL Pitcher of the Month.
- Finished in top five of NL Cy Young voting twice.
- Two-time NL All-Star selection (1981 and 1985).
- Number 41 on the *Sporting News'* 1999 list of Baseball's 100 Greatest Players.
- #34 retired by Astros.
- Inducted into Astros Hall of Fame in 2019.
- Elected to Baseball Hall of Fame by members of BBWAA in 1999.

17

JUSTIN VERLANDER

A three-time Cy Young Award winner and onetime league MVP, Justin Verlander has performed so brilliantly over the course of his 18-year career that he is virtually guaranteed induction into the Baseball Hall of Fame the very first time his name appears on the ballot. Having most of his finest seasons for the Detroit Tigers, Verlander earned six All-Star selections, six top-five finishes in the AL Cy Young voting, his first Cy Young Award, and his lone MVP trophy during his time in the Motor City. However, Verlander pitched just as well for the Astros from 2017 to 2022, winning more than 20 games once, striking out more than 250 batters twice, and compiling an ERA under 3.00 four times, en route to posting the lowest ERA in franchise history. Making an enormous impact during his five-year stint in Houston, Verlander earned three All-Star nominations and won two Cy Young Awards, in helping the Astros win four division titles, three pennants, and two World Series, before returning to Texas for a second tour of duty with the club during the latter stages of the 2023 campaign.

Born in Manakin Sabot, Virginia, on February 20, 1983, Justin Brooks Verlander got his start in organized baseball in the Tuckahoe Little League in nearby Richmond. Later developing into a top performer at Goochland High School after his father enrolled him in the Richmond Baseball Academy, Verlander registered 86 mph on the radar gun with his fastball by his senior year. Following his graduation from Goochland High, Verlander spent three seasons excelling on the mound for Old Dominion University in Norfolk, Virginia, establishing himself as the all-time strikeout leader in Commonwealth of Virginia (Division I) history by fanning 427 batters in 335⅔ total innings of work.

Selected by the Detroit Tigers with the second overall pick of the June 2004 MLB Draft after helping the USA win a silver medal in the 2003 Pan American Games, Verlander spent less than one full season in Detroit's farm system before earning his first big-league callup in July 2005. Returned to the minors after appearing in two games with the parent club, Verlander rejoined the Tigers for good in 2006, earning AL Rookie of the Year honors by compiling a record of 17-9 and an ERA of 3.63 for a Detroit team that posted its first winning mark in more than a decade.

Impressed with the poise that the 23-year-old right-hander displayed on the mound his first year in the league, Rays manager Joe Maddon commented, "That kid has so much potential, and he doesn't look a bit like a rookie. He has everything and can be as good as he wants."

Tigers catcher Iván Rodríguez said of his battery-mate, "He's going to be a superstar in this game for a long time."

Detroit outfielder Craig Monroe added, "He's confident, halfway cocky, which is good. Maybe that is what gives him the edge."

Meanwhile, Cleveland Indians slugging DH/first baseman Travis Hafner noted, "He throws 99, which you see very rarely. He throws strikes, and he has a great curveball and changeup. He has a great future."

Verlander followed his outstanding rookie season with an equally impressive sophomore campaign, earning All-Star honors by going 18-6 with a 3.66 ERA. Less effective in 2008, Verlander won just 11 of his 28 decisions and posted an ERA of 4.84. However, he rebounded in 2009 to begin an outstanding four-year run during which he compiled an overall record of 78-31 and a composite ERA of 2.95. Performing especially well in 2011, Verlander earned Cy Young and AL MVP honors by capturing the pitcher's version of the Triple Crown, leading the league with 24 victories (against five losses), a 2.40 ERA, and 250 strikeouts, while also finishing first in the circuit with a WHIP of 0.920 and 251 innings pitched.

Verlander spent most of the next five seasons in Detroit, winning another 59 games, before being dealt to the Astros for three minor-league prospects just prior to the August 31, 2017, trade deadline. Verlander, who left Detroit with a career record of 183-114, an ERA of 3.49, a WHIP of 1.191, and 2,373 strikeouts in 2,511 total innings of work, ended up paying huge dividends for his new team the rest of the year, winning all five of his regular-season starts and compiling an ERA of 1.06 for the Astros, before helping them win their first world championship by going 4-1 during the postseason. Meanwhile, Verlander, who started the Wins for Warriors Foundation for veterans of the US military in 2016, raised nearly a quarter of a million dollars through his foundation to help Houston recover from Hurricane Harvey, which struck the city in August 2017.

Continuing to perform at an elite level the next two seasons, Verlander earned All-Star honors and a runner-up finish in the AL Cy Young voting in 2018 by going 16-9 with a 2.52 ERA and a league-leading 290 strikeouts and 0.902 WHIP, before winning his second Cy Young Award the

Justin Verlander won two Cy Young Awards as a member of the Astros.
Courtesy of Keith Allison

following year by compiling a record of 21-6, leading the league with 223 innings pitched and a WHIP of 0.803, and finishing second in the circuit with 300 strikeouts and an ERA of 2.58.

Showing no signs of slowing down at 36 years of age, the 6'5", 235-pound Verlander retained the same velocity and movement on his mid-to-upper-90s four-seam fastball, which typically breaks inside to right-handed batters and away from lefties. Verlander's unusual ability to "add" or "sub-tract" from the velocity on his signature pitch over the course of a game as the situation dictates is one of the things that has made him so difficult for opposing batters to face. Known to reach 100 mph on the radar gun during the latter stages of contests, Verlander has tremendous stamina, with former

Tigers manager Jim Leyland once marveling, "I've never had a starting pitcher who can throw 99 (mph) in the ninth inning."

Verlander's repertoire of pitches also includes a mid-to-high 80s slider that moves very much like a cutter, a 12-6 curveball that averages about 80 mph, and an 85–88 mph changeup.

Extremely competitive, Verlander described his approach to pitching by saying, "I like to challenge hitters with a 'Here it is, hit it' mentality. It's definitely a big part of my game, especially when I get in situations where I need it. I usually save a little bit so it's there for me."

Meanwhile, in elaborating on his pitching style, Verlander stated, "I'm a power guy. Good fastball; a knuckle-curve that I can throw for strikes; a changeup that sinks down and away from lefties and I can also throw for strikes."

Verlander added, "When an artist wants to paint a painting, they have all those things in their head that they want to portray on a canvas. It's the same thing when I'm pitching. I have all these thoughts going through my head about how I want to pitch: which pitch I want to throw here, and why do I want to throw it?"

Coming off his magnificent performance in 2019, Verlander missed virtually all of the next two seasons due to injury. After being shut down for most of 2020 with a forearm strain, Verlander underwent Tommy John surgery in late September that forced him to sit out the entire 2021 campaign as well. Returning to action in 2022, the 39-year-old Verlander miraculously had one of his finest seasons, earning Cy Young honors for the third time by compiling a record of 18-4 and a league-leading 1.75 ERA and 0.829 WHIP, while being placed on a strict pitch count. Although Verlander subsequently struggled somewhat in the postseason, getting hit hard in his lone start against Seattle in the ALDS and his first start against Philadelphia in the World Series, he helped the Astros capture their second world championship by turning in solid performances against the Yankees in Game 1 of the ALCS and the Phillies in Game 5 of the Fall Classic, winning both decisions.

Choosing to become a free agent by declining a $25 million option with the Astros at the end of the year, Verlander inked a two-year, $86.7 million deal with the New York Mets that brought his time in Houston to an end. Paying tribute to the city and its fans shortly thereafter, Verlander posted a message on Instagram that read: "To Houston: Thank you from the bottom of my heart for being so positive, generous, and accepting. You made me and my family feel at home, and I'll always be grateful for that. We have all shared lots of amazing moments together since the trade in 2017. My family and I will forever cherish our time in the 🤘 and the memories created that will last a lifetime!"

Following his arrival in New York, Verlander missed the first month of the 2023 campaign with a "low-grade teres major strain," before returning to action in early May. However, with the Mets failing to live up to pre-season expectations, they elected to part ways with Verlander at the trade deadline, dealing him back to the Astros for a pair of minor-league prospects after he compiled a record of 6-5 and an ERA of 3.15 for them. Upon his return to Houston Velander went 7-3 with a 3.31 ERA and a WHIP of 1.118, in helping the Astros capture their sixth division title in the last seven years. Over parts of six seasons in Houston, Verlander has compiled an overall record of 68-22, an ERA of 2.36, and a WHIP of 0.860, thrown three complete games and two shutouts, and recorded 888 strikeouts in 720 total innings of work. Meanwhile, over the course of his big-league career, Verlander has posted a record of 257-141, an ERA of 3.24, and a WHIP of 1.118, thrown 26 complete games and 9 shutouts, and struck out 3,342 batters in 3,325.1 innings pitched.

ASTROS CAREER HIGHLIGHTS

Best Season

Although Verlander performed magnificently in 2022, earning Cy Young honors and a 10th-place finish in the AL MVP voting by posting a record of 18-4, leading the league with a 1.75 ERA and a WHIP of 0.829, and striking out 185 batters in 175 innings pitched, he made a slightly greater overall impact in 2019, when, in addition to leading all AL hurlers with 21 victories, a WHIP of 0.803, and 223 innings pitched, he finished second in the league with a 2.58 ERA and 300 strikeouts.

Memorable Moments/Greatest Performances

Verlander performed brilliantly against the Yankees in the 2017 ALCS, earning series MVP honors by winning both his starts, compiling an ERA of 0.56, and allowing just 10 hits and two walks in 16 innings of work, while recording 21 strikeouts. After yielding just five hits and striking out 13 batters during a complete-game 2–1 victory in Game 2, Verlander returned to the mound for Game 6, tying the series at three games apiece by allowing five hits and no runs, walking one batter, and striking out eight over the first seven innings of a 7–1 Astros win.

Although the Astros ended up losing to the Yankees, 4–0, on May 1, 2018, Verlander continued to dominate New York's lineup, allowing just three hits, issuing no walks, and recording 14 strikeouts over eight scoreless innings.

Verlander tossed a five-hit shutout on May 16, 2018, walking just one batter and striking out seven during a 2–0 win over the Anaheim Angels.

Verlander recorded 12 strikeouts and yielded just one hit and one walk over the first eight innings of a 5–1 win over the White Sox on May 21, 2019, surrendering only a solo home run to José Abreu.

Verlander dominated the Cleveland lineup on July 30, 2019, registering 13 strikeouts and allowing just two hits over the first seven innings of a 2–0 Astros win.

Verlander threw the third no-hitter of his career on September 1, 2019, recording 14 strikeouts and yielding just a first-inning walk to Cavan Biggio during a 2–0 win over the Blue Jays.

Verlander turned in another dominant performance on April 16, 2022, allowing just three hits, issuing no walks, and striking out eight batters over the first eight innings of a 4–0 win over the Seattle Mariners.

Verlander came up a few outs short of tossing his fourth no-hitter on May 10, 2022, yielding just two walks and an eighth-inning single to Gio Urshela during a 5–0 win over the Twins, before being replaced on the mound prior to the start of the final frame.

Verlander nearly matched that effort on June 29, 2022, allowing just two hits and one walk over the first eight innings of a 2–0 win over the Mets.

Verlander continued his dominance of the Twins on August 23, 2022, working six perfect innings and recording 10 strikeouts during a 4–2 Astros win, before turning the game over to the bullpen in the top of the seventh.

Notable Achievements

- Won 21 games in 2019.
- Won at least 16 games two other times.
- Posted winning percentage above .750 three times.
- Compiled ERA under 3.00 four times, finishing with mark under 2.00 twice.
- Posted WHIP under 1.000 four times.

- Struck out more than 250 batters twice, amassing 300 strikeouts in 2019.
- Threw more than 200 innings twice.
- Threw no-hitter vs. Toronto on September 1, 2019.
- Led AL in wins twice, winning percentage once, ERA once, WHIP three times, strikeouts once, strikeouts-to-walks ratio twice, shutouts once, innings pitched once, and starts twice.
- Finished second in AL in ERA once, strikeouts once, and innings pitched once.
- Holds Astros career records for best winning percentage (.756), ERA (2.36), WHIP (0.860), and strikeouts-to-walks ratio (6.938).
- Holds Astros single-season records for best winning percentage (.850 in 2022), WHIP (0.803 in 2019), and strikeouts-to-walks ratio (7.838 in 2018).
- Six-time division champion (2017, 2018, 2019, 2021, 2022, and 2023).
- Four-time AL champion (2017, 2019, 2021, and 2022).
- Two-time world champion (2017 and 2022).
- Three-time AL Player of the Week.
- May 2018 AL Pitcher of the Month.
- 2017 ALCS MVP.
- 2017 Babe Ruth Award winner.
- Two-time AL Cy Young Award winner (2019 and 2022).
- Finished second in 2018 AL Cy Young voting.
- Finished 10th in 2018 AL MVP voting.
- 2019 All-MLB First Team.
- Three-time AL All-Star selection (2018, 2019, and 2022).

18

MOISÉS ALOU

An outstanding offensive performer who excelled at the plate for six different teams during a lengthy major-league career that spanned parts of 17 seasons, Moisés Alou overcame a litany of injuries to establish himself as one of the finest all-around hitters of his era. A lifetime .303 hitter who also amassed more than 330 home runs and close to 1,300 RBIs, Alou surpassed 30 homers three times, knocked in more than 100 runs five times, and batted over .330 on five separate occasions, earning six All-Star nominations and three top-10 finishes in the NL MVP voting. Having some of his finest seasons for the Astros, Alou topped 20 homers, knocked in more than 100 runs, and batted over .300 in each of his three years in Houston, en route to compiling the highest career batting average and OPS of any player in franchise history. A two-time All-Star for the Astros, Alou proved to be a huge contributor to teams that won three division titles, before splitting his final seven seasons between the Chicago Cubs, San Francisco Giants, and New York Mets.

Born in Atlanta, Georgia, on July 3, 1966, Moisés Rojas Alou grew up in the Dominican Republic after his parents divorced shortly after he turned two years of age. Raised by his mother, Maria, young Moisés seemed destined for a career in baseball from his early childhood. The son of star outfielder and longtime major-league manager Felipe Alou, and the nephew of big-league outfielders Matty and Jesús Alou, Moisés received a considerable amount of help in developing his baseball skills during his formative years, although he spent more time on the basketball court as a youngster, recalling, "Actually, I had no choice but to play basketball because the schools here in the Dominican didn't have baseball programs or baseball fields. But they do have basketball, like every school, and they have basketball courts."

Alou continued, "I started playing organized baseball right after high school because I wanted to get a scholarship to go to school in the United States, and that was my only way out. My brother had a scholarship from this Latin American foundation. . . . I played some baseball—street ball or pickup games—and I'd play some with my uncle. But I didn't play organized ball until after high school."

After arriving in the United States at the age of 18, Alou enrolled at Cañada College, a small public community college located in Redwood City, California, where, over the course of the next two seasons, he hit 17 homers, knocked in 84 runs, and batted well over .400. Impressed with Alou's tremendous bat speed and quickness on the basepaths, the Pittsburgh Pirates selected him with the second overall pick of the 1986 MLB Amateur Draft. Alou subsequently spent the next four years in the minor leagues, before being traded to the Montreal Expos on August 16, 1990. After appearing in 14 games with the Expos during the season's final month, Alou missed the entire 1991 campaign with a badly injured shoulder. Returning to action in 1992, Alou earned a runner-up finish in the NL Rookie of the Year voting by hitting nine homers, driving in 56 runs, and batting .282

Moisés Alou helped lead the Astros to three division titles during his brief stint in Houston.

for an Expos team that finished second in the NL East under new manager Felipe Alou.

Continuing to thrive under his father's direction the next four seasons, Alou averaged 19 homers and 79 RBIs, batted over .300 once, and won his first Silver Slugger, despite suffering a severe ankle injury in 1993 that robbed him of much of his speed, and undergoing surgery on both shoulders before the 1995 season ended. Particularly outstanding during the strike-shortened 1994 campaign, Alou earned All-Star honors and a third-place finish in the NL MVP voting by hitting 22 homers, driving in 78 runs, scoring 81 times, and finishing fourth in the league with a .339 batting average.

A free agent at the end of 1997, Alou signed with the Florida Marlins; he helped lead them to the world championship by hitting 23 homers, knocking in 115 runs, batting .292, and compiling an OPS of .866. But with Marlins owner Wayne Huizenga choosing to dismantle his team the following offseason, Florida traded Alou to the Astros for three minor-league prospects on November 11, 1997.

Commenting on the deal afterwards, Marlins general manager Dave Dombrowski said, "It's not what you prefer to do. But, in this situation, we're looking for young quality players that are ready to step in. You don't want to trade a player like Moisés Alou. That's no question."

Meanwhile, Astros GM Gerry Hunsicker gushed, "Moisés Alou obviously is one of the premier players in the game today. It's unusual that anybody can acquire a player of this magnitude. Adding him to our lineup makes us a force to be reckoned with. When you put Bagwell, Biggio, and Alou in the middle of your order, it's a pretty awesome trio, no matter what the order is."

Performing brilliantly his first year in Houston, Alou helped lead the Astros to a regular-season record of 102-60 and the second of their three straight NL Central Division titles by hitting 38 homers, driving in 124 runs, scoring 104 times, batting .312, and posting an OPS of .981, earning in the process All-Star honors, his second Silver Slugger, and a third-place finish in the NL MVP balloting. Alou subsequently missed the entire 1999 campaign with a torn ACL he sustained when he slipped and fell off his treadmill while working out at home in the Dominican Republic the following offseason. Despite being limited by an assortment of injuries to 126 games in 2000, Alou had another big year, hitting 30 homers, knocking in 114 runs, batting .355, and compiling an OPS of 1.039. Alou followed that by hitting 27 homers, driving in 108 runs, batting .331, and posting an

OPS of .949 in 2001, with his superb offensive display gaining him All-Star recognition for the fourth of six times.

The right-handed-hitting Alou, who, after entering the majors at a lean 6'3" and 185 pounds added some 15–20 pounds of muscle onto his frame, possessed a short, compact swing that enabled him to drive the ball with authority to all fields. Known for his quick wrists, Alou rarely overswung, never striking out more than 87 times in a season. Though not a dead-pull hitter, Alou learned how to adjust his swing to take better advantage of the inviting left field wall at Enron Field after the Astros moved there in 2000.

Also known for his calm demeanor at the plate, Alou said, "The way I hit, my swing and everything was low maintenance. I didn't have very much movement because I had quick hands. My bat speed was pretty good, and I remember my dad telling me, and I agreed with it, that the guy that can hit the fastball is going to stay in the game as long as they want."

A solid defender as well, Alou, who manned both corner outfield positions during his time in Houston, possessed a strong throwing arm and decent range, although the injuries he sustained earlier in his career reduced his speed considerably.

Despite the prolific offensive numbers Alou posted the previous few seasons, the budget-conscious Astros chose not to offer him a contract extension at the end of 2001, allowing him to become a free agent. Electing to sign with the Chicago Cubs, Alou left Houston having hit 95 homers, driven in 346 runs, scored 265 times, collected 513 hits, 93 doubles, and eight triples, batted .331, compiled a .403 on-base percentage, and posted a .585 slugging percentage as a member of the team.

Alou played three years in Chicago, earning All-Star honors in 2004 by hitting 39 homers, driving in 106 runs, and batting .293, before signing with the San Francisco Giants when he became a free agent again at the end of the year. After two seasons in San Francisco, Alou spent a year-and-a-half assuming a part-time role in New York, posting batting averages of .341 and .347 for the Mets before announcing his retirement midway through the 2008 campaign with career totals of 332 home runs, 1,287 RBIs, 1,109 runs scored, 2,134 hits, 421 doubles, 39 triples, 106 stolen bases, a .303 batting average, a .369 on-base percentage, and a .516 slugging percentage.

After remaining away from the game for a few years following his retirement, Alou accepted a position with the San Diego Padres, for whom he has worked as a special assistant in player development since 2015.

ASTROS CAREER HIGHLIGHTS

Best Season

Alou performed magnificently his entire time in Houston, driving in more than 100 runs and batting well over .300 in each of his three full seasons, with his .355 batting average in 2000 representing the second-highest single-season mark in franchise history. Nevertheless, Alou posted his best overall numbers as a member of the Astros in 1998, when he earned a third-place finish in the NL MVP balloting and *Sporting News* NL All-Star honors by hitting 38 homers, driving in 124 runs, scoring 104 times, collecting 182 hits and 34 doubles, batting .312, compiling an on-base percentage of .399, and posting a slugging percentage of .582.

Memorable Moments/Greatest Performances

Alou had a huge game against his former team on April 26, 1998, when he went 3-for-6, with a homer, double, five RBIs, and three runs scored during a 15–0 win over the Montreal Expos.

Alou helped lead the Astros to a 17–2 rout of the Chicago White Sox on June 30, 1998, by homering twice, driving in four runs, and scoring three times.

Alou contributed to a 16–7 victory over the Pirates on September 15, 2000, by scoring four times and knocking in four runs with a homer and a pair of doubles.

Alou led the Astros to an 11–6 win over the Braves on April 24, 2001, by going 4-for-5, with two homers, four RBIs, and three runs scored.

Alou hit safely in 23 straight games from June 22 to July 18, 2001, going 36-for-89 (.405), with seven homers, seven doubles, 11 walks, 24 RBIs, and 18 runs scored over that stretch.

Notable Achievements

- Hit more than 20 home runs three times, topping 30 homers twice.
- Knocked in more than 100 runs three times.
- Scored more than 100 runs once (104 in 1998).
- Batted over .300 three times, topping the .330-mark twice.
- Surpassed 30 doubles twice.
- Compiled on-base percentage over .400 once (.416 in 2000).

- Posted slugging percentage over .500 three times, topping the .600-mark once.
- Posted OPS over .900 three times, topping the 1.000-mark once.
- Finished second in NL with .355 batting average in 2000.
- Finished third in NL with .331 batting average in 2001.
- Holds Astros career records for highest batting average (.331) and OPS (.988).
- Ranks among Astros career leaders with .585 slugging percentage (2nd) and .403 on-base percentage (3rd).
- Three-time division champion (1998, 1999, and 2001).
- May 31, 1998, NL Player of the Week.
- 1998 Silver Slugger Award winner.
- 1998 Astros team MVP.
- Finished third in 1998 NL MVP voting.
- Two-time NL All-Star selection (1998 and 2001).
- 1998 *Sporting News* NL All-Star selection.

19

GLENN DAVIS

The first Astros player to hit more than 30 home runs in a season three times, Glenn Davis established himself as one of the NL's top sluggers during his time in Houston, despite having to play half his games in the cavernous Astrodome. Also the first player in franchise history to surpass 20 round-trippers six straight times, Davis accomplished the feat from 1985 to 1990, a period during which he also knocked in more than 90 runs on three separate occasions. The foremost power threat on Houston's 1986 Western Division championship team, Davis earned a runner-up finish in the league MVP voting with his prodigious slugging—one of three times he placed in the top 10 in the balloting. A two-time NL All-Star as well, Davis accomplished all he did after enduring a difficult childhood that often left him contemplating suicide.

Born in Jacksonville, Florida, on March 28, 1961, Glenn Earle Davis grew up barely knowing his father, Gene Davis, a minor-league player who left his wife and children shortly after Glenn turned seven years of age. In discussing his dad years later, Davis said, "He was the type of person that couldn't handle pressure. He had all the ability, but he wasn't able to deal with failure. I think that's what started the problems between him and my mother."

Bitter over the problems that baseball caused her, Davis's mother, Margaret, who eventually divorced her husband and remarried, refused to allow her son to follow a similar path, with Glenn's older sister, Diane, remembering, "When Daddy was playing ball, he got involved in drinking. Momma was determined to protect Glenn from that."

Forbidden to see his father once his parents divorced, Davis recalled, "I didn't understand what was going on for a while, but I began to see that something was wrong, that I was being used as a tool of jealousy against my father. I was always made fun of in the neighborhood because I had to sneak down and meet my father at the end of the block if I wanted to see him."

Glenn Davis earned a runner-up finish in the 1986 NL
MVP voting.

Revealing that her younger brother grew increasingly resentful as he
became more involved in sports, Diane stated, "Glenn was very bitter about
the divorce, much more so than the rest of us. He wanted his daddy there
to see him do all these things."

Further troubled by a lack of self-esteem, Glenn suffered from acne as
a child and grew into much of his 6'3", 210-pound frame while still in elementary school, causing him to become the frequent target of jokes made
by the other neighborhood children. Slow and ponderous, Glenn was also
teased on the ballfield, with his sister remembering, "He was always so fat
that they would kid him in Little League that he had to hit a home run just
to get to first base."

Reaching his emotional nadir as a teenager, Davis recalled, "All through
my teenage years I constantly thought about committing suicide. I would
hold a knife to my stomach and think about stabbing myself, or sometimes

I'd consider running out into the street in front of a car. Many nights, I would sit in my room crying and ask God why He was letting these things happen to me. I felt like an ugly duckling, unloved and alone in the world . . . "

Davis continued, "I would put a gun to my head with no bullets in the chamber and just sit there on the bed and pull the trigger over and over. . . . I knew that if I did that, it would hurt my mother and father, that they would be sorry for what they had done to me. They would have to live with that for the rest of their lives."

Finally finding some relief from his suffering after George Davis (no relation), the athletic director at University Christian High School, and his wife took him into their home, Glenn became like one of the family. Also developing an extremely strong bond with their son, Storm, who later became a major-league pitcher, Glenn combined with his newfound "brother" to lead the Christians to back-to-back Florida state titles in 1978 and 1979.

Subsequently selected by Baltimore in the 31st round of the 1979 MLB June Amateur Draft, Davis chose not to sign for a bonus of $2,700 when he learned that the Orioles viewed him primarily as a pitcher, later saying, "I had a good arm and all, but I told them I wanted to hit."

Electing instead to accept a baseball scholarship to the University of Georgia, Davis spent one season playing for the Bulldogs, before transferring to Manatee Junior College in Florida to make himself eligible for the MLB Draft sooner. Ultimately selected by the Astros with the fifth overall pick of the draft's Secondary Phase in 1981, Davis inked a deal worth $50,000, after which he spent the next four seasons advancing through Houston's farm system.

Developing into a top power-hitting prospect during that time, Davis hit a total of 71 home runs, earning in the process a callup to the parent club in September 1984. Although Davis batted just .213 in 18 games and 61 official at-bats during the season's final month, he made a favorable impression on team brass by homering twice and knocking in eight runs. Named the Astros' starting first baseman the following year, Wilson earned a fifth-place finish in the NL Rookie of the Year voting by hitting 20 homers, driving in 64 runs, scoring 51 times, batting .271, and compiling an OPS of .807, despite appearing in only 100 games and garnering just 350 official at-bats.

Emerging as one of the NL's premier sluggers in 1986, Davis helped lead the Astros to the Western Division title by placing near the top of the league rankings with 31 home runs, 101 RBIs, and a .493 slugging percentage, while also scoring 91 runs, collecting 32 doubles, batting .265, and compiling an OPS of .837. Davis, who earned All-Star honors and finished second in the NL MVP voting to Philadelphia's Mike Schmidt, drew favorable comparisons to the Hall of Fame third baseman from Houston batting coach Denis Menke, who stated at one point during the season, "He [Davis] has a home run hitter's swing and a better stroke, I think, than Mike Schmidt's. But Glenn doesn't just want to be a power hitter; he wants to be a hitter."

Davis continued his assault against NL pitching the next three seasons, earning another All-Star selection and two more top-10 finishes in the league MVP balloting by averaging 30 homers and 94 RBIs from 1987 to 1989. Particularly outstanding in 1988 and 1989, Davis hit 30 homers, knocked in 99 runs, scored 78 times, batted .271, and compiled an OPS of .818 in the first of those campaigns, before reaching the seats 34 times, driving in 89 runs, scoring 87 others, batting .269, and posting an OPS of .842 in the second.

The Astros' only true power threat throughout the period, Davis typically led the team in home runs by a wide margin, annually ranking among the league leaders in that category even though he had the misfortune of playing his home games in the Astrodome. And despite being a free swinger who never drew more than 69 bases on balls in any single season, the right-handed-hitting Davis made more consistent contact than most sluggers, striking out more than 80 times just twice his entire career. Meanwhile, Davis gradually developed into a solid defensive first baseman, consistently ranking among the top players at his position in putouts, assists, and fielding percentage.

Plagued by a rib injury in 1990, Davis appeared in only 93 games. Nevertheless, he managed to put up respectable numbers, concluding the campaign with 22 homers, 64 RBIs, a .251 batting average, and a career-high OPS of .880. But with the Astros seeking to reduce their payroll, they completed a trade with the Orioles the following offseason that sent Davis to Baltimore for youngsters Steve Finley, Pete Harnisch, and Curt Schilling.

Davis, who left Houston with career totals of 166 homers, 518 RBIs, 427 runs scored, 795 hits, 150 doubles, and 10 triples, a .262 batting average, a .337 on-base percentage, and a .483 slugging percentage, ended up spending three injury-marred years in Baltimore, hitting only 24 home runs in a total of just 185 games, before being released during the latter stages of the 1993 campaign following an argument with Birds manager Johnny Oates. Davis subsequently spent one season playing in the minors and another two in Japan, before retiring from baseball at the end of 1996.

Following his playing days, Davis settled with his wife, Teresa, in Columbus, Georgia, where he became the CEO of the Cascade Group, which develops hotels in the southeast region of the country. Davis also continued his work with The Carpenter's Way home for disadvantaged children that he and his wife first established in 1992. Davis, who also helped found the Arabella Home for Girls in 2008, currently serves as an elected city councilman for the City of Columbus.

ASTROS CAREER HIGHLIGHTS

Best Season

Although Davis hit three more homers and batted a few points higher in 1989, the 1986 campaign proved to be his most impactful season. Serving as the primary power threat on an Astros team that won the NL West title, Davis finished second in the league with 31 homers, placed fourth in the circuit with 101 RBIs, scored 91 times, batted .265, compiled a slugging percentage of .493, and posted an OPS of .837.

Memorable Moments/Greatest Performances

Davis helped lead the Astros to a 12–1 win over the Montreal Expos on July 7, 1986, by homering twice and knocking in five runs.

Davis gave the Astros a 1–0 win over Montreal on July 22, 1986, when he led off the bottom of the 10th inning with a home run.

Davis plated all four runs the Astros scored during a 4–2 win over the Braves on July 28, 1986, delivering the game's big blow in the bottom of the eighth inning, when he homered off Doyle Alexander with two men out and two men on base.

Davis gave Mike Scott the only run he needed to defeat the Mets, 1–0, in Game 1 of the 1986 NLCS when he homered off Dwight Gooden in the bottom of the second inning.

Davis delivered the decisive blow of a 7–6 win over the Phillies on July 2, 1987, when he hit a three-run homer off ace reliever Steve Bedrosian in the top of the ninth inning.

Davis starred in defeat on September 10, 1987, hitting three homers and driving in five runs during an 8–7 loss to the San Diego Padres.

Davis gave the Astros a 7–6 victory over the Padres on June 8, 1989, when he homered off reliever Mark Davis with one man aboard in the bottom of the 10th inning.

. Davis feasted off San Diego pitching again on August 8, 1989, homering twice and knocking in five runs during a 12–3 Astros win.

Although the Astros lost to the Giants in 11 innings by a score of 6–5 on June 1, 1990, Davis had a big day at the plate, driving in all five Houston runs with three homers.

Notable Achievements

- Hit at least 20 home runs six times, topping 30 homers on three occasions.
- Knocked in more than 100 runs once (101 in 1986).
- Surpassed 30 doubles twice.
- Posted slugging percentage over .500 once (.523 in 1990).
- Hit three home runs in one game twice (vs. San Diego on September 10, 1987, and vs. San Francisco on June 1, 1990).
- Finished second in NL in home runs twice.
- Led NL first basemen in fielding percentage once.
- Ranks among Astros career leaders in home runs (7th), slugging percentage (9th), and intentional bases on balls (tied for 5th).
- 1986 division champion.
- July 16, 1989, NL Player of the Week.
- 1986 Silver Slugger Award winner.
- 1990 Lou Gehrig Memorial Award winner.
- Two-time Astros team MVP (1986 and 1988).
- Finished in top 10 of NL MVP voting three times, placing as high as second in 1986.
- Two-time NL All-Star selection (1986 and 1989).

20

CARLOS CORREA

One of the outstanding young players that helped turn the Astros into perennial pennant contenders, Carlos Correa spent seven seasons in Houston, establishing himself as the finest shortstop in franchise history. Despite being plagued by injuries, Correa hit at least 20 homers five times, knocked in more than 90 runs twice, and batted over .300 once, while also winning one Gold Glove for his exceptional work in the field. A major contributor to Astros teams that won four division titles, three pennants, and one World Series, Correa earned two All-Star nominations and one top-five finish in the AL MVP voting, before signing with the Minnesota Twins as a free agent following the conclusion of the 2021 campaign.

Born in Ponce, Puerto Rico, on September 22, 1994, Carlos Javier Correa grew up some 20 miles east, in Barrio Velázquez, a fishing village located in the town of Santa Isabel. Displaying an affinity for baseball at an early age, Correa often played catch in an alley adjacent to his home, before enrolling in a youth league shortly after he celebrated his fifth birthday.

Trained by his father during his formative years, Correa began to exhibit superior ability by the time he turned 11 years of age, prompting his family to move to the municipality of Caguas, where he further honed his skills by practicing with higher-level teams, while also attending Raham Baptist Academy on an academic scholarship. Eventually offered a scholarship to the Puerto Rico Baseball Academy and High School in the town of Gurabo, Correa developed into one of the region's best players with the help of his coaches, who worked with him extensively on improving his batting skills.

After graduating from the PRBAHS, Correa initially signed a letter of intent to attend the University of Miami on a baseball scholarship. However, he changed his plans when the Astros selected him with the first overall pick of the 2012 MLB Amateur Draft, making him the highest-selected player ever to be drafted directly from a Puerto Rican high school, and just the third Latin player to be chosen first overall. After agreeing with the

Astros on a $4.8 million signing bonus on June 7, 2012, Correa spent parts of the next four seasons in the minor leagues, performing well at every stop, despite having his 2014 campaign cut short by a fractured right fibula that required season-ending surgery.

Promoted to the majors on June 8, 2015, Correa spent the next four months starting for the Astros at shortstop, earning AL Rookie of the Year honors by hitting 22 homers, driving in 68 runs, scoring 52 times, batting .279, and compiling an OPS of .857, in 99 games and just under 400 official at-bats. Correa followed that up by hitting 20 homers, knocking in 96 runs, scoring 76 times, batting .274, and posting an OPS of .811 in 2016, before earning his first All-Star nomination in 2017 by hitting 24 homers, driving in 84 runs, scoring 82 times, batting .315, and compiling an OPS

Before departing for Minnesota, Carlos Correa helped lead the Astros to four division titles, three pennants, and one world championship.
Courtesy of Keith Allison

of .941, despite missing nearly two months of action with a torn ligament in his left thumb. Correa subsequently excelled for the Astros in the post-season, helping them win their first world championship by hitting a pair of homers and driving in six runs against Boston in the ALDS, homering once and batting .333 against the Yankees in the ALCS, and driving in five runs with a pair of homers against the Dodgers in the World Series.

One of the game's bigger shortstops at 6'4" and 220 pounds, the right-handed-hitting Correa has good power and does an excellent job of driving the ball to the outfield gaps. Correa also runs the bases well and possesses soft hands and a strong throwing arm in the field, where he relies on good footwork and a more upright ready position to get to the ball. Typically utilizing a one-handed pickup to leverage his long arms, Correa also employs a jump hop on his throws to first base while fading toward third.

Plagued by injuries that limited him to 110 games in 2018, Correa turned in a subpar performance, finishing the season with just 15 homers, 65 RBIs, and a .239 batting average. Correa then missed half of the ensuing campaign as well after suffering a rib fracture while getting a massage at home. Nevertheless, he managed to hit 21 homers, drive in 59 runs, bat .279, and compile an OPS of .926. Meanwhile, Correa began to assume more of a leadership role in Houston, taking it upon himself to apologize for his teammates after the Astros sign-stealing scandal broke the following offseason. Admitting that his team illegally stole signs to gain an advantage over their opponents during their championship campaign of 2017, Correa told reporters, "We were wrong for everything we did in 2017. It's not what we stand for. It's not what we want to portray as an organization, and we were definitely wrong about all that, and we feel really sorry. We affected careers, we affected the game in some way, and, looking back at it, it was just bad."

Correa, who helped children in Houston after Hurricane Harvey struck the area in 2017 and aided people in his hometown in Puerto Rico after Hurricane Maria damaged the island that same year, also continued to display his generosity, donating $500,000 in medical equipment to help the city of Houston during the COVID-19 pandemic.

Posting modest numbers during the pandemic-shortened 2020 campaign, Correa hit just five homers, knocked in only 25 runs, and batted just .264. But he committed just one error in 57 games at shortstop, giving him a .995 fielding percentage that ranked first among players at his position.

Establishing himself as arguably the AL's finest shortstop in 2021, Correa earned his second All-Star selection and a fifth-place finish in the league MVP voting by hitting 26 homers, driving in 92 runs, scoring 104 times, batting .279, and compiling an OPS of .850. Excelling on defense as well, Correa received his first Gold Glove after committing just 11 errors in the field all year.

A free agent at season's end, Correa chose not to accept the Astros' qualifying offer of $18.4 million for one year, and instead signed a three-year contract worth $105.3 million with the Minnesota Twins that included opt-out provisions after the first and second seasons. Upon learning the terms of Correa's new deal, Alex Bregman said, "He deserves it. Nobody is a smarter baseball player, works harder, is more of a leader. Every quality that you look for in a baseball player."

Correa, who left Houston with career totals of 133 homers, 489 RBIs, 438 runs scored, 781 hits, 162 doubles, eight triples, and 33 stolen bases, a .277 batting average, a .356 on-base percentage, and a .481 slugging percentage, performed well his first year in Minnesota, hitting 22 homers, driving in 64 runs, scoring 70 times, and batting .291, despite missing nearly a month of action due to injury. Electing to opt out of the final two years of his contract and become a free agent again at the end of the year, Correa subsequently agreed to lucrative long-term deals, first with the San Francisco Giants, and then with the New York Mets, only to have both teams express an interest in renegotiating after finding fault with his physical exam. Ultimately choosing to remain in Minnesota, Correa inked a six-year, $200 million deal with the Twins that promises to keep him in the Minneapolis area through 2028.

ASTROS CAREER HIGHLIGHTS

Best Season

Before departing for Minnesota at the end of the year, Correa had his finest season for the Astros in 2021, when he earned his second All-Star selection and a fifth-place finish in the AL MVP voting by hitting 26 homers, driving in 92 runs, scoring 104 times, batting .279, and posting an OPS of .850.

Memorable Moments/Greatest Performances

Correa contributed to a 21–5 rout of the Arizona Diamondbacks on October 2, 2015, by going 3-for-4, with a homer, triple, four RBIs, and four runs scored.

Although the Astros lost Game 4 of the 2015 ALDS to Kansas City, 9–6, Correa collected four hits, homered twice, and knocked in four runs.

After homering earlier in the game, Correa gave the Astros a 3–2 win over the Angels on June 21, 2016, when he delivered a two-run bases-loaded double in the bottom of the ninth inning.

Correa helped lead the Astros to a lopsided 19–1 victory over the Toronto Blue Jays on July 9, 2017, by going 4-for-5, with two homers, five RBIs, and three runs scored.

Correa knocked in both runs the Astros scored during their 2–1 victory over the Yankees in Game 2 of the 2017 ALCS, hitting a solo homer off Luis Severino in the bottom of the fourth inning, before plating the game's winning run with a double off Aroldis Chapman in the ninth.

Correa evened the 2019 ALCS at a game apiece when he hit a solo homer in the bottom of the 11th inning of Game 2 that gave the Astros a 3–2 win over the Yankees.

Correa came up big for the Astros against Oakland in Games 1 and 4 of the 2020 ALDS, homering twice and knocking in four runs during a 10–5 win in the opener, before going 3-for-4, with a homer and five RBIs during an 11–6 win in the series clincher.

Although the Astros subsequently lost to Tampa Bay in seven games in the 2020 ALCS, Correa helped them stave off elimination in Game 5 by hitting a game-winning solo home run in the bottom of the ninth inning.

Notable Achievements

- Hit at least 20 home runs five times.
- Scored more than 100 runs once (104 in 2021).
- Batted over .300 once (.315 in 2017).
- Surpassed 30 doubles twice.
- Posted slugging percentage over .500 three times.
- Posted OPS over .900 twice.
- Led AL with 11 sacrifice flies in 2018.
- Led AL shortstops in fielding percentage once.
- Ranks among Astros career leaders in slugging percentage (10th) and OPS (10th).
- Four-time division champion (2017, 2018, 2019, and 2021).
- Three-time AL champion (2017, 2019, and 2021).
- 2017 world champion.
- Three-time AL Player of the Week.
- June 2015 AL Rookie of the Month.

- May 2017 AL Player of the Month.
- 2015 AL Rookie of the Year.
- 2021 Gold Glove Award winner.
- 2021 Platinum Glove Award winner.
- 2021 Astros team MVP.
- Finished fifth in 2021 AL MVP voting.
- Two-time AL All-Star selection (2017 and 2021).
- 2021 *Sporting News* AL All-Star selection.

21

GEORGE SPRINGER

One of the key figures in the Astros' return to prominence that began in 2015, George Springer spent seven seasons in Houston, excelling both at the bat and in the field for teams that won three division titles, two pennants, and one World Series. A high-energy player who served as the Astros' offensive catalyst from his leadoff spot in the batting order, Springer hit at least 20 homers five times and surpassed 80 RBIs and 100 runs scored three times each, while also compiling an OPS over .900 once. An outstanding defender as well, Springer did an excellent job in both center field and right, with his strong all-around play earning him three All-Star selections and one top-10 finish in the AL MVP voting.

Born in New Britain, Connecticut, on September 19, 1989, George Chelston Springer acquired his love of baseball from his father, George Sr., who, after leaving his home in Panama at the age of 17 to pursue his dream of becoming a professional baseball player, sustained an arm injury that forced him to eventually live vicariously through his son.

Suffering through a difficult childhood, George Jr. developed a stuttering problem that caused him to withdraw in social settings, with his father later saying, "It can be painful when people view you as less intelligent and make you the subject of ridicule. He experienced his share of bullying. I don't say *teasing* because that connotes something benign. It was something he was dealing with every day. In the back of the classroom, he would be afraid to answer. You're talking about a kid who abounds with enthusiasm."

Although Springer's stutter gradually became less pronounced with the help of a speech therapist, the joy he derived from playing baseball also contributed greatly to his improvement. In addition to practicing his swing in a batting cage that his dad built for him in the backyard, Springer developed his ball-hawking skills by shagging pop flies his father hit to him with a tennis ball on windy days. Young George also frequently attended games of the New Britain Rock Cats, the Double-A affiliate of the Minnesota Twins, where he and his friends scavenged for batting practice home run balls.

George Springer served as the offensive catalyst for Astros
teams that won three division titles, two pennants, and one
World Series.
Courtesy of Keith Allison

Experiencing a life-changing event at one such contest in 1998 when
future Twins star Torii Hunter asked him to play catch, Springer recalled,
"He changed my life. I got a chance to play catch at the time with what I
thought was a big leaguer. I didn't know any better. He's playing on a big
diamond in a stadium with lights and a big scoreboard. It made me want
to play baseball even more."

Springer continued, "There was something about the way he played,
the style of his game, that I became interested in. He was always having fun,
climbing a wall if he had to, sliding into home plate headfirst. I gravitated
toward that stuff. He became my idol that day."

Evolving into an outstanding player himself as a teenager, Springer
played baseball his freshman year at New Britain High School, before

transferring to Avon Old Farms School in nearby Avon after moving there with his family prior to the start of his sophomore year. Despite standing just 5'2" and weighing only 100 pounds in his one year at New Britain High, Springer excelled on the diamond, with varsity baseball coach, Ken Kezer, recalling, "He was a great athlete. He'd play JV in the afternoon, and at night he'd play varsity, coming into the game in the fifth or sixth inning. He was the fastest kid on the team. He just knew how to go after a ball. And I just loved how humble he was with everybody."

Continuing his outstanding play at Avon Old Farms School the next three years, Springer established himself as one of the finest players in the state after he grew 12 inches and added nearly 100 pounds during his junior and senior years, prompting the University of Connecticut to offer him a baseball scholarship. Springer subsequently garnered several individual accolades during his time at UConn, earning a spot on *Baseball America's* Freshman All-America First Team in 2009, before gaining Second-Team All-America recognition from that same publication and Big East Conference Player of the Year honors in 2011.

Impressed with Springer's exceptional play at the collegiate level, the Astros selected him in the first round of the 2011 MLB Amateur Draft, with the 11th overall pick. Rising quickly through Houston's farm system, Springer spent just two full seasons in the minors, earning Texas League Player of the Year honors with Double-A Corpus Christi in 2013, before being promoted to the parent club during the early stages of the ensuing campaign after compiling a .353 batting average and a .647 slugging percentage at Triple-A Oklahoma City.

In discussing the 24-year-old Springer's promotion to Houston, Astros general manager Jeff Luhnow told reporters, "We don't want to rest all our hopes on one player, but he's a pretty good player, and there's more behind him. If he does well, I think it will lift our team, which is now struggling a little bit, and lift our city's spirits, and give us hope that there's more like him coming. That's exciting. That's what we've been working for."

Joining an Astros team that had failed to win as many as 60 games in any of the three previous seasons, Springer performed well as a rookie, batting just .231, but hitting 20 homers, driving in 51 runs, and scoring 45 times, despite being limited by injuries to 78 games and 345 total plate appearances. Plagued by injuries again in 2015, Springer appeared in only 102 games. Nevertheless, he managed to hit 16 homers, drive in 41 runs, score 59 times, steal 16 bases, and raise his batting average to .276, while also doing an excellent job in right field for an Astros team that posted its first winning record in seven years.

Remaining healthy throughout the 2016 campaign, Springer hit 29 homers, knocked in 82 runs, ranked among the league leaders with 116 runs scored, and compiled a batting average of .261 and an OPS of .815. He followed that by hitting 34 homers, driving in 85 runs, finishing second in the league with 112 runs scored, batting .283, and posting an OPS of .889 in 2017, earning in the process the first of his three consecutive All-Star nominations and his first Silver Slugger. Meanwhile, after spending his first three seasons playing right field almost exclusively, Springer saw a significant amount of action in both center field and right, performing extremely well at both posts. Springer subsequently capped his finest season to date with an MVP performance against the Dodgers in the World Series, leading the Astros to their first world championship by going 11-for-29 (.379), with five homers, seven RBIs, and eight runs scored.

Considered by many to be the man who ignited Houston's offense, the right-handed-swinging Springer possessed the ability to put the Astros on top early by driving the ball into the seats from his leadoff spot in the batting order. Hardly a prototypical leadoff hitter, the 6'3", 220-pound Springer possessed outstanding power, struck out often, and did not steal very many bases. Yet, he gradually learned to cut down on his strikeouts, became more selective at the plate, ran the bases well, and provided a spark to his teammates with his enthusiasm and aggressive style of play, with then-Astros manager A. J. Hinch stating, "George's energy, personality, and enthusiasm set the tone for this team. He's so important for this team because he is so likable and relatable. He connects with everyone, whether they are Latin American, pitchers, coaches, front office. . . . Everyone has a comfort level with George. They take their cue from George. Ask Altuve."

Agreeing with his skipper, José Altuve said, "One hundred percent. George is the heart and soul because of who he is on and off the field. We feed off his personality and his energy."

Springer had another solid season for the Astros in 2018, hitting 22 homers, driving in 71 runs, scoring 102 times, and batting .265, before earning a seventh-place finish in the AL MVP voting the following year by scoring 96 runs and establishing career-high marks with 39 homers, 96 RBIs, a .292 batting average, and an OPS of .974. Springer subsequently hit 14 homers, knocked in 32 runs, scored 37 times, and batted .265 during the pandemic-shortened 2020 campaign, before signing with the Toronto Blue Jays for six years and $150 million when he became a free agent at the end of the year.

In his seven seasons with the Astros, Springer hit 174 homers, knocked in 458 runs, scored 567 times, collected 832 hits, 137 doubles, and 13 triples, stole 48 bases, and compiled a .270 batting average, a .361 on-base percentage, and a .491 slugging percentage. Known for his ability to perform well under pressure, Springer also hit 19 homers, knocked in 38 runs, scored 43 times, batted .269, and compiled an OPS of .891 in 58 postseason contests.

Since leaving Houston, Springer has been somewhat less productive at the plate, averaging 23 homers, 66 RBIs, and 78 runs scored over the past three seasons, while posting a composite batting average of .262. Nevertheless, he earned his fourth All-Star nomination in 2022 by hitting 25 homers, driving in 76 runs, scoring 89 times, and batting .267. Heading into the 2024 campaign, Springer boasts career totals of 242 homers, 656 RBIs, 802 runs scored, 1,206 hits, 203 doubles, 19 triples, and 86 stolen bases, a lifetime batting average of .267, an on-base percentage of .354, and a slugging percentage of .482.

In addition to the many contributions Springer has made to his teams on the playing field, he has maintained a strong presence within the community, spending much of his time in Houston working with the Astros Community Leaders program and the Urban Youth Academy. Springer, who still stutters slightly, also serves as a national spokesperson for the Stuttering Association for the Young (SAY), hosts an annual bowling event in Houston, and participated in a baseball clinic held at the Newtown, Connecticut, Youth Academy for elementary school students in the aftermath of the Sandy Hook Elementary School shooting.

ASTROS CAREER HIGHLIGHTS

Best Season

Despite appearing in fewer games and garnering far fewer plate appearances than he did in any of the three previous seasons, Springer posted the best overall numbers of his career in 2019, when he earned a seventh-place finish in the AL MVP voting by hitting 39 homers, driving in 96 runs, scoring 96 times, batting .292, compiling an on-base percentage of .383, and posting a slugging percentage of .591.

Memorable Moments/Greatest Performances

Springer led the Astros to a 9–4 win over Seattle on May 24, 2014, by homering twice and knocking in five runs.

Springer continued his hot hitting two days later, going 4-for-4, with a homer, two doubles, three RBIs, and five runs scored during a 9–2 win over Kansas City on May 26, 2014.

Springer gave the Astros a 5–4 win over the Arizona Diamondbacks on June 1, 2016, when he homered with two men out and no one on base in the bottom of the 11th inning.

Springer came up big in the clutch again on April 5, 2017, when he gave the Astros a 5–3 win over Seattle by homering with two men out and two men on in the bottom of the 13th inning.

Springer helped lead the Astros to a lopsided 12–2 victory over the Toronto Blue Jays on July 7, 2017, by going 4-for-4, with two homers, a double, five RBIs, and four runs scored.

An outstanding big-game player throughout his career, Springer earned 2017 World Series MVP honors by hitting five homers, driving in seven runs, scoring eight times, batting .379, and compiling an OPS of 1.471 during the Astros' seven-game win over the Dodgers, with his five home runs tying the single-series record previously held by Reggie Jackson and Chase Utley.

Springer contributed to a 16–2 win over Oakland on May 7, 2018, by going a perfect 6-for-6 at the plate, with a homer, double, three RBIs, and four runs scored.

Springer helped the Astros complete their three-game sweep of Cleveland in the 2018 ALDS by hitting a pair of solo home runs during an 11–3 victory in Game 3.

Springer helped lead the Astros to a 15–5 rout of the Texas Rangers on May 12, 2019, by going 5-for-5, with two homers, four RBIs, and five runs scored.

Springer starred during a 13–5 win over the Anaheim Angels on September 22, 2019, hitting three homers and knocking in four runs.

Springer flexed his muscles again in Game 2 of the 2020 ALDS, when, after collecting four hits in the previous contest, he homered twice during a 5–2 win over Oakland.

Notable Achievements

- Hit at least 20 home runs five times, surpassing 30 homers twice.
- Scored more than 100 runs three times.
- Posted slugging percentage over .500 three times.
- Posted OPS over .900 once (.974 in 2019).

- Hit three home runs in one game vs. Anaheim Angels on September 22, 2019.
- Led AL with 162 games played and 744 plate appearances in 2016.
- Finished second in AL with 112 runs scored in 2017.
- Led AL outfielders in fielding percentage once.
- Ranks among Astros career leaders in home runs (6th), slugging percentage (7th), and OPS (tied for 7th).
- Three-time division champion (2017, 2018, and 2019).
- Two-time AL champion (2017 and 2019).
- 2017 world champion.
- Two-time AL Player of the Week.
- May 2014 AL Rookie of the Month.
- Two-time Silver Slugger Award winner (2017 and 2019).
- 2017 World Series MVP.
- Finished seventh in 2019 AL MVP voting.
- Three-time AL All-Star selection (2017, 2018, and 2019).

22

JOE MORGAN

Although he is remembered more for his years in Cincinnati, Joe Morgan began his major-league career in Houston, where he spent parts of nine seasons manning second base for the Astros. The team's primary starter at that post from 1965 to 1971, Morgan gained All-Star recognition twice by stealing more than 40 bases three times and scoring at least 100 runs twice, before being included in a trade with the Reds that is generally considered to be one of the poorer ones in franchise history. Establishing himself as one of the greatest second basemen in the history of the game during his time in Cincinnati, Morgan helped lead the Reds to two world championships, earning in the process two NL MVP awards and an eventual place in the Baseball Hall of Fame. Nevertheless, Morgan, who returned to Houston for one more season during the latter stages of his career, accomplished enough as a member of the Astros to also gain induction into their Hall of Fame following his playing days.

Born in Bonham, Texas, on September 19, 1943, Joe Leonard Morgan moved with his family at the age of five to Oakland, California, where his father worked for a tire and rubber company. Looking back on his childhood, Morgan, who grew up with five younger siblings, said, "I had a great childhood. My parents always made sure that I was able to enjoy the fruits of being a child, you know? I didn't have to mature too quickly. I was not expected to know everything at the age of 10 or 12. I could be a kid and enjoy, you know, just enjoy life."

After getting his start in organized sports in the local Babe Ruth League at the age of 13, Morgan went on to star in baseball at Castlemont High School, where he also played basketball and ran track. Failing to receive any college scholarship offers, Morgan spent one season playing baseball at Merritt Community College, before signing with the expansion Houston Colt .45s as an amateur free agent at only 19 years of age on November 1, 1962.

Morgan subsequently spent the next two years advancing through Houston's farm system, performing well enough at every stop to earn brief

Before establishing himself as a future Hall of Famer in Cincinnati, Joe Morgan earned two All-Star selections as a member of the Astros.

callups to the parent club at the end of each season. Yet even though Morgan garnered Carolina League All-Star honors by batting .332 in 95 games with the Durham Bulls, he seriously considered quitting due to the racism he encountered as the team's only Black player. Ultimately electing to continue to pursue his dream of playing in the majors, Morgan recalled, "It would be nice to say that I changed my mind because of the example of earlier Black players who had it tougher, like Jackie Robinson. . . . But my decision came from my own sense of shame and embarrassment. When I thought of facing my father and telling him that I had quit—I simply could not go ahead."

Joining the newly named Astros for good in 1965 after earning Texas League MVP honors the previous season by batting .323, driving in 90 runs, and stealing 47 bases at Double-A San Antonio, Morgan immediately laid claim to the team's starting second base job. Excelling in his first full big-league season, Morgan hit 14 homers, collected 12 triples, knocked in 40 runs, scored 100 times, stole 20 bases, led the NL with 97 walks, batted .271, and compiled an OPS of .791, while spending most of the season hitting out of either the first or second spot in the batting order. Although Morgan ended up finishing runner-up in the NL Rookie of the Year voting to fellow second sacker Jim Lefebvre, who played for the pennant-winning Dodgers, Astros manager Luman Harris disagreed strongly with the results of the balloting, saying, "If Joe Morgan isn't Rookie of the Year, they'd better stop giving the award."

Despite being limited to 122 games, five homers, 60 runs scored, and 11 stolen bases by a broken kneecap he suffered during batting practice, Morgan posted solid numbers again in 1966, earning All-Star honors by batting .285, drawing 89 bases on balls, finishing second in the league with a .410 on-base percentage, and compiling an OPS of .801. After batting .275, scoring 73 runs, and swiping 29 bags the following year, Morgan missed almost all of 1968 with torn ligaments in his knee that he sustained when Tommie Agee of the Mets slid in hard at second base trying to break up a double play. Although fully recovered by the start of the ensuing campaign, Morgan batted just .236 as he struggled to recapture his stroke. Nevertheless, he established new career-highs with 15 homers and 43 RBIs, scored 94 runs, compiled a very respectable .365 on-base percentage, and ranked among the NL leaders with 49 steals and 110 walks. Regaining his All-Star form in 1970, Morgan earned his second trip to the Midsummer Classic by raising his batting average to .268, scoring 102 runs, driving in 52 others, stealing 42 bases, and drawing 102 bases on balls.

Though diminutive in stature, the 5'7", 160-pound Morgan, who spent much of his career hitting leadoff, possessed good power at the plate, surpassing 20 homers in a season four times after leaving the cavernous Astrodome. A left-handed hitter who flapped his back elbow like a chicken to keep it from dipping while awaiting the pitcher's offering, Morgan also drove the ball well to the outfield gaps, finishing in double digits in triples on three separate occasions. However, Morgan's greatest strengths as a hitter proved to be his tremendous patience and keen batting eye. Consistently working his way deep into the count, Morgan rarely swung at bad pitches, striking out more than 70 times in a season just twice in his career, while drawing more than 100 bases on balls on eight separate occasions. A terror on the basepaths as well, Morgan scored more than 100 runs eight times and stole at least 40 bases nine straight times, consistently ranking among the NL leaders in both categories.

While not as strong defensively during the early stages of his career, Morgan gradually developed into one of the NL's top fielding second basemen, leading all players at his position in putouts three times, assists once, double plays turned once, and fielding percentage three times. In discussing the importance that he placed on being a complete player, Morgan said, "Growing up in California, my father would take me to the minor league games, the Oakland Oaks. We would see the players, and my father would say, 'Well, he's a good player. He can hit, but he doesn't field very well. He can field, but he doesn't hit.' And my father always impressed upon me to try to be a complete player. So, I think I worked harder on my defense than I did on any other part of the game. Everyone loves to hit, and usually that's where they channel their energies. With me, I channeled my energies toward my weaknesses. If I was a good hitter, which I was all during my minor-league career, but I was not as good defensively, so I worked very hard on my defense. Then I worked very hard on my stolen bases. I did everything to make myself a complete player."

Despite appearing in all but two games the Astros played in 1971, Morgan posted slightly subpar numbers, concluding the campaign with 13 homers, 56 RBIs, 87 runs scored, 40 stolen bases, a .256 batting average, and an OPS of .757. Spending most of the season feuding with Astros manager Harry "The Hat" Walker, who accused him of being selfish, moody, and a troublemaker, Morgan defended himself by suggesting that the southern-bred Walker based his beliefs on his association with outfielder Jim Wynn, saying, "It seemed like anyone who was friendly with Jimmy was labeled a troublemaker by Harry. Well, I was friends with him before Harry got to Houston, and I'll be friends with him when Harry's gone."

The subject of frequent trade rumors during the early stages of the following offseason, Morgan saw his time in Houston come to an end when the Astros completed a trade with the Reds on November 29, 1971, that sent him, infielder Denis Menke, pitcher Jack Billingham, and outfielders César Gerónimo and Ed Armbrister to Cincinnati for first baseman Lee May, second baseman Tommy Helms, and utilityman Jimmy Stewart.

Stating that he looked forward to becoming more of a table-setter at the top of Cincinnati's powerful lineup upon learning of the deal, Morgan said, "Now I can just try to get on base. I set a goal of scoring 100 runs every year, getting 100 walks, and driving in 50 runs. I want to hit .300, too, but I haven't been able to do that yet."

Given a free hand by Reds manager Sparky Anderson, who took note of his superior athletic ability and tremendous baseball acumen, Morgan reached a level of excellence in Cincinnati that he never attained during his years with the Astros. Emerging as arguably the finest all-around player in the game, Morgan surpassed 100 runs scored and 100 walks six straight times, stole more than 50 bases five times, hit more than 20 homers four times, batted over .300 twice, and knocked in more than 100 runs once from 1972 to 1977, helping the Reds win four division titles, three pennants, and two World Series. In addition to gaining All-Star recognition in each of those campaigns, Morgan won five Gold Gloves and earned five top-10 finishes in the NL MVP voting, winning the award in both 1975 and 1976.

Finally beginning to show signs of aging in 1978, the 34-year-old Morgan batted just .236, although he still managed to hit 13 homers, knock in 75 runs, and score 68 times. After another rather mediocre performance the following year, Morgan signed with the Astros as a free agent on January 31, 1980, telling the *Sporting News* that winter, "I wanted to play for a contender, and that's a big reason why I'm here. I like what's been happening in Houston."

Meanwhile, Astros GM Tal Smith gushed, "I don't know of any player who is more intelligent, more competitive, and more dedicated than Joe Morgan."

Expressing his glee upon learning of the impending arrival of Morgan, Astros third baseman Enos Cabell stated, "What this means is that, for the first time in my career, I'm playing on a team that should be picked to win its division."

Although Morgan batted just .243 and scored only 66 runs for the Astros in 1980, he helped them win their first division title by stealing 24 bases, compiling an on-base percentage of .367, and finishing first in the league with 93 walks, while also providing veteran leadership to a team that came within one game of advancing to the World Series. Released by the Astros at the end of the year, Morgan signed with the Giants, with whom he spent the next two seasons starting at second base, before splitting his final two big-league seasons between the Phillies and Oakland Athletics. Announcing his retirement following the conclusion of the 1984 campaign, Morgan ended his playing career with 268 homers, 1,133 RBIs, 1,650 runs scored, 2,517 hits, 449 doubles, 96 triples, 689 stolen bases, 1,865 walks and only 1,015 strikeouts, a .271 batting average, a .392 on-base percentage, and a .427 slugging percentage, with his 1,865 bases on balls representing the fifth-highest total in MLB history. Morgan also amassed the third-most assists (6,967) and the fourth-most putouts (5,742) of any second baseman in the history of the game. As a member of the Astros, Morgan hit 72 homers, knocked in 327 runs, scored 597 times, collected 972 hits, 153 doubles, and 63 triples, stole 219 bases, batted .261, compiled an on-base percentage of .374, and posted a slugging percentage of .393.

After retiring as an active player, Morgan began a lengthy career in broadcasting, serving as a television color analyst for the Reds, ABC, NBC, and ESPN, where he partnered with Jon Miller on *Sunday Night Baseball* for more than two decades. Morgan also wrote several books on baseball and worked for many years as a businessman and philanthropist.

Inducted into the Baseball Hall of Fame the first time his name appeared on the ballot in 1990, Morgan said during his acceptance speech, "I take my vote as a salute to the little guy, the one who doesn't hit 500 home runs. I was one of the guys that did all they could to win. I'm proud of my stats, but I don't think I ever got on for Joe Morgan. If I stole a base, it was to help us win a game, and I like to think that's what made me special."

Diagnosed with myelodysplastic syndrome (a form of cancer) in 2015, Morgan received a bone marrow transplant from one of his daughters that allowed him to live another five years, until October 11, 2020, when he died at his home in Danville, California, at the age of 77 from a nerve condition called polyneuropathy.

Upon learning of his passing, the Astros released a statement that read: "This is a huge loss for our game. Joe Morgan was a true superstar in every sense of the word. In the early part of his career, he was one of our first stars, a cornerstone for the Houston Colt .45s and Astros, and a significant reason for the success of the franchise. His contributions will never be forgotten."

Meanwhile, Johnny Bench said of his former Reds teammate, "Joe wasn't just the best second baseman in baseball history, he was the best player I ever saw, and one of the best people I've ever known. He was a dedicated father and husband, and a day won't go by that I won't think about his wisdom and friendship. He left the world a better, fairer, and more equal place than he found it, and he inspired millions along the way."

ASTROS CAREER HIGHLIGHTS

Best Season

Before establishing himself as a Hall of Fame player in Cincinnati, Morgan had some excellent years for the Astros, with the 1970 campaign ranking as arguably his finest. In addition to hitting eight homers, driving in 52 runs, batting .268, compiling an on-base percentage of .383, and posting a slugging percentage of .396, Morgan ranked among the NL leaders with 102 runs scored, nine triples, 102 bases on balls, and 42 stolen bases, earning in the process his second All-Star nomination.

Memorable Moments/Greatest Performances

Morgan starred in defeat on July 8, 1965, going 6-for-6, with two homers, a double, a stolen base, three RBIs, and four runs scored during a 9–8 loss to the Milwaukee Braves in 12 innings.

Morgan again homered twice and knocked in three runs during a 10–1 win over the Mets on July 10, 1965.

Morgan contributed to a 17–4 pasting of the Cubs on May 26, 1967, by hitting safely in four of his six trips to the plate, homering once, driving in four runs, and scoring three times.

Morgan led the Astros to an 11–6 victory over the Cardinals on June 5, 1969, by going 4-for-4, with a homer, walk, stolen base, and four runs scored.

Morgan helped lead the Astros to a 9–4 win over the Padres on September 7, 1970, by going 5-for-6 at the plate, with two doubles and two RBIs.

Notable Achievements

- Scored at least 100 runs twice.
- Finished in double digits in triples three times.
- Stole more than 20 bases six times, topping 40 thefts on three occasions.
- Drew more than 100 bases on balls twice.
- Compiled on-base percentage over .400 twice.
- Led NL in triples once and walks twice.
- Finished second in NL in on-base percentage once, walks twice, and stolen bases three times.
- Led NL second basemen in assists once.
- Ranks among Astros career leaders in triples (2nd), stolen bases (5th), bases on balls (6th), on-base percentage (7th), and runs scored (12th).
- 1980 division champion.
- 1965 *Sporting News* NL Rookie of the Year.
- Two-time NL All-Star selection (1966 and 1970).
- Number 60 on the *Sporting News*' 1999 list of Baseball's 100 Greatest Players.
- Inducted into Astros Hall of Fame in 2019.
- Elected to Baseball Hall of Fame by members of BBWAA in 1990.

23

YORDAN ÁLVAREZ —

One of the finest all-around hitters in the game today, Yordan Álvarez has excelled at the plate for the Astros ever since he arrived in Houston in June 2019. An elite home-run hitter and RBI-man who also hits for a high batting average, Álvarez has surpassed 30 homers three times, driven in more than 100 runs once, and batted over .300 twice, en route to earning one top-10 finish in the AL MVP voting, one Silver Slugger, and a pair of All-Star selections. The most feared member of Houston's starting lineup, Álvarez has served as one of the central figures on teams that have won four division titles, three pennants, and one World Series. And, at only 26 years of age as of this writing, Álvarez has likely only scratched the surface of what he is capable of accomplishing.

Born in Las Tunas, Cuba, on June 27, 1997, Yordan Ruben Álvarez grew up in central-eastern Cuba, where he made a name for himself as a member of the Leñadores de Las Tunas, the local baseball team that competes in the Cuban National Series—the 16-team league that provides the nation's stiffest baseball competition. Playing for Las Tunas for two years, Álvarez developed into one of the league's top hitters in his second season, compiling a batting average of .351 in 40 games and 125 total plate appearances.

Defecting from Cuba in 2016, Álvarez established residency in Haiti, where he met future Houston Astros teammate Yuli Gurriel, who had previously emigrated there from Cuba. Subsequently signed by the Los Angeles Dodgers as an international free agent, Álvarez remained in the organization for less than two months, before the Astros acquired him for minor-league reliever Josh Fields on August 1, 2016. Later acknowledging that he made a big mistake by trading Álvarez to the Astros, Dodgers president of baseball operations Andrew Friedman stated, "I obviously wish I would have said yes to other names the Astros asked for before him."

Álvarez subsequently spent nearly three full years in the minor leagues, excelling at the plate for six different teams at various levels of the Houston

Yordan Álvarez ranks among the most dangerous hitters in the game today.
Courtesy of Ken Lund

farm system, while gradually transitioning from first base to the outfield. Performing especially well for the Pacific Coast League's Triple-A Round Rock Express in 2019, Álvarez hit 23 homers, knocked in 71 runs, batted .343, and posted an OPS of 1.185 in 56 games and 253 total plate appearances, earning him a promotion to the parent club on June 9.

Assuming the role of designated hitter following his arrival in Houston, Álvarez went on to earn AL Rookie of the Year honors by hitting 27 homers, driving in 78 runs, batting .313, posting a slugging percentage of .655, and compiling an OPS of 1.067 in just over 300 official at-bats, setting all-time records for qualified rookies in each of the last two categories.

Extremely impressed with the 22-year-old Álvarez's approach at the plate, then-Astros manager A. J. Hinch told *Baseball America*: "He's got great presence in the batter's box. He controls his body in the batter's box pretty well, and he takes some really big swings. He hits the ball hard, draws a fair share of walks. He's been very disciplined at the plate, which I've liked, and his timing seems good."

Limited to just two games by ailing knees that forced him to undergo multiple surgeries in late August 2020, Álvarez garnered only nine plate appearances during the pandemic-shortened campaign. However, he made a triumphant return to the Astros' starting lineup the following year, helping them capture their fourth division title in five seasons by hitting 33 homers, driving in 104 runs, scoring 92 times, batting .277, and compiling an OPS of .877, while splitting his time between left field and DH. Seeing a significant amount of action at both posts again in 2022, Álvarez compiled even better overall numbers, earning his first All-Star nomination and a third-place finish in the AL MVP voting by ranking among the league leaders with 37 homers, 97 RBIs, 95 runs scored, a .306 batting average, a .406 on-base percentage, and a .613 slugging percentage, despite missing several games in July and another five in early September due to inflammation in both hands.

The left-handed-hitting Álvarez, who stands 6'5" and weighs close to 230 pounds, possesses tremendous power to all fields. Capable of driving the ball out of any part of the ballpark, Álvarez hits many of his homers to the opposite field, often using his long arms and great strength to take full advantage of the inviting left field wall at Minute Maid Park. More than just a home-run hitter, though, Álvarez knows how to use the entire field, has good knowledge of the strike zone, and rarely overswings, with teammate Alex Bregman stating, "I think a lot of people, like, try and amp up to get power. But he knows that he just needs to stay within himself and stay within his swing. When he makes contact, it goes. And he can do it from line to line too. He can hit it to left field, he can hit it to right field. He hit three homers in one game to center field this year. So, it has an effortless feel to the swing, but it's powerful."

José Altuve also spoke highly of Álvarez, saying, "I think he's the best hitter I've ever played with. It's amazing what he can do. . . . He's a natural hitter. But, on top of that, he works hard every day. He goes to the cage and works with a purpose. He has an approach every day to get to home plate (to score). He doesn't give at-bats away. He cares every day about winning. About being better."

Despite missing 39 games in 2023 with a right oblique strain, Álvarez had another excellent year, earning his second consecutive All-Star selection by hitting 31 homers, driving in 97 runs, batting .293, and placing near the top of the league rankings with a .407 on-base percentage and a .583 slugging percentage. Heading into the 2024 campaign, Álvarez boasts career totals of 129 home runs, 380 RBIs, 324 runs scored, 513 hits, 114 doubles, and 4 triples, a batting average of .295, an on-base percentage of .390, and a slugging percentage of .588.

With Álvarez having signed a six-year contract extension worth $115 million with the Astros on June 2, 2022, he seems likely to remain in Houston until at least the end of the 2028 season, giving him an excellent opportunity to add significantly to those totals and claim an even more prominent place in these rankings.

CAREER HIGHLIGHTS

Best Season

Although Álvarez has posted excellent numbers in each of the last three seasons, he made his greatest overall impact in 2022, when he earned All-MLB First Team honors and a third-place finish in the AL MVP voting by ranking in the league's top five in home runs (37), RBIs (97), runs scored (95), batting average (.306), on-base percentage (.406), slugging percentage (.613), OPS (1.019), and walks (78).

Memorable Moments/Greatest Performances

Álvarez helped lead the Astros to a 23–2 rout of the Orioles on August 10, 2019, by hitting three homers, driving in seven runs, and scoring four times, with one of his homers coming with the bases loaded.

Álvarez contributed to a lopsided 15–1 victory over the Tampa Bay Rays on August 27, 2019, by homering twice, knocking in four runs, and scoring three times.

Álvarez led the Astros to a 7–4 win over the Yankees on May 6, 2021, by hitting a pair of solo home runs off Gerrit Cole.

Álvarez gave the Astros a 2–1 win over the White Sox on June 18, 2021, when he drove home Yuli Gurriel from first base with an RBI double in the bottom of the ninth inning.

Álvarez helped lead the Astros to a 9–6 victory over Oakland on July 6, 2021, by scoring three times and driving in five runs with a single and a pair of homers.

Álvarez earned 2021 ALCS MVP honors by going 12-for-23 (.522), with a homer, triple, three doubles, two walks, six RBIs, seven runs scored, and an OPS of 1.408. Particularly outstanding in Games 5 and 6, Álvarez led the Astros to a 9–1 win over the Red Sox in the first of those contests by scoring twice and driving in three runs with a homer, double, and single, before going 4-for-4, with a triple, two doubles, one RBI, and two runs scored in the 5–0 Game 6 clincher.

Álvarez led the Astros to an 8–3 victory over the Angels on April 18, 2022, by going 3-for-5 and knocking in four runs with a pair of two-run homers.

Álvarez gave the Astros a 7–6 win over the Kansas City Royals on July 4, 2022, by homering off Scott Barlow with two men out in the bottom of the ninth inning.

Álvarez led the Astros to a 5–0 win over Oakland on September 16, 2022, by hitting three solo home runs off Adrián Martínez.

Álvarez came up big in Game 1 of the 2022 ALDS, driving in two runs with a third-inning double, before giving the Astros a dramatic 8–7 come-from-behind victory over the Seattle Mariners by hitting a game-winning three-run homer in the bottom of the ninth.

Álvarez helped the Astros clinch their second world championship with a 4–1 win over the Phillies in Game 6 of the 2022 World Series when he hit a two-out, three-run homer off José Alvarado in the bottom of the sixth inning.

Álvarez helped lead the Astros to a 12–2 mauling of the Milwaukee Brewers on May 22, 2023, by going 3-for-4 at the plate, with two home runs, five RBIs, and three runs scored, with one of his homers coming with the bases loaded.

Álvarez contributed to a 13-5 rout of the Red Sox on August 28, 2023, by going a perfect 4-for-4 at the plate, with a homer, two walks, four RBIs, and two runs scored.

Álvarez performed magnificently in the 2023 ALDS, leading the Astros to a four-game victory over Minnesota by hitting four homers, driving in six runs, scoring seven times, batting .438, and posting an OPS of 1.783. Particularly outstanding in Houston's 6-4 Game 1 win, Álvarez homered twice, knocked in three runs, and scored three times.

Although the Astros subsequently lost the ALCS to Texas in seven games, Álvarez continued his hot hitting, homering twice, driving in nine runs, batting .481, and posting an OPS of 1.309.

Notable Achievements

- Hit more than 20 home runs four times, topping 30 homers three times.
- Knocked in more than 100 runs once.
- Batted over .300 twice.
- Surpassed 30 doubles once.
- Compiled an on-base percentage over .400 three times.
- Posted a slugging percentage over .600 three times.
- Posted an OPS over 1.000 twice.
- Hit three home runs in one game twice (vs. Baltimore on August 10, 2019, and vs. Oakland on September 16, 2022).
- Finished second in AL in on-base percentage and OPS once each.
- Finished third in AL in slugging percentage twice and home runs, on-base percentage, and OPS once each.
- Four-time division champion (2019, 2021, 2022, and 2023).
- Three-time AL champion (2019, 2021, and 2022).
- 2022 world champion.
- Three-time AL Rookie of the Month.
- Two-time AL Player of the Week.
- June 2022 AL Player of the Month.
- 2019 AL Rookie of the Year.
- 2021 ALCS MVP.
- 2022 Silver Slugger winner.
- 2022 Astros team MVP.
- Third in 2022 AL MVP voting.
- 2022 All-MLB First Team selection.
- Three-time All-MLB Second Team selection (2019, 2021, and 2023).
- Two-time AL All-Star selection (2022 and 2023).

24

DAVE SMITH

One of the first true one-inning closers, Dave Smith spent 11 seasons in Houston, appearing in more games during that time than any other pitcher in franchise history. Known for his calm demeanor that allowed him to remain unfazed in even the most pressure-packed situations, Smith compiled an ERA under 2.50 six times and saved more than 20 games on six separate occasions, en route to amassing the second most saves in team annals. A member of the Astros from 1980 to 1990, Smith proved to be a key contributor to teams that won two division titles, with his excellent work out of the bullpen earning him two All-Star selections and one top-20 finish in the NL MVP voting.

Born in Richmond, California, on January 21, 1955, David Stanley Smith grew up some 455 miles southeast, in the city of Poway, where he practically lived on the beach as a teenager. Looking back on his high school years, Smith said, "I'd get up early, and I'd go to the beach. And then I'd go to school (Poway High School), and then I'd go to the beach, and then I'd go to (baseball) practice."

A surfer boy at heart, Smith remained obsessed with riding the waves after he enrolled at nearby San Diego State University, remembering, "Well, I was always late for practice. I'd show up with a surfboard on top of my van, and I'd be wearing a wet bathing suit, you know. And I'd stroll into the ballpark. I guess that ticked him [his coach] off a little bit."

Recalling the rather precarious situations in which Smith sometimes put his teammates, former San Diego State infielder Armen Keteyian recounted, "See, Smitty was always the first one to say, 'Let's party, boys.' We'd get in his van. Dave's van was like our mobile home. We'd take it everywhere the team would play. And we'd be at the first 7-Eleven or beer place we could find."

Keteyian continued, "One time, he and I were driving in his Z down El Cajon Boulevard to some strip place. He comes around the block and pulls up behind two guys in a van. They don't make their turn properly, so

Smitty yells something and they come out of the van. I say, 'Oh, no, we're gonna fight,' but it gets broken up. So, we keep driving, and, to my left, I see the van again, and they've got the doors open, and they've got guns. They took two shots and knocked out a tire on my side. I'm under the seat now, but Dave floors it. . . . We get stopped by cops, who pull guns on us, too. We explained, and they ended up catching these guys. They had just robbed something. I had to go testify. So, that's what happened when you hung around with Smitty."

Ultimately selected by the Astros in the eighth round of the 1976 MLB Amateur Draft, Smith spent the next four years in the minors, before joining the parent club at the beginning of the 1980 campaign. Serving as a right-handed complement to lefty reliever Joe Sambito his first year in Houston, Smith performed exceptionally well, earning a fifth-place finish in

Dave Smith appeared in more games than any other pitcher in franchise history.

the NL Rookie of the Year voting by compiling a record of 7-5 and an ERA of 1.93, saving 10 games, and registering 85 strikeouts in 102⅔ innings pitched over 57 relief appearances.

Continuing to serve the Astros in a similar capacity the next four seasons, Smith pitched effectively, posting an overall record of 18-12, twice compiling an ERA under 3.00, and accumulating a total of 30 saves. But Smith really came into his own after he assumed the role of closer in 1985, going 9-5 with a 2.27 ERA and finishing third in the league with 27 saves. Although Smith won just four of his 11 decisions the following year, he helped the Astros capture the NL West title by collecting 33 saves, earning All-Star honors and a 17th-place finish in the league MVP balloting.

Claiming that Smith's disposition set him apart from other closers, former Astros catcher Alan Ashby said, "He was a surfer boy who wasn't crazy like most closers are supposed to be. He was quiet, and I think he was thinking about surfing most of the time. That's kind of who Smitty was, but he was very effective."

Although Smith, who stood 6'1" and weighed close to 200 pounds, lacked a high-octane heater, typically registering somewhere between 88 and 90 mph on the radar gun with his fastball, he possessed a superb change-up, which he used as his "out" pitch. In discussing the effectiveness of Smith's favorite offering, Ashby stated, "He had one of the great change-ups in the game—such an effective pitch. He could almost tell hitters it was coming, and they still couldn't hit it."

Astros infielder Enos Cabell said of his former teammate, "His best pitch was his change-up, and he'd throw it any time. People don't understand that. He got outs with the change-up and threw it all the time, and they still couldn't hit it. He was different. He was very different."

Meanwhile, Bill Doran spoke of the confidence Smith inspired in his teammates, saying, "When you fight your tail off for eight innings, and you come up one run ahead, and to have Smitty come in and have the rate of success he had, it keeps you in the game. It keeps you going, that, 'Hey, if we just claw one out here, we have somebody dependable who's going to come in and not give it away.'"

Smith remained one of the NL's top closers for another four years, averaging 25 saves from 1987 to 1990, while also compiling an ERA well under 3.00 each season. But, after going 6-6 with a 2.39 ERA and 23 saves in 1990, Smith decided to leave Houston and sign with the Chicago Cubs when he became a free agent at the end of the year. Smith, who, as a member of the Astros compiled a record of 53-47, an ERA of 2.53, and a WHIP of 1.189, registered 199 saves, and struck out 529 batters in 762 total innings of work, proved to be far less successful in Chicago, saving only 17 games over the next season-and-a-half, before announcing his retirement after the Cubs released him midway through the 1992 campaign.

Following his playing days, Smith spent eight seasons working for the San Diego Padres as a pitching coach at both the minor- and major-league levels, before resigning in June 2001 after undergoing alcohol rehabilitation. Smith, who also served as one of the directors of The San Diego School of Baseball for nearly 30 years, lived until December 17, 2008, when he passed away at only 53 years of age after suffering a heart attack.

Upon learning of his former Houston teammate's passing, Charlie Kerfeld said, "Our lockers were right next to each other for all the years I was there. He was a great teammate. He always seemed to be able to take things in stride, probably better than all of us. . . . A California dude, that was what he was. He would relax and let things happen. It shakes you up a little bit. You realize how short life is and how you should enjoy every moment of it."

Astros president of baseball operations, Tal Smith, who served as the team's GM during part of Smith's tenure in Houston, said, "He was a very tough competitor. He was fearless on the mound and went out and had a great career. Until Billy Wagner broke his record, he was our all-time saves leader. He had a very, very fine career. . . . This is certainly a tough loss."

Meanwhile, former San Diego Padres infielder Tim Flannery said of his longtime friend, "He was the most giving, unconditionally compassionate man anyone ever came across. Everybody's got Dave Smith stories. Usually, it's him reaching into his pocket and pulling out $100 to give to someone selling newspapers for a quarter. . . . Going back to his playing days, he was one of the great closers and a fierce competitor. He also had a zest for life, reckless abandon at times. He's gone at 53. He earned every moment of his life. He packed a lot into it."

ASTROS CAREER HIGHLIGHTS

Best Season

Smith proved to be one of the NL's most dominant relief pitchers from 1985 to 1990, compiling an ERA well under 3.00 and saving more than 20 games six straight times. While Smith excelled in each of those seasons, the 1987 campaign stands out as his finest since, in addition to recording 24 saves, he established career-best marks in ERA (1.65), WHIP (1.000), strikeouts-to-walks ratio (3.48), and strikeouts per nine innings pitched (11.0), fanning 73 batters in 60 innings of work.

Memorable Moments/Greatest Performances

Smith earned a victory over the Padres on August 15, 1980, by recording eight strikeouts and allowing four hits and no runs over the final five frames of a game the Astros won in 20 innings by a score of 3–1.

Smith got credit for a 5–3 win over the Dodgers on October 4, 1981, after he recorded four strikeouts and allowed no one to reach base over the final two innings.

Smith earned a save by surrendering just one hit and recording three strikeouts over the final four innings of a 7–5 win over the Montreal Expos on July 12, 1983.

Smith turned in another impressive performance on June 14, 1984, when he saved a 3–1 win over the Dodgers by allowing just one hit and striking out four batters in 3⅓ innings of work.

Smith saved a 4–3 victory over the Phillies on July 12, 1986, by recording four strikeouts in three perfect innings of work.

Smith threw 27⅔ consecutive scoreless innings from April 6 to June 18, 1987.

Notable Achievements

- Posted winning percentage over .700 once.
- Compiled ERA under 3.00 nine times, finishing with mark below 2.50 five times and 2.00 twice.
- Saved more than 20 games six times, topping 30 saves once.
- Threw more than 100 innings once.
- Finished third in NL in saves twice.
- Holds Astros career record for most pitching appearances (563).
- Ranks among Astros career leaders in saves (2nd), ERA (tied for 4th), and WHIP (10th).
- Two-time division champion (1980 and 1986).
- Two-time NL All-Star selection (1986 and 1990).

25

DON WILSON

The only pitcher in franchise history to throw multiple no-hitters as a member of the team, Don Wilson spent his entire nine-year major-league career in Houston, combining with Larry Dierker much of that time to give the Astros a formidable one-two punch at the top of their starting rotation. A hard-throwing right-hander who depended primarily on the movement of his fastball and slider to retire opposing batters, Wilson won at least 15 games three times, despite pitching for mostly losing teams. Capable of shutting down even the league's best offenses, Wilson also compiled an ERA under 3.00 three times, recorded more than 200 strikeouts once, and threw more than 200 innings on six separate occasions, earning in the process one All-Star selection and an eventual place in the Astros Hall of Fame. Nevertheless, Wilson remains a tragic figure due to the circumstances surrounding his death at only 29 years of age.

Born in Monroe, Louisiana, on February 12, 1945, Donald Edward Wilson moved with his family at an early age to Compton, California, a city located just south of Los Angeles. After getting his start in baseball in the local Little League, Wilson developed into a star at Centennial High School, where, in addition to playing shortstop and third base, he occasionally filled in at pitcher for his older brother, Willy, recalling years later, "Willy was getting mighty tired, so he asked me to pitch a few games to spell him. I did, and I've been hooked on pitching ever since."

Continuing to hone his skills on the diamond at Compton Community Junior College, Wilson drew the attention of pro scouts his first few years there with his exceptional mound work, telling a reporter in 1967, "When I was a junior at Compton, there'd be maybe 10–15 scouts come out to watch me pitch."

But Wilson quickly added, "Then I tore a ligament in my arm, and nobody came out when I was a senior. They said I was through. A scout for the California Angels said I'd never make it to the big leagues."

Tragedy brought Don Wilson's life and career to a premature end.

Proving the scouts wrong, Wilson began competing semiprofessionally following his graduation from CCC, performing well enough on the mound to be offered a $450-a-month contract by the Astros. After signing with Houston, Wilson spent less than two full seasons in the minor leagues, compiling a record of 18-6 and registering 197 strikeouts in 187 innings of work at Double-A Amarillo (Texas) in 1966, before being summoned to the majors in late September. Appearing in one game with the Astros, Wilson earned his first big-league victory by recording seven strikeouts and allowing five hits and two runs in six innings of relief during a 3–2 win over the Cincinnati Reds. Impressed with Wilson's strong performance, Astros manager Grady Hatton told beat writer John Wilson the following offseason, "When you have a real good arm and can throw strikes, you can move up to the majors."

Displaying tremendous confidence in Wilson, Hatton inserted him into the starting rotation during the early stages of the 1967 campaign, after which the 22-year-old right-hander went on to compile a record of 10-9, post an ERA of 2.79, register 159 strikeouts in 184 innings of work, and throw the first of his two no-hitters for an Astros team that finished ninth in the 10-team NL with only 69 wins. Despite receiving poor run support much of the time, Wilson never once complained, with John Wilson reporting in the *Sporting News*, "Wilson is glad to be in the majors this season, at least a year ahead of schedule, and despite the things that have happened, he is proving to himself and everybody else that he can pitch in the big leagues."

Meanwhile, Wilson, who relied almost exclusively on his fastball and slider his first full season in Houston, looked ahead to bigger and better things, telling the *Sporting News* in November 1967, "If I can come up with one other pitch, or even two, I think it would help me a lot because the hitter couldn't just lay back and wait for the fastball and slider. . . . In the minors, I had confidence I could get the batters out with a fastball. You know, I was 18 years old before I ever threw a curve. But in the big leagues, you need more than a fastball and a curve. Maybe I'll be a pretty good pitcher when I master the change-up."

Although the 6'2", 200-pound Wilson never developed either an outstanding curve or changeup, the movement on his fastball made him one of the league's more difficult pitchers to hit, with Bill James later writing in *The Neyer/James Guide to Pitchers*, "His fastball was fast, about 93, and it had fantastic movement—sometimes diving, sometimes sailing, sometimes breaking sharply out on a right-handed hitter. When his fastball was moving, he just aimed for the middle of the plate and threw fastballs."

In discussing Wilson's favorite offering, author and baseball historian Craig Wright stated, "Wilson had a lot of movement on his fastball, but it was not like he was a sinker-baller. He was getting a lot of lateral movement, kind of like Kerry Wood in his early days. He was not a big strikeout pitcher when he was at his best. It was his movement that got people out."

After Grady Hatton stated during the early stages of the 1968 campaign, "Don has a great arm. He has a high-riding fastball and a short, hard slider. He's young, strong, and eager. He should be a dandy." Wilson went on to compile a record of 13-16 for the last-place Astros, while also posting an ERA of 3.28, tossing three shutouts, completing nine of his 30 starts, and striking out 175 batters in 208⅔ innings of work. Wilson followed that by going 16-12, with an ERA of 4.00, 13 complete games, and a career-high 235 strikeouts in 1969, before developing an acute case of tendinitis in his right elbow the following spring. Limited to 27 starts and 184 innings after spending the first three weeks of the season on the disabled list, Wilson, who relied heavily on offspeed pitches to retire opposing batters in 1970, ended up compiling a record of 11-6 and an ERA of 3.91, throwing just three complete games and registering only 94 strikeouts.

Commenting on Wilson's diminished velocity and the change in his approach on the mound the following offseason, John Wilson wrote in the January 2, 1971, issue of the *Sporting News*, "The big smoke was gone. Wilson was giving them soft stuff and curves. There were only a few games he had enough of a fastball to keep the hitters off balance."

Although Wilson regained the zip on his fastball in 1971, his dependence on the breaking ball the previous year enabled him to do a better job of mixing his pitches, making him a more complete pitcher. Turning in the finest performance of his career, Wilson earned team MVP honors and his lone All-Star nomination by compiling a record of 16-10, throwing 268 innings, and ranking among the league leaders with an ERA of 2.45, a WHIP of 1.022, 180 strikeouts, and 18 complete games.

Wilson would have had a significantly better won-lost record had he received more run support from his teammates. Nevertheless, he chose not to focus on the negative at the end of the season, saying, when asked about his failure to win 20 games, "I'm not really all that concerned about it. My big goal is just to be consistent. I've been working all year on it and feel I have that consistency now. Once that is established, the wins will take care of themselves."

Extremely impressed with Wilson's outstanding performance, the *Chicago Defender* wrote, "If Houston's Don Wilson ever strikes the mother lode in his long search for consistency, he's bound to become one of baseball's golden pitchers."

Meanwhile, John Wilson noticed a change in Wilson's disposition, writing in the *Sporting News*, "There appears to be another change in Wilson this year. He doesn't seem to be quite as tied up inside. His moody periods, pronounced during the time he was worried about his arm, almost have disappeared."

Admitting that his attitude had changed somewhat, Wilson, who Doc Young of the *Los Angeles Sentinel* once called "Intelligent, articulate, concerned, and competitive," said, "In the past, I kind of kept to myself. I didn't really become quite as close to the other fellows as I have this year. It wasn't that I was unfriendly, but just that I kind of went my way. But this year, we've gotten closer, especially with the other pitchers. We talk more, maybe play cards together sometimes, and it's just a little closer thing."

Wilson had another excellent year for the Astros in 1972, going 15-10, with a 2.68 ERA, 172 strikeouts, three shutouts, 13 complete games, and 228⅓ innings pitched. Although Wilson compiled an overall mark of just 22-29 over the course of the next two seasons, he continued to perform well on the mound, posting ERAs of 3.20 and 3.08, while also tossing seven shutouts and 15 complete games.

Still only 29 years old at the end of the 1974 season, Wilson, who to that point had compiled a record of 104-92, an ERA of 3.15, and a WHIP of 1.212, registered 1,283 strikeouts, and thrown 20 shutouts, 78 complete games, and 1,748⅓ innings, appeared to have several more good seasons left in his right arm. But Wilson's career and, sadly, his life ended abruptly on January 5, 1975, when police found his body in the passenger seat of his Ford Thunderbird, which had been left running in his garage. Some of the carbon monoxide from the vehicle also seeped into Wilson's home, killing his young son. After initial news reports indicated that Wilson had committed suicide, the coroner determined that he had died accidentally from carbon monoxide inhalation, claiming that he had been drinking and likely fell asleep after turning on the car.

Some three months after Wilson's passing, the Astros retired his number 40 in a special ceremony held at the Astrodome. His teammates also honored him throughout the year by wearing a black patch on the left arm of their jerseys that displayed his number.

Several years later, two of the Astros players closest to Wilson recalled the complex nature of their former teammate, with Bob Watson saying, "A lot of people didn't like Don Wilson because he spoke his mind. That was his way of letting people know he was a man. He had his opinions, and he stuck to them."

Meanwhile, Doug Rader, who played with Wilson in the minors before spending another eight seasons with him in Houston, claimed that several bad experiences had caused his longtime teammate to become somewhat bitter, stating, "I'd say he was a little disillusioned with people. He was a very sensitive, warm person, and very often the bad element in some people would disappoint him tremendously. . . . A lotta people thought Don Wilson was a militant, but it wasn't true. He was just a very defensive individual."

Rader then added, "The most heartbreaking thing to me, the shame of it all, is that he had overcome his bitterness, and he was now again the man he used to be, the one I knew at first . . . I've heard all kinds of crazy things, rumors, about how Don Wilson died. I don't care what anyone says,

I'll never believe he killed himself. He loved life too much. His death simply had to be an accident. I'd stake my life on that."

CAREER HIGHLIGHTS

Best Season

Wilson pitched his best ball for the Astros in 1971 and 1972, posting a total of 31 victories over the course of those two seasons. Performing slightly better in 1971, Wilson earned his only trip to the All-Star Game by going 16-10 with 180 strikeouts and establishing career-best marks in ERA (2.45), WHIP (1.022), complete games (18), and innings pitched (268).

Memorable Moments/Greatest Performances

Wilson threw the first no-hit, no-run game in franchise history on June 18, 1967, when he allowed no hits, issued three walks, and recorded 15 strikeouts during a 2–0 win over the Braves. Recalling Wilson's extraordinary effort some 15 years later, former Braves first baseman Tito Francona stated in the May 1982 issue of *Baseball Digest*, "Everybody always talks about Koufax's no-hitters, and especially that perfect game he pitched against the Cubs in 1965. I faced Koufax and, no doubt about it, he was great, but I don't quite remember another pitcher who threw the ball as hard as Wilson did that day."

Wilson tossed 29⅔ consecutive scoreless innings from July 9 to July 26, 1967, highlighting his scoreless streak with a 7–0, two-hit shutout of the Mets on July 20.

Wilson tied the then-MLB record by registering 18 strikeouts during a complete-game 6–1 victory over the Reds on July 14, 1968, yielding just five hits and two walks along the way.

Wilson hit the only home run of his career during a 6–2 victory over the Cubs on August 31, 1968, in which he allowed two runs on seven hits in six innings of work.

Wilson dominated the Cincinnati lineup again on September 10, 1968, recording 16 strikeouts and yielding just six hits and two walks during a 3–2 complete-game win.

On May 1, 1969, just one day after Cincinnati's Jim Maloney no-hit the Astros, Wilson returned the favor, allowing no hits, issuing six walks, and recording 13 strikeouts during a 4–0 win over the Reds. Still seething over the poor sportsmanship that the Reds displayed when they routed the Astros, 14–0, nine days earlier, Wilson said following the contest, "There were a couple of times my legs were shaking so much I had to step off the mound. I never wanted anything so bad in all my life as to pitch that no-hitter."

Wilson continued his dominance of the Reds on September 17, 1971, yielding just four walks and a second-inning double to Tony Pérez during a 4–1 Astros win.

Wilson displayed his mettle on September 7, 1972, working all 13 innings of a 5–1 win over the Giants in which he allowed 10 hits and two walks, while striking out seven batters.

Wilson again went the distance when the Astros defeated the Reds, 1–0, in 10 innings on August 3, 1973, recording nine strikeouts and yielding just four hits and two walks.

In addition to surrendering just five hits during a 3–0 shutout of the Braves on July 1, 1974, Wilson drove in a run with an RBI double.

Notable Achievements

- Won at least 15 games three times.
- Compiled ERA under 3.00 three times.
- Struck out more than 200 batters once (235 in 1969).
- Threw more than 200 innings six times.
- Tossed 18 complete games in 1971.
- Threw two no-hitters (vs. Atlanta on June 18, 1967, and vs. Cincinnati on May 1, 1969).
- Finished second in NL with WHIP of 1.022 in 1971.
- Finished third in NL with 2.45 ERA in 1971.
- Ranks among Astros career leaders in wins (7th), ERA (tied for 8th), strikeouts (7th), shutouts (4th), innings pitched (5th), complete games (3rd), and starts (8th).
- July 7, 1974, NL Player of the Week.
- 1971 NL All-Star selection.
- #40 retired by Astros.
- Inducted into Astros Hall of Fame in 2019.

26

BILL DORAN

A steady and dependable player who performed well both at the bat and in the field, Bill Doran spent parts of nine seasons in Houston, starting at second base for the Astros in eight of those. The team's regular second-sacker from 1983 to 1990, Doran proved to be an excellent table-setter at the top of the batting order, hitting more than .280 three times and compiling an on-base percentage over .360 five times, while also stealing more than 20 bases on five separate occasions. An outstanding fielder as well, Doran led all players at his position in putouts once and fielding percentage twice, with his strong all-around play earning him team MVP honors twice. And, more than three decades after he donned an Astros uniform for the last time, Doran received the additional honor of gaining induction into the team's Hall of Fame.

Born in Cincinnati, Ohio, on May 28, 1958, William Donald Doran starred in multiple sports at Mount Healthy High School, excelling in baseball, basketball, and football. An All-League quarterback in high school, Doran chose to focus exclusively on baseball after he accepted an athletic scholarship to Miami University of Ohio in Oxford, where he spent three seasons playing for the RedHawks, before turning pro when the Astros selected him in the sixth round of the 1979 MLB Amateur Draft.

Gradually advancing through Houston's farm system over the course of the next four seasons, Doran batted .302, scored 100 runs, and stole 48 bases at Triple-A Tucson in 1982, earning him a late-season callup to the parent club. Appearing in 26 games with the Astros during the month of September, Doran batted .278, scored 11 runs, and stole five bases, prompting manager Bob Lillis to name him the team's starting second baseman prior to the start of the ensuing campaign.

Rewarding Lillis for the faith he placed in him, Doran earned a fifth-place finish in the NL Rookie of the Year voting by hitting eight homers, driving in 39 runs, scoring 70 times, batting .271, and compiling an on-base percentage of .371, while also leading all NL second sackers with

347 putouts. Doran followed that with a similarly productive 1984 season, hitting four homers, knocking in 41 runs, scoring 92 others, stealing 21 bases, ranking among the league leaders with 11 triples, batting .261, and posting an on-base percentage of .341, before earning team MVP honors for the first of two times in 1985 by hitting 14 homers, driving in 59 runs, scoring 84 times, swiping 23 bags, batting .287, and compiling an OPS of .797 that represented the second-highest mark of his career. Although Doran's overall numbers fell off slightly in 1986 (he finished the season with six homers, 37 RBIs, a .276 batting average, and an OPS of .741), he helped lead the Astros to the division title by scoring 92 runs and ranking among the league leaders with 81 walks and 42 stolen bases, earning in the process an 11th-place finish in the NL MVP voting.

The switch-hitting Doran, who stood 5'11" and weighed 175 pounds, played an integral role in any success the Astros experienced during the

Bill Doran started at second base for the Astros for eight seasons.

1980s. Generally assuming either the first or second spot in the batting order, Doran helped ignite Houston's offense with his aggressive baserunning and all-out style of play, with former Astros announcer Bill Brown saying, "He was one of my favorite players. . . . If you talk to anybody that covered him, anybody who knew him, he played as hard as anybody ever has for this franchise."

In discussing everything Doran brought to the team, former Astros shortstop Dickie Thon stated, "He was very underrated. To me, he was maybe the best second baseman in the league—even when (Ryne) Sandberg was there. The one year (1987), Billy had only six errors the whole year, and they gave the Gold Glove to Sandberg, who had more errors (10). Billy had better range and a lot of double plays. He could hit and run the bases very well. He could bunt. He could do everything. He was a very good player. They don't say enough about Billy in Houston."

Longtime Astros broadcaster Milo Hamilton also had high praise for Doran, saying in *Making Airwaves: 60 Years at Milo's Microphone*, a 2006 book he co-authored with Dan Schlossberg, "Bill Doran was another of our valuable young veterans. He was one of those little guys—a real battler—who got his uniform dirty every game. He had a little pop in his bat as well, and he could steal some bases, too. He was a victim of playing in the Ryne Sandberg era. Doran was overshadowed by Sandberg, whose reputation made sure he kept winning the Gold Glove Award year after year. There were a couple of years when Doran should have won it."

One such year was 1987, when, after losing an arbitration hearing the previous offseason that he hoped would raise his annual salary to $825,000 (he had to settle for $625,000), Doran committed only six errors in the field, en route to leading all NL second basemen in fielding percentage for the first of two straight times. In perhaps his finest all-around season, Doran also hit 16 homers, knocked in 79 runs, scored 82 times, stole 31 bases, drew 82 bases on balls, batted .283, compiled an on-base percentage of .365, and posted a slugging percentage of .406 for an Astros team that finished a disappointing third in the NL West, with a record of 76-86.

Plagued by a torn rotator cuff for much of the following season, Doran hit seven homers, knocked in 53 runs, scored only 66 times, and batted just .248. Failing to regain his earlier form after undergoing offseason surgery to repair his injured shoulder, Doran posted extremely similar numbers in 1989, although his batting average slipped to just .219. Rebounding somewhat in 1990 despite being hampered by a bad back that required surgery during the latter stages of the campaign, Doran scored 49 runs and batted .288 in 109 games with the Astros, before being traded to his hometown

Cincinnati Reds for three prospects as part of a payroll purge on August 30. Leaving Houston with career totals of 69 homers, 404 RBIs, 611 runs scored, 1,139 hits, 180 doubles, 35 triples, 191 stolen bases, and 585 walks, a .267 batting average, a .355 on-base percentage, and a .374 slugging percentage, Doran scored more runs, stole more bases, and walked more times than any other Astros player during the 1980s.

Doran ended up spending the next two years serving the Reds as a part-time player, before announcing his retirement midway through the 1993 campaign after assuming a backup role with the Milwaukee Brewers the first half of the season. Over parts of 12 big-league seasons, Doran hit 84 homers, knocked in 497 runs, scored 727 times, collected 1,366 hits, 220 doubles, and 39 triples, stole 209 bases, batted .266, compiled an on-base percentage of .354, and posted a slugging percentage of .373.

Following his retirement as an active player, Doran returned to Cincinnati, where he has spent most of the last three decades serving the Reds in one capacity or another. A minor-league instructor, minor-league field coordinator, director of player development, and major-league coach at different times, Doran moved into the role of special assistant to the general manager in 2019—a position he currently holds.

Yet, despite his lengthy tour of duty in Cincinnati, Doran continues to retain a strong connection with the fans of Houston, saying, "The fans were always wonderful. You get around the other places and you see how certain guys are treated, and that was just never an issue in Houston. Through the good times, through the bad times, the people were always great and supportive. I look back, and, of course, it's been a long time, but I have nothing but fond memories of the entire time that I was there. It was just a full package."

ASTROS CAREER HIGHLIGHTS

Best Season

Doran played his best ball for the Astros from 1984 to 1987, finishing in double digits in homers twice, while also scoring more than 80 runs and stealing more than 20 bases each season. It's an extremely close call, but with Doran scoring 82 runs, stealing 31 bases, batting .283, posting an OPS of .772, and establishing career-high marks with 16 homers, 79 RBIs, 177 hits, and a .992 fielding percentage in 1987, we'll identify that as his finest season.

Memorable Moments/Greatest Performances

Although the Astros lost to the Montreal Expos, 7–5, on July 6, 1984, Doran went a perfect 5-for-5 at the plate.

Doran collected five hits again during a 4–3 win over the Mets on July 11, 1985, driving home Dickie Thon with the winning run from second base with an RBI single in the bottom of the 12th inning.

Doran contributed to an 11–4 win over the Cubs on August 27, 1985, by knocking in a career-high five runs with a triple, double, and single.

Doran helped lead the Astros to a 7–3 victory over the Reds on April 19, 1987, by homering twice in one game for one of two times in his career.

Doran tied his career high by knocking in five runs during a 10–6 win over the Braves on July 11, 1989, with four of his ribbies coming on a second-inning grand slam off Charlie Puleo.

Notable Achievements

- Compiled on-base percentage over .400 once (.405 in 1990).
- Amassed 11 triples in 1984.
- Topped 30 doubles once (31 in 1985).
- Stole more than 20 bases five times, topping 30 thefts twice and 40 steals once (42 in 1986).
- Led NL in games played once.
- Led NL second basemen in putouts once and fielding percentage twice.
- Ranks among Astros career leaders in runs scored (11th), hits (10th), triples (10th), total bases (12th), bases on balls (7th), stolen bases (tied for 9th), plate appearances (10th), and at-bats (10th).
- 1986 division champion.
- Two-time NL Player of the Week.
- Two-time Astros team MVP (1985 and 1987).
- Inducted into Astros Hall of Fame in 2023.

27

CARLOS LEE

One of the game's top sluggers for nearly a decade, Carlos Lee hit more than 30 homers five times and knocked in more than 100 runs six times over the course of a 14-year major-league career that included stints with five different teams. Having some of his finest seasons for the Astros, Lee batted over .300 and surpassed 25 homers and 100 RBIs three times each during his time in Houston, proving to be one of the few bright spots on some of the worst teams in franchise history. The Astros' primary starter in left field from 2007 to 2011, Lee also saw a significant amount of action at first base, before being dealt to the Miami Marlins midway through the 2012 campaign.

Born in Aguadulce, Panama, on June 20, 1976, Carlos Lee developed a love for baseball at an early age, while also acquiring a passion for cattle ranching from his grandfather. After excelling on the diamond at Rodolfo Chiari High School, Lee competed in the local semipro leagues until the Chicago White Sox signed him as an amateur free agent in 1997.

Lee subsequently spent two years advancing through Chicago's farm system, before joining the parent club early in 1999. Performing well in his first big-league season, Lee earned Rookie of the Year consideration by hitting 16 homers, driving in 84 runs, and batting .293. After averaging 25 home runs and 85 RBIs the next three seasons, Lee established himself as a true force to be reckoned with in 2003, when he hit 31 homers, knocked in 113 runs, batted .291, and compiled an OPS of .830. Yet, even though Lee posted a similarly impressive stat-line in 2004, the White Sox sent him to Milwaukee as part of a five-player trade they completed with the Brewers at the end of the year.

Continuing to put up excellent numbers in Milwaukee, Lee earned All-Star honors in 2005 by hitting 32 homers, driving in 114 runs, and batting .265, before reaching the seats 28 times, knocking in 81 runs, batting .286, and compiling an OPS of .896 through the first four months of the ensuing campaign. Once again, though, Lee found himself heading elsewhere when the Brewers traded him and Nelson Cruz to the Texas Rangers for four players on July 28, 2006.

After finishing out the season in Texas, Lee signed with the Astros for six years and $100 million when he became a free agent at the end of the year, making him the highest paid player in team annals, to that point. Giving the Astros a solid return on their investment his first year in Houston, Lee hit 32 homers, knocked in 119 runs, scored 93 times, batted .303, and compiled an OPS of .882, earning All-Star and Silver Slugger honors. Lee followed that with two more extremely productive seasons, hitting 28 homers, driving in 100 runs, batting .314, and posting an OPS of .937 in 2008 despite being limited by injuries to 115 games, before hitting 26 homers, knocking in 102 runs, batting .300, and compiling an OPS of .831 in 2009.

The right-handed-hitting Lee, who stood 6'2" and weighed more than 270 pounds, presented an imposing figure to opposing pitchers when standing in the batter's box. Nicknamed "El Caballo" ("The Horse") for

Carlos Lee knocked in more than 100 runs three times as a member of the Astros.

his great size and strength, Lee possessed tremendous power to all fields, although he pulled almost all his homers to left. Not particularly selective at the plate, Lee walked more than 60 times in a season just once his entire career. However, he also struck out more than 90 times just twice, never fanning more than 63 times as a member of the Astros. Excellent with men on base, Lee homered with the bases loaded 17 times, tying him with Jimmie Foxx and Ted Williams for the seventh-most grand slams in MLB history. Meanwhile, Lee's seven grand slams with the Astros represent a club record.

Yet, despite his outstanding offensive production, Lee became a polarizing figure among the Astros fanbase during his time in Houston. Often criticized for his defensive shortcomings, Lee, who possessed decent speed earlier in his career (he stole at least 17 bases three times between 2001 and 2006) before adding some 20 or 25 pounds onto his frame after he joined the Astros, displayed very little range in the outfield, forcing the team to eventually move him to first base. Lee also drew the rancor of the hometown fans by often jogging down to first base, rather than running out groundballs. More than anything, though, Lee and his massive contract handcuffed a struggling Astros team that had aging players and a decimated farm system.

Although Lee batted just .246 for the Astros in 2010, he finished second on the team with 24 home runs and 89 RBIs. Improving upon those numbers slightly the following year, Lee hit 18 homers, knocked in 94 runs, and batted .275. After being shifted to first base in 2012, Lee hit five homers, knocked in 29 runs, and batted .287 during the season's first three months, before being traded to the Florida Marlins on July 4 for infield prospect Matt Dominguez and minor-league pitcher Rob Rasmussen.

Upon announcing the deal, Astros general manager Jeff Luhnow said, "Carlos has been an important part of our team and our community in Houston for almost six seasons, and he will be missed. We made this move with an eye towards the future and are very excited about adding Dominguez and Rasmussen to our talent base. Both players have a bright future."

Lee, who during his time in Houston hit 133 homers, knocked in 533 runs, scored 376 times, collected 894 hits, 187 doubles, and eight triples, stole 26 bases, batted .286, compiled a .338 on-base percentage, and posted a .479 slugging percentage, spent the rest of 2012 starting at first base for the Marlins, before becoming a free agent again at the end of the year. After failing to receive a contract offer from any team, Lee officially announced his retirement on June 21, 2013, ending his career with 358 homers, 1,363 RBIs, 1,125 runs scored, 2,273 hits, 469 doubles, 19 triples, 125 stolen bases, a .285 batting average, a .339 on-base percentage, and a .483 slugging percentage.

Since retiring from baseball, Lee, who donated $25,000 and over 300 bales of hay to support Texas ranchers whose properties were ravaged by Hurricane Ike in 2010, has become more heavily involved with his favorite pursuit of raising cattle. A cattle rancher with properties in Texas and his hometown of Aguadulce, Panama, Lee owns and operates close to a dozen ranches, where he raises bulls, cows, and horses.

ASTROS CAREER HIGHLIGHTS

Best Season

A productive hitter his entire time in Houston, Lee had his best year for the Astros in 2007, when he won his second Silver Slugger by hitting 32 homers, scoring 93 runs, batting .302, posting a slugging percentage of .528 and an OPS of .882, finishing third in the NL with 119 RBIs, and ranking among the league leaders with 190 hits, 43 doubles, and 331 total bases.

Memorable Moments/Greatest Performances

Lee led the Astros to a 9–6 win over the Phillies on April 13, 2007, by hitting three homers and knocking in six runs, reaching the seats once with the bases loaded.

After hitting a solo home run earlier in the game, Lee gave the Astros a 6–5 win over the Giants on May 15, 2007, when he homered again with no one aboard in the bottom of the 10th inning.

Lee provided further heroics on June 28, 2007, when his two-out grand slam home run in the bottom of the 11th inning gave the Astros an 8–5 victory over the Colorado Rockies.

Lee delivered the big blow of a 6–2 win over the Reds on July 29, 2008, when he homered off Bronson Arroyo with the bases loaded in the bottom of the fifth inning.

Lee helped lead the Astros to a 9–5 victory over the Reds on August 8, 2009, by going 4-for-5, with a homer, double, three RBIs, and three runs scored, driving in what proved to be the game-winning runs with a two-run double in the top of the 10th inning.

Lee delivered the decisive blow of a 6–2 win over the Colorado Rockies on June 9, 2010, when he homered with two men out and the bases loaded in the top of the 10th inning.

Notable Achievements

- Hit more than 20 home runs four times, topping 30 homers once (32 in 2007).
- Knocked in at least 100 runs three times.
- Batted .300 or better three times.
- Surpassed 30 doubles three times, topping 40 two-baggers once (43 in 2007).
- Posted slugging percentage over .500 twice.
- Posted OPS over .900 once (.937 in 2008).
- Hit three home runs in one game vs. Philadelphia on April 13, 2007.
- Led NL with 13 sacrifice flies in 2007.
- Finished third in NL with 119 RBIs in 2007.
- Led NL left fielders with nine assists in 2009.
- Ranks among Astros career leaders in RBIs (12th) and slugging percentage (tied for 11th).
- August 10, 2008, NL Player of the Week.
- 2007 Silver Slugger Award winner.
- 2007 NL All-Star selection.
- 2007 *Sporting News* NL All-Star selection.

28

TERRY PUHL

A member of the first three Astros playoff teams, Terry Puhl spent 14 seasons in Houston, establishing himself during that time as one of the better hitters and outfielders in franchise history. Known for his outstanding speed, exceptional defense, and ability to make consistent contact at the plate, Puhl batted over .300 three times, stole more than 20 bases six times, and led all NL outfielders in fielding percentage twice, en route to earning one All-Star selection and an eventual place in the Astros Hall of Fame. Yet, had Puhl not been plagued by injuries for much of his career and been misused by the Astros, he likely would have accomplished a good deal more.

Born in Melville, Saskatchewan, on July 8, 1956, Terry Stephen Puhl grew up north of the border, where he starred in multiple sports while attending Melville Comprehensive High School. A standout in baseball, football, volleyball, and track, Puhl proved to be especially proficient on the diamond, pitching his team to four championships and winning two most valuable player awards. An excellent hitter as well, Puhl batted .575 during the 1973 Midget League Championship series, prompting Houston Astros scout Wayne Morgan to sign him as an undrafted free agent outfielder for $1,000, even though he had never played the outfield before.

Puhl subsequently began his professional career with the rookie-league Covington Astros in the spring of 1974, remembering, "I left the 12th grade with one semester to go and went away to spring training. Then, I returned to Melville and finished school after playing in the Rookie League."

Puhl ended up spending three-and-a-half years in the minor leagues, playing for Class A Dubuque in 1975, Double-A Columbus and Triple-A Memphis in 1976, and Triple-A Charleston in 1977, before being promoted to the parent club midway through the 1977 campaign. Performing well for the Astros over the season's final three months while spending most of his time in left field, Puhl batted .301, scored 40 runs, collected five triples, and stole 10 bases in 60 games and 265 total plate appearances, although he failed to hit a homer and knocked in only 10 runs.

Terry Puhl spent parts of 14 seasons patrolling the outfield for the Astros.

Impressed with Puhl's approach at the plate, Astros hitting coach Deacon Jones called the 21-year-old rookie "the best student I've encountered," adding, "He has good instincts, and he is the best young hitter I've seen at knowing the strike zone."

Named the Astros starting left fielder prior to the start of the 1978 season, Puhl spent the first two months of the campaign manning that post, before moving to center in mid-June after César Cedeño sustained a season-ending injury. Doing a creditable job in Cedeño's absence, Puhl committed just three errors in the field and finished fourth among all NL outfielders with 386 putouts. Meanwhile, after being inserted into the leadoff spot in the batting order, Puhl batted .289, scored 87 runs, stole 32 bases, and compiled an on-base percentage of .343, earning All-Star honors for the only time in his career.

Continuing to bat leadoff and play center field for much of 1979, Puhl had another solid season, compiling a batting average of .287 and an on-base percentage of .352, scoring 87 runs, and stealing 30 bases, prompting teammate Enos Cabell to refer to him as "the guy who'll be the best player on the team in a couple of years." Assuming a somewhat different role in 1980, Puhl moved to right field and, after batting either first or second since he became a regular member of the starting lineup two years earlier, spent the final two months of the campaign hitting out of the number three spot in the batting order. Performing well over the course of the season, Puhl helped lead the Astros to their first division title by batting .282, posting an OPS of .776, establishing career-high marks with 13 homers and 55 RBIs, scoring 75 runs, and stealing 27 bases. Although the Astros subsequently suffered a heartbreaking five-game defeat at the hands of the Philadelphia Phillies in the NLCS, Puhl turned in a memorable performance, going 10-for-19 (.526), with three walks, two stolen bases, three RBIs, and four runs scored.

The left-handed-hitting Puhl, who possessed a wiry 6'2", 195-pound frame, had very little power at the plate. However, he compensated for his shortcomings in that area with good speed, excellent defense, and a healthy batting average. One of the league's better contact hitters (he fanned just 507 times in almost 5,500 total plate appearances over the course of his career), Puhl employed a short, compact swing that enabled him to slap the ball to all fields. Meanwhile, Puhl used his speed to leg out at least seven triples three straight times and steal more than 20 bases in five of six seasons at one point. And, as for his defense and character, former Astros GM Tal Smith called Puhl "A true professional who hardly ever made mistakes. He was an excellent right fielder and became an excellent center fielder . . . just a true professional; conducted himself in every respect in a first-class way."

After getting off to a slow start in 1981, Puhl rebounded somewhat to finish the season with a .251 batting average. He followed that by batting .262, hitting eight homers, driving in 50 runs, and scoring 64 times in 1982, before missing a significant amount of playing time in each of the next two seasons with injuries. Nevertheless, Puhl performed well in both 1983 and 1984, batting .292, scoring 66 runs, and stealing 24 bases in the first of those campaigns, before batting .301, hitting nine homers, driving in 55 runs, and scoring 66 times in the second.

The 1984 season proved to be Puhl's last as an everyday player. Plagued by injuries in each of the next three seasons that included a pulled hamstring in 1985 and a sprained ankle in 1986, Puhl failed to garner more than 220 total plate appearances, limiting him to totals of just seven homers, 52 RBIs, 60 runs scored, and 10 stolen bases. Meanwhile, with the Astros seeking to fill their power void by asking Puhl to alter his style of hitting, the slender outfielder posted batting averages of just .244 and .230 in 1986 and 1987, prompting one local newspaper to write, "Puhl is a proven .300 hitter whose average has plummeted partly because of a need to swing for the fences . . . and in the process became so confused that he hit neither for power nor average."

Although Puhl assumed the role of a part-time player in both 1988 and 1989, he experienced something of a resurgence, compiling a batting average of .303 and stealing 22 bases in the first of those campaigns, before batting .271 in the second. Used almost exclusively as a pinch-hitter in 1990 after sustaining another injury early in the year, Puhl batted .293 in just 49 total plate appearances. Released by the Astros at season's end, Puhl signed with Kansas City, for whom he appeared in 15 games, before announcing his retirement when the Royals released him on June 9. Over parts of 15 big-league seasons, Puhl hit 62 homers, knocked in 435 runs, scored 676 times, collected 1,361 hits, 226 doubles, and 56 triples, stole 217 bases, batted .280, and compiled an on-base percentage of .349 and a slugging percentage of .388, posting virtually all those numbers as a member of the Astros. Puhl also committed a total of just 18 errors in the field, with his lifetime fielding percentage of .994 as a right fielder giving him the second-highest mark in MLB history among players who manned that position.

Following his playing days, Puhl returned to his adopted hometown of Houston, where, having secured a stockbroker's license, he entered the world of wealth management. While functioning in that capacity, Puhl also became the head baseball coach at the University of Houston-Victoria in 2006—a position he maintained until the end of the 2022 season, when he retired from coaching.

ASTROS CAREER HIGHLIGHTS

Best Season

Although Puhl earned his lone All-Star nomination two years earlier, he posted his best overall numbers in 1980, when, appearing in more than 140 games for one of just four times, he established career-high marks with 13 homers and 55 RBIs, scored 75 runs, collected 24 doubles, stole 27 bases, batted .282, and compiled an OPS of .776.

Memorable Moments/Greatest Performances

Puhl starred in defeat on May 9, 1980, homering twice in one game for one of just two times in his career during a 5–4 loss to the Braves.

Puhl contributed to a 12–5 victory over the Pirates on August 21, 1980, by going 4-for-5, with a double, a stolen base, two RBIs, and four runs scored.

Although the Astros lost the 1980 NLCS to the Phillies in five games, Puhl performed brilliantly, batting .526, with 10 hits in 19 official at-bats, compiling an OPS of 1.222, walking three times, stealing two bases, knocking in three runs, and scoring four times. Particularly outstanding in the series finale, which the Phillies won in 10 innings, 8–7, Puhl collected four hits, stole a base, and scored three runs.

Puhl starred in defeat again on May 22, 1982, driving in a career-high five runs with a homer and triple during a 6–5, 12-inning loss to the Mets, with his grand slam home run off Neil Allen in the bottom of the ninth sending the game into extra innings.

Puhl helped lead the Astros to an 11–5 win over the Dodgers on September 28, 1987, by going a perfect 4-for-4 at the plate, with a homer and four RBIs.

Notable Achievements

- Batted over .300 three times.
- Stole more than 20 bases six times, topping 30 thefts twice.
- Finished second in NL with nine triples in 1982.
- Led NL outfielders in fielding percentage twice.
- Led NL right fielders in fielding percentage three times and double plays turned once.
- Led NL center fielders in fielding percentage once.
- Ranks among Astros career leaders in runs scored (8th), hits (8th), extra-base hits (11th), triples (4th), doubles (10th), total bases (9th), stolen bases (6th), walks (12th), sacrifice hits (tied for 9th), games played (6th), plate appearances (9th), and at-bats (9th).
- Ranks second in MLB history among right fielders with career fielding percentage of .994.
- 1978 NL All-Star selection.
- Inducted into Astros Hall of Fame in 2022.

29

— DOUG RADER —

A hard-hitting third baseman who spent his first nine big-league seasons in Houston, Doug Rader proved to be the finest player at his position in team annals prior to the arrival of Alex Bregman. Houston's primary starter at third from 1968 to 1975, Rader provided excellent power and run production in the middle of the Astros' batting order throughout the period, hitting more than 20 homers three times and knocking in more than 80 runs on four separate occasions. Even better in the field, Rader led all NL third sackers in putouts, assists, fielding percentage, and double plays turned twice each, en route to winning five consecutive Gold Gloves. As much as anything else, though, Rader became known during his time in Houston for his occasionally bizarre behavior and offbeat sense of humor.

Born in Chicago, Illinois, on July 30, 1944, Douglas Lee Rader grew up some 30 miles northwest, in the Chicago suburb of Northbrook, where he acquired the nickname "The Red Rooster" because of the color of his hair. Adopted at an early age, Rader credited his parents for instilling in him a strong sense of values, saying, "I was very fortunate to fall in the lap of a couple who cared for me and structured me in a decent way."

A standout shortstop at Glenbrook North High School, Rader drew interest from several major colleges, before ultimately choosing to enroll at Illinois Wesleyan University, a small NAIA school located in Bloomington, Illinois. In explaining his decision, Rader recalled, "We got to play as freshmen against Big-10 schools and others like Ole' Miss and Tulane. Then we played a 50-game schedule in the summer, and we were all provided jobs over the summer. So, basically, I got to play 100 games as a freshman in college. That wouldn't have happened at an NCAA school. Plus, it was a really good school."

Performing exceptionally well at Illinois Wesleyan, Rader received high praise from head baseball coach Jack Horenberger, who told the school newspaper, *The Argus*, in May 1963 that Rader was "one of the best prospects we ever had here, and, by prospect, I mean professional prospect. He's

196

a good hitter with fine power, but what I especially like about him at the plate is his attitude. He can look bad on one pitch but turns around and fights you on the next pitch. He's a real competitor."

After failing to make the US Olympic team earlier in the year, Rader signed with the Houston Colt .45s as an amateur free agent in September 1964, remembering, "I had a chance to make the Olympic team in 1964, and, at that point, it was still an exhibition event. Scouts were evaluating everyone in conjunction with the Olympic committee, and I was one of the last ones to get cut. At the end of 1964, I decided to start my journey. I was one of the last guys to sign before the [MLB] draft."

Rader continued, "Everyone knew the draft was going to happen, but I tried out that summer, and there were a number of teams looking at me. I worked out with Houston for scout Wally Laskowski in Chicago and did well. They wanted me to go to the Instructional League and play against

Doug Rader won five consecutive Gold Gloves for his outstanding defensive work at third base.

other players who had already signed. I did, and I went 5-for-5. [Houston GM] Paul Richards was there and offered me a contract."

After verbally agreeing to terms with Houston, Rader received news from his father that both the Braves and Cardinals had called with substantially larger offers. However, being a man of honor, Rader remained true to his word, recalling, "My dad had principles that were terribly old school but ethical. I had already agreed to sign for $30,000 with Richards. So, when my dad asked me what I was going to do, I knew exactly what I was going to do. I didn't have a choice. We didn't have much money but, to me, money has never been a big issue in my life. It wasn't at that point, and it still isn't. . . . So, I signed with the Colt .45s, and I was scheduled to go to Modesto of the California League. But by the time I got to spring training, they had changed their name to the Astros, and I was headed to Durham [of the Carolina League]."

Rader subsequently spent the next two-and-a-half seasons advancing through Houston's farm system, before joining the parent club for good midway through the 1967 campaign after hitting nine homers, driving in 44 runs, and batting .293 in 75 games with Triple-A Oklahoma City. Recalling how he felt when he took the field for the first time as a member of the Astros, Rader said, "It was unbelievable to walk into the dome. I had been there before, after the 1965 season they had a few of us come in and work out while the club was there. Being on the field with that many people there was thrilling. I was floating on air."

Acquitting himself extremely well the rest of the year while spending most of his time at first base, Rader batted .333, hit two homers, and collected 26 RBIs in 47 games and 162 official at-bats. Moved across the diamond to third base the following year, Rader found himself sharing playing time with veteran third sacker Bob Aspromonte. But after Rader hit six homers, knocked in 43 runs, batted .267, and compiled an OPS of .721 in 98 games and 333 at-bats, he became the full-time starter at third when the Astros dealt Aspromonte to Atlanta at season's end.

Posting decent numbers in his first full season, Rader concluded the 1969 campaign with 11 homers, 83 RBIs, 62 runs scored, a .246 batting average, and an OPS of .684. Improving upon his performance the following year, Rader hit 25 homers, knocked in 87 runs, scored 90 times, batted .252, and compiled an OPS of .758, while also earning Gold Glove honors for the first of five straight times by leading all players at his position in putouts, assists, fielding percentage, and double plays turned. Hampered by injuries in 1971 that limited him to 135 games, Rader hit just 12 homers, knocked in only 56 runs, and batted just .244. But even though

Rader posted batting averages of just .237 and .254 the next two seasons, he proved to be far more productive at the plate, totaling 43 home runs and 179 RBIs.

Although the right-handed-hitting Rader, who stood 6'2" and weighed close to 210 pounds, never hit more than 25 home runs in a season, he possessed outstanding power at the plate, becoming in 1970 the first player to drive a ball into the fourth deck at the Astrodome, a notoriously bad park for sluggers.

In discussing the problems that the Astrodome presented to him and the other members of Houston's lineup, Rader said, "The original Dome was horrendous. Jimmy Wynn was barely recognized for what he was able to do because of that park. Take a look at the power numbers for visiting clubs in the Dome. The Cubs would come in with 32-ounce bats, and they couldn't get it to the warning track. We had to use logs to get the damn thing out of there. . . . Then, you would go to Atlanta and Wrigley Field, and I think that's where the jealousy sets in. They get to play 81 games in these places, and we're just trying to get the ball to the wall in our place."

Also finding fault with the Astrodome's artificial surface, Rader stated, "Fielding in the Dome changed from year to year. It was the worst dirt in the history of the world. It was a very unpredictable infield. There was a reason why they had turf. They couldn't grow grass or tend to it properly. It was not a good infield. They had groundskeepers that wore space suits, so how could they take care of it."

Playing under such conditions, Rader often found it necessary to let off steam by conducting himself in an atypical manner. A noted prankster, Rader once delivered the Astros' starting lineup to the umpires in a skillet. On another occasion, he suggested to youngsters during a media interview that they eat their baseball cards to help them remember all the information that appeared on the back. Also known to greet visitors to his home completely naked and to defecate on a teammate's birthday cake, Rader often found himself being described in the local newspapers as a "flake," to which he responded, "I imagine that is correct. I did some flaky, stupid things. But it was because of youthful exuberance, so I look for special dispensation. We had fun, though."

Rader had one more solid season for the Astros, hitting 17 homers, driving in 78 runs, batting .257, compiling an OPS of .749, and winning his fifth straight Gold Glove in 1974, before age and injuries began to take their toll. After Rader hit just 12 homers, knocked in only 48 runs, and batted just .223 in 1975, the Astros traded him to the San Diego Padres for pitchers Joe McIntosh and Larry Hardy on December 11, 1975, ending his lengthy association with the organization.

Rader, who left Houston with career totals of 128 homers, 600 RBIs, 520 runs scored, 1,060 hits, 197 doubles, 30 triples, and 32 stolen bases, a batting average of .250, an on-base percentage of .318, and a slugging percentage of .402, ended up spending just one full season in San Diego, hitting nine homers, driving in 55 runs, and batting .257 for the Padres in 1976, before being dealt to the Toronto Blue Jays midway through the ensuing campaign. After finishing out the season in Toronto, Rader announced his retirement when the Blue Jays released him the following spring.

Looking back on his final days as an active player, Rader said, "I never really thought about the end, but by that point, my feet were shot, my elbows were shot, my shoulders hurt, and it wasn't pleasant playing any-more. I was also back on turf (in Toronto) and my legs were destroyed to begin with. And of all the destinations, Toronto would have been down the line for me because of the surface. And being on another expansion team was no fun. When I got released, I didn't care. I came home and started something else."

Following his playing days, Rader, who over parts of 11 big-league seasons hit 155 homers, knocked in 722 runs, scored 631 times, collected 1,302 hits, 245 doubles, 39 triples, batted .251, and compiled an OPS of .725, spent several years managing at both the minor- and major-league levels, piloting the Texas Rangers from 1983 to 1985, the Chicago White Sox in 1986, and the California Angels from 1989 to 1991, before retiring from baseball in 1994 after spending the previous year serving as the Florida Marlins first hitting coach.

Although the 79-year-old Rader never had the good fortune of being part of a division-winning team as either a player or manager, his biggest disappointment from baseball comes from his lack of familiarity with many of the men he competed against. In discussing his greatest regret, Rader says, "I was raised and played in a time when fraternization between play-ers and teams was forbidden. I think about all the wonderful guys I played against, all the tremendous people, and I never got a chance to know any of them because we were forced into this fake familiarity breeds contempt mindset. I don't know if anyone from my era feels strongly about that. . . . It's bothered me forever not being allowed to interact with people that I played against. You see how guys are now. That was absolutely forbidden. I think about people I never got to know or say two words to during my career is my biggest regret."

ASTROS CAREER HIGHLIGHTS

Best Season

Although Rader posted extremely comparable numbers in one or two other seasons, he had his finest all-around year in 1970, when, in addition to driving in 87 runs, batting .252, and winning his first Gold Glove, he established career-high marks with 25 homers, 90 runs scored, and 251 total bases.

Memorable Moments/Greatest Performances

Rader helped lead the Astros to a 16–3 victory in the first game of their doubleheader split with the Pirates on August 10, 1968, by going 5-for-5 at the plate, with three doubles, four RBIs, and three runs scored.

Rader gave the Astros a 6–2 win over the Phillies on May 27, 1969, when he homered off reliever Luis Peraza with the bases loaded in the bottom of the ninth inning.

Rader led the Astros to a lopsided 12–4 victory over the Cardinals on May 16, 1971, by collecting a career-high six RBIs, with four of those coming on a first-inning grand slam.

Rader contributed to an 11–7 win over the Cubs on May 14, 1975, by knocking in five runs with a pair of homers.

Rader helped lead the Astros to an 8–7, 12-inning victory over the Expos on May 25, 1975, by going 5-for-6, with three doubles, one RBI, and three runs scored.

Notable Achievements

- Hit more than 20 home runs three times.
- Batted over .300 once.
- Led NL third basemen in putouts twice, assists twice, double plays turned twice, and fielding percentage twice.
- Ranks among Astros career leaders in RBIs (9th), hits (12th), total bases (11th), sacrifice flies (tied for 9th), games played (11th), plate appearances (11th), and at-bats (11th).
- Five-time Gold Glove Award winner (1970, 1971, 1972, 1973, and 1974).

30

LEE MAY

A feared slugger who surpassed 30 home runs and 100 RBIs three times each over the course of an 18-year major-league career that included stints with four different teams, Lee May proved to be one of the most intimidating hitters of his generation. Nicknamed the "Big Bopper" for his size and ability to deliver the long ball, May homered at least 20 times in 11 straight seasons, while also driving in at least 94 runs in eight of those. Having his finest seasons for the Reds, Astros, and Orioles, May spent three extremely productive years in Houston, earning one All-Star selection and one top-10 finish in the NL MVP voting, before moving on to Baltimore, where he helped lead the Orioles to the AL pennant in 1979.

Born in Birmingham, Alabama, on March 23, 1943, Lee Andrew May grew up in the segregated South, where he held several jobs as a youngster, including delivering newspapers and cleaning offices. The son of a semipro ballplayer, May suffered through the divorce of his parents at a relatively early age, forcing him, his younger brother, and his mom to move in with his grandmother.

An excellent all-around athlete during his teenage years, May starred in football, basketball, and baseball at A.H. Parker High School, excelling as a fullback on the gridiron and a forward on the hardwood. But baseball remained the first love of the tall and husky May, who recalled years later, "They called me the 'Big Bopper.' That was fine with me. I always wanted to be a home run hitter when I was growing up. My favorite player was Harmon Killebrew. . . . I wanted to be just like Killebrew and hit a lot of homers."

Recruited by several colleges for both baseball and football as graduation neared, May received an offer to play football for the University of Nebraska. However, he instead chose to sign with the Cincinnati Reds for $12,000, later explaining, "Well, the Reds offered me money, and I felt I had a better chance in baseball. Plus, I felt I'd have a longer career in baseball . . . and it was safer."

Lee May hit more than 20 home runs in each of his three seasons in Houston.

May spent the next few years advancing through Cincinnati's farm system, making a successful conversion from the outfield to first base during that time. In discussing his switch in positions, May stated, "I threw sidearm too much for an outfielder, and my throw would move too much from the target."

While playing minor-league ball, May also attended Miles College in Fairfield, Alabama, for one semester and spent his winters further honing his skills in Venezuela and Puerto Rico, remembering, "I actually planned on going to college (in the offseason), but I was always busy playing winter ball, and it just got squeezed out. They paid you better in Puerto Rico and Venezuela than your own club paid you. . . . I made $350 a month in my first year in the minors and $1,500 a month in Venezuela that same winter."

While coming up through the minors, May received a piece of advice from one of his managers, John "Red" Davis, that enabled him to better harness his power at the plate. Recalling the correction that Davis made to his batting stance, May said, "I was uppercutting the ball, and Red had me go into a semicrouch. The result was 18 home runs at Rocky Mount in 1963, 25 at Macon in 1964, and 34 at Triple-A San Diego in 1965."

After making brief appearances with the Reds in both 1965 and 1966, May finally arrived in the majors to stay in 1967, when, splitting his time between first base and the outfield, he earned *Sporting News* NL Rookie of the Year honors by hitting 12 homers, driving in 57 runs, and batting .265 in 127 games and 438 official at-bats. Named the team's starting first baseman the following year, May hit 22 homers, knocked in 80 runs, and batted .290, before establishing himself as one of the NL's top sluggers in 1969, when he earned the first of his three All-Star nominations by batting .278 and ranking among the league leaders with 38 homers and 110 RBIs. Continuing his assault on NL pitching the next two seasons, May totaled 73 home runs and 192 RBIs for Cincinnati teams that became known as "The Big Red Machine."

Perhaps the most underappreciated member of a star-studded lineup that also included Johnny Bench, Tony Pérez, and Pete Rose, May later received high praise from Bench, who said, "A lot of people never realized how important he was to us when we won the pennant in '70. . . . We were stumbling around late in the year because we were all tired, but Lee was hitting home runs almost every day. And when we died in the [World] Series, he was a one-man gang."

Despite the outstanding numbers that May posted for them the previous four seasons, the Reds elected to include him in a trade they completed with the Astros on November 29, 1971, that sent him, slick-fielding second baseman Tommy Helms, and utilityman Jimmy Stewart to Houston for second sacker Joe Morgan, shortstop Denis Menke, pitcher Jack Billingham, and outfielders César Gerónimo and Ed Armbrister. Later admitting to being very much surprised by the deal, May claimed that it caught him off guard "because I had such a good year in '71 and had been named the MVP of the Reds."

The key player in the trade from Houston's perspective, May possessed the kind of power at the plate that management believed would enable him to succeed even in the cavernous Astrodome. And succeed May did, as he earned All-Star honors and a ninth-place finish in the NL MVP balloting in his first year with the Astros by ranking among the league leaders with 29 home runs, 98 RBIs, and 290 total bases, batting .284, compiling an on-base percentage of .343, and posting a slugging percentage of .490. Similarly productive in each of the next two seasons, May hit 28 homers, knocked in 105 runs, and batted .270 in 1973, before reaching the seats 24 times, driving in 85 runs, and batting .268 the following year.

An imposing figure at the plate, May, who stood 6'3" and weighed close to 220 pounds, wagged his bat back and forth as he awaited the pitcher's offering, all the while glaring out toward him as he stood on the mound. Extremely strong, the right-handed-hitting May possessed tremendous power to all fields, although he pulled most of his homers to left. Commenting on May's ability to reach the seats, onetime Reds batting coach Ted Kluszewski stated, "He may be fooled on a certain pitch but the next time up he'll hit the same pitch out of the park."

Despite his size, May also proved to be surprisingly nimble in the field, consistently ranking among the NL's top first basemen in putouts, assists, double plays turned, and fielding percentage. An outstanding team leader as well, May earned the respect of his teammates wherever he went, often using his pragmatic personality and comical sense of timing to put out clubhouse fires.

With the Astros seeking to move Bob Watson in from the outfield to his more natural position of first base, they traded May and minor-league outfielder Jay Schlueter to the Baltimore Orioles for infielder-outfielder Enos Cabell and top infield prospect Rob Andrews on December 3, 1974. May, who left the Astros having hit 81 homers, driven in 288 runs, scored 211 times, collected 464 hits, 81 doubles, and five triples, batted .274, compiled a .317 on-base percentage, and posted a .471 slugging percentage as a member of the team, ended up spending the next six seasons in Baltimore, during which time he proved to be a perfect fit for the offensive philosophy employed by manager Earl Weaver, who believed in "waiting for the three-run homer." In discussing May on one occasion, Weaver said, "He's a guy who likes to hit the ball as hard as he can every time he goes up there . . . and when he's doing it, he can be destructive."

Continuing his string of 11 straight seasons with at least 20 home runs in Baltimore, May surpassed 20 round-trippers in each of his first four seasons with the Orioles, while also driving in 109 runs once and collecting 99 RBIs twice. A free agent at the end of 1980, May signed with the Kansas City Royals, with whom he assumed a backup role the next two seasons, before announcing his retirement following the conclusion of the 1982 campaign. Over parts of 18 big-league seasons, May hit 354 homers, knocked in 1,244 runs, scored 959 times, amassed 2,031 hits, 340 doubles, 31 triples, batted .267, compiled a .313 on-base percentage, and posted a .459 slugging percentage. A free swinger who readily admitted, "I deliberately try to hit a home run every time up," May also drew only 487 bases on balls and struck out 1,570 times over the course of his career.

After retiring as an active player, May spent several years coaching at the major-league level, first serving as hitting coach in Kansas City and later coaching first base for the Reds, Royals, Orioles, and Tampa Bay Devil Rays. Ending his career in baseball with the organization that first signed him, May said in 2011, "I now do PR with the Reds and have eight grandchildren who keep me and my wife pretty busy." May lived another six years, dying of pneumonia in a Cincinnati hospital at the age of 74 on July 29, 2017.

Upon learning of his passing, former Reds announcer Al Michaels, who car-pooled to Riverfront Stadium with May during their time together in Cincinnati, said of his old friend, "He was a big presence with zero bombast. Just a rock-solid guy with a great, understated sense of humor."

ASTROS CAREER HIGHLIGHTS

Best Season

While May hit well in each of his three seasons in Houston, he performed best as a member of the Astros in 1972, earning All-Star honors and a ninth-place finish in the NL MVP voting by hitting 29 homers, driving in 98 runs, scoring a career-high 87 runs, collecting 31 doubles, batting .284, and posting an OPS of .833.

Memorable Moments/Greatest Performances

May contributed to a 17–5 pasting of the Montreal Expos on August 17, 1972, by going 4-for-6 at the plate, with two homers, four RBIs, and three runs scored.

May had an extremely productive afternoon against the Dodgers on September 17, 1972, driving in five runs with a homer, double, and pair of singles during a 15–11 Astros win.

May hit safely in 21 straight games from May 30 to June 22, 1973, going 35-for-86 (.407), with three homers, one triple, four doubles, 16 RBIs, and 10 runs scored.

May led the Astros to a 12–2 victory over the Padres on June 21, 1973, by hitting three home runs, driving in five runs, and scoring four times, homering off three different pitchers.

May had five hits in one game for the only time in his career on April 29, 1974, when he went a perfect 5-for-5, with two home runs, four RBIs, and three runs scored during an 18–2 rout of the Cubs, hitting both his homers in the sixth inning.

Notable Achievements

- Hit more than 20 home runs three times.
- Knocked in more than 100 runs once.
- Surpassed 30 doubles once (31 in 1972).
- Hit three home runs in one game vs. San Diego on June 21, 1973.
- Finished second in NL with 105 RBIs in 1973.
- Led NL first basemen in putouts once and double plays turned once.
- May 5, 1974, NL Player of the Week.
- Finished ninth in 1972 NL MVP voting.
- 1972 NL All-Star selection.

31

BOB KNEPPER

In discussing his Giants teammate at one point during the 1979 season, pitcher John Montefusco stated, "[Bob] Knepper might be another Sandy Koufax. He's got everything. The guys don't even want to face him in batting practice. A cinch 25-game winner someday."

Although the left-handed-throwing Knepper failed to live up to the unrealistic expectations his fellow hurler set for him, he experienced a considerable amount of success during a 15-year career that included lengthy stints in San Francisco and Houston. A member of the Astros for parts of nine seasons, Knepper served as one of the mainstays of their starting rotation from 1981 to 1989, winning at least 15 games three times, while also compiling an ERA under 3.00 once and throwing more than 200 innings on four separate occasions. Among the franchise's all-time leaders in several statistical categories, Knepper earned two All-Star selections during his time in Houston, helping the Astros win one division title in the process. Yet Knepper will always be remembered for squandering a three-run, ninth-inning lead he held over the Mets in Game 6 of the 1986 NLCS and for his ultraconservative comments that overshadowed his many accomplishments on and off the field.

Born in Akron, Ohio, on May 25, 1954, Robert Wesley Knepper moved with his family at the age of nine to the tiny city of Calistoga, in Napa Valley, California. Knowing early on that he wanted to pursue a career in baseball, Knepper recalled, "I got a lot of support from my parents. My mother always said I would pitch for the Giants. My father took a lot of heat for letting me pass up college to play ball."

Excelling in multiple sports at Calistoga High School, Knepper proved to be especially gifted in baseball, drawing the attention of several major-league clubs with his exceptional mound work. Scouted most heavily by the San Francisco Giants, Knepper turned in his most dominant performance with Hall of Fame southpaw Carl Hubbell (then a Giants scout) in attendance, striking out 22 batters during a victory over St. Helena High School.

Selected by the Giants in the second round of the 1972 MLB Amateur Draft, Knepper spent nearly five full seasons in the minors, before finally joining the parent club during the latter stages of the 1976 campaign. After starting four games for the Giants in the season's final month, Knepper became a regular member of their starting rotation the following year, when he went 11-9, with a 3.36 ERA and 100 strikeouts in 166 innings of work. Improving upon those numbers significantly in 1978, Knepper compiled a record of 17-11, led all NL hurlers with six shutouts, and ranked among the league leaders with a 2.63 ERA, 16 complete games, and 260 innings pitched, with his stoic nature, smooth delivery, and outstanding movement on his pitches prompting Cincinnati Reds manager Sparky Anderson to proclaim, "Knepper is a cross between Tommy John and Vida Blue."

Far less successful the next two seasons, Knepper compiled an overall record of just 18-28 and an ERA over 4.00 each year, causing the Giants to begin entertaining trade offers for him. Further fueling San Francisco's

Bob Knepper won 17 games for the Astros'
1986 NL Western Division championship team.

willingness to part ways with Knepper was the criticism he drew from the media and some of his teammates for his deep Christian faith that resulted in him becoming a member of the Giants' "God Squad" of fundamentalists. Often exhibiting his obsession with his religion when reporters asked him about his performance at the end of games, Knepper simply replied, "It's God's will."

Ultimately dealt to the Astros on December 8, 1980, for infielder Enos Cabell, Knepper welcomed the trade, stating at the time that he believed Houston's clubhouse to be strongly spiritual, and calling the Bay Area "such a liberal, almost anti-Christian society."

Meanwhile, Astros management expressed little concern over Knepper's struggles the previous two seasons, with GM Al Rosen saying, "Our scouting reports on Knepper were excellent. Some of our people felt he may have had a (correctable) problem with his delivery."

Performing exceptionally well his first year in Houston, Knepper earned NL All-Star and Comeback Player of the Year honors during the strike-shortened 1981 campaign by compiling a record of 9-5, finishing second in the league with a 2.18 ERA, placing third in the circuit with a WHIP of 1.060, and tossing five shutouts. Knepper subsequently suffered through two dismal seasons that saw him compile an overall record of just 11-28, before rebounding in 1984 to go 15-10 with a 3.20 ERA and rank among the league leaders with three shutouts, 11 complete games, and 233⅔ innings pitched. Knepper followed that with two more solid seasons, compiling a record of 15-13 and an ERA of 3.55 in 1985, before helping the Astros capture the NL West title in 1986 by going 17-12 with a 3.14 ERA, leading all NL hurlers with five shutouts, and ranking among the league leaders with a WHIP of 1.040, eight complete games, and 258 innings pitched.

A control pitcher who depended primarily on the location and movement of his pitches to retire opposing batters, the 6'3", 200-pound Knepper employed a three-quarters-to-sidearm throwing motion that helped him keep his pitches low and constantly moving. Although Knepper's fastball typically registered somewhere between 85 and 90 mph on the radar gun, it appeared faster since it seemed to explode out of his easy throwing motion. Knepper's repertoire of pitches also included a sharp-breaking curveball and an above-average changeup.

Claiming that he needed to feel relaxed on the mound to be effective, Knepper said, "If I relax and throw the ball over the plate, they'll probably pop it up."

A remarkably cool and unemotional athlete, Knepper often drew criticism for his seemingly uncaring attitude. Responding to such charges, Knepper stated, "When I'm pitching good, the word is 'unflappable,' and that means good. When I'm pitching bad, it's said, 'He doesn't care because he doesn't scream and throw his glove on the mound.' . . . I see myself as Bob Knepper, the guy with the potential to be a great pitcher."

Although Knepper had one of the finest seasons of his career in 1986, Astros fans tend to remember him more for his failure to close out Game 6 of that year's NLCS. After yielding just two hits and no runs to the Mets over the first eight innings, Knepper allowed three runs to cross the plate in the top of the ninth, thereby sending the contest into extra innings. Seven frames later, the Mets pushed across another three runs, enabling them to record a 7–6, 16-inning victory that ended the Astros' hopes of advancing to the World Series.

Looking back on the outing nearly a decade later, Knepper told author Mike Sowell in the latter's book, *One Pitch Away*, "In that ninth inning, when I just ran out of gas, or lost a little concentration, or whatever happened, that was the lowest point in my career. . . . It was just a real major disappointment for us not to win that ball game. We had worked so hard, we had played so hard, and in the playoffs, we had come through so many things that just seemed to be against us. And we felt the Mets had such a psychological thing against trying to hit Mike Scott, who would have pitched Game 7, that, if we had won Game 6, we'd have won Game 7, and we'd be in the World Series."

Perhaps experiencing something of a hangover, Knepper pitched poorly in 1987, going just 8-17 with a 5.27 ERA. Blaming his regression on mechanics, Knepper stated following one of his early exits, "I was trying too hard to throw the ball hard. I can't pitch that way. I was rushing my delivery."

Returning to top form in 1988, Knepper earned All-Star honors by compiling a record of 14-5 and an ERA of 3.14, causing him to say, "My mechanics are so much better. I can put the ball where I want it each time."

However, prior to the start of the 1988 regular season, Knepper became embroiled in controversy when, following a spring training start during which Pam Postema served as home plate umpire, he told reporters, "I just don't think a woman should be an umpire. There are certain things a woman shouldn't be, and an umpire is one of them. It's a physical thing. God created women to be feminine. I don't think they should be competing with men. It has nothing to do with her ability. I don't think women should be in any position of leadership. I don't think they should be presidents or politicians. I think women were created not in an inferior position, but in a role of submission to men. You can be a woman umpire if you want, but that doesn't mean it's right. You can be a homosexual if you want, but that doesn't mean that's right either."

Knepper also berated the National Organization for Women, saying, "They are a bunch of lesbians. Their focus has nothing to do with women's rights. It has everything to do with women wanting to be men."

Unfortunately, Knepper's comments, which drew widespread condemnation, helped overshadow his kinder, more compassionate side. Someone who cared deeply for his fellow players, Knepper received praise for his efforts as Houston's player representative, being described as a "model player representative . . . informed and open-minded." Knepper also proved to be a pillar of strength to Giants teammate Dave Dravecky when the latter attempted to mount his comeback from cancer in 1989.

Knepper's decline in popularity made it easier for the Astros to part ways with him when he got off to a horrific 4-10 start in 1989. After refusing an assignment to Triple-A Tucson on July 28, Knepper suffered the indignity of being released by the Astros. Knepper, who compiled an overall record of 93-100, an ERA of 3.66, and a WHIP of 1.306, threw 41 complete games and 18 shutouts, and struck out 946 batters in 1,738 total innings of work during his time in Houston, subsequently signed with the Giants, with whom he ended his career nearly one year later. Released by San Francisco on June 26, 1990, Knepper announced his retirement, leaving the game with a career record of 146-155, a 3.68 ERA, a WHIP of 1.327, 78 complete games, 30 shutouts, and 1,473 strikeouts in 2,708 innings pitched.

Following his playing days, Knepper traveled north with his wife and three children to the 1,300-acre ranch in southwest Oregon he had purchased in 1982. The family remained there for several years, before eventually moving to Denver, Colorado.

Waxing philosophical on his playing career some years later, Knepper said, "I learned a lot from the 1986 NLCS Game Six playoff game. I learned a lot about myself. I learned a lot about the value and the lasting value—or the lack of lasting value—that the game of baseball has. And I'm not sure I'd give up that lesson for anything. . . . It really helped put my life in perspective, to realize what's really important in life. Is it winning a game? Is it pleasing people who really don't care about me at all? The majority of the fans and the press don't really care about you as a person. All they care about is how you perform for them. So, do I want to put that much emphasis on pleasing those people versus pleasing my God?"

Knepper continued, "I've learned that anything you do in baseball—all the records or all the games you've won—really has no lasting value. My relationship with Christ and my relationship with my family—that has lasting value. . . . So, I think as I worked through all that, I realized that game, it was just a game, I gave it my best shot. And as I got out of baseball, I was able to see things a little more focused, a little clearer, and not be involved so emotionally in it. It was just a matter of coming to the right conclusion."

ASTROS CAREER HIGHLIGHTS

Best Season

Knepper won 15 games in both 1984 and 1985, and he earned his only All-Star selection as a member of the Astros in 1988, when he compiled a record of 14-5 and an ERA of 3.14. However, Knepper made his greatest overall impact in 1986, when he helped lead the Astros to the NL West title by going 17-12 with a 3.14 ERA, posting a WHIP of 1.140, leading the league with five shutouts, and finishing third in the circuit with 258 innings pitched.

Memorable Moments/Greatest Performances

Knepper won a 1–0 pitchers' duel with Dodgers left-hander Jerry Reuss on April 21, 1981, tossing a three-hit shutout and scoring the game's only run in the bottom of the third inning on an RBI single by César Cedeño after leading off the frame with a double.

Knepper threw another three-hit shutout on September 2, 1981, also issuing just one walk, recording nine strikeouts, and driving in two runs with a double during an 8–0 win over the Mets.

Knepper turned in another outstanding all-around effort on June 9, 1983, yielding just two hits and striking out 10 batters during a 3–0 shutout of the Giants in which he also knocked in a run with a triple.

Knepper shut out the Dodgers, 3–0, on April 18, 1984, allowing just four hits, issuing no walks, and registering five strikeouts.

Knepper beat the Giants with both his arm and his bat on June 29, 1985, recording seven strikeouts and allowing just four hits during a complete-game 8–1 win, while also knocking in four runs with a single and one of his six career homers.

Knepper threw a three-hit shutout on July 18, 1986, registering nine strikeouts and issuing just one walk during a 3–0 win over the Mets.

Knepper turned in arguably the most dominant performance of his career on September 21, 1988, when he struck out seven and allowed just a second-inning single to Dale Murphy and a ninth-inning walk to catcher Bruce Benedict during a 1–0 win over the Braves.

Notable Achievements

- Won at least 15 games three times.
- Posted winning percentage over .700 once.
- Compiled ERA under 3.00 once (2.18 in 1981).
- Threw more than 200 innings four times.
- Led NL pitchers in shutouts once and assists once.
- Finished second in NL in ERA once and shutouts once.
- Ranks among Astros career leaders in wins (9th), shutouts (6th), innings pitched (6th), complete games (tied for 6th), and starts (5th).
- 1986 division champion.
- April 26, 1981, NL Player of the Week.
- 1981 *Sporting News* NL Comeback Player of the Year.
- Two-time NL All-Star selection (1981 and 1988).

32
YULI GURRIEL

standout on the Cuban National team that won World Cup Championships in 2003 and 2005 and Olympic Gold in 2004, Yuli Gurriel
spent several years starring in his homeland, before joining the Astros
during the latter stages of the 2016 campaign at the rather advanced age
of 32. Establishing himself as Houston's primary starter at first base shortly
thereafter, Gurriel spent the next six seasons manning that post for the
Astros, proving to be one of the more unheralded members of teams that
won five division titles, four pennants, and two World Series. A solid contact hitter who won the 2021 AL batting crown, the right-handed-swinging
Gurriel batted over .290 four times, surpassed 40 doubles three times, and
topped 30 homers and 100 RBIs once each, before signing with the Miami
Marlins prior to the start of the 2023 campaign.

Born in Sancti Spiritus, Cuba, on June 9, 1984, Yulieski Gurriel grew
up around baseball, acquiring his love of the game from his father, Lourdes
Gurriel, who starred in the Cuban Leagues for many years. Following in
his father's footsteps, Gurriel developed into one of his native country's
best players during the first decade of the 21st century, excelling at different times for the Sancti Spiritus and Industriales ballclubs of the Cuban
National Series. Particularly outstanding in 2005–2006, Gurriel batted
.327 and led the CNS with 27 homers, 92 RBIs, 89 runs scored, and 11
triples, compiling those numbers during a 90-game season. Gurriel posted
another extremely impressive stat-line in 2009–2010, when he reached the
seats 30 times, knocked in 105 runs, scored 90 others, and batted .363.
Demonstrating the ability to excel in big games, Gurriel also performed
well in the World Baseball Classic, leading all players with eight homers in
2005 and earning All-Tourney honors the following year as a second baseman with his exceptional all-around play, prompting several MLB scouts
to project him as a potential first-round pick were he eligible for the draft.

After competing in the CNS for 13 seasons, Gurriel spent one year
playing for the Yokohama DeNA BayStars of the Nippon Professional

Baseball League, before returning to Cuba in 2015. However, one year later, Gurriel and his younger brother, Lourdes Jr., defected to Haiti after competing in the Caribbean Series in the Dominican Republic. Subsequently declared a free agent by MLB, Gurriel signed with the Astros for five years and $47.5 million on July 16, 2016, after which he spent just one month in the minor leagues, before joining the parent club in late August. Playing mostly third base the rest of the year, Gurriel appeared in a total of 36 games, hitting three homers, driving in 15 runs, and batting .262.

Named Houston's starting first baseman prior to the start of the 2017 campaign, Gurriel acquitted himself extremely well in his first full big-league season, earning a fourth-place finish in the AL Rookie of the Year voting by hitting 18 homers, driving in 75 runs, scoring 69 times, collecting 43 doubles, batting .299, and compiling an OPS of .817 for the eventual world champions. Continuing to perform well in the postseason, Gurriel batted .529 against Boston in the ALDS, knocked in four runs against the

Yuli Gurriel won the AL batting title with a mark of .319 in 2021.
Courtesy of Keith Allison

Yankees in the ALCS, and homered twice and knocked in four runs against the Dodgers in the World Series.

Despite his strong play, Gurriel found himself embroiled in controversy after he made a racist gesture toward Dodgers pitcher Yu Darvish after homering against him in Game 3 of the Fall Classic. After Gurriel returned to the dugout following his solo blast off the Japanese right-hander, cameras caught him smiling and raising his hands as if to stretch the sides of his eyes, while also mouthing the Spanish word "chinito," which translates to "little Chinese Boy." Gurriel later apologized for his actions and said that anyone from Asia is called "chino" in Cuba. However, he acknowledged that the time he spent in Japan made him aware that Asians consider the term offensive. Meanwhile, Darvish issued a statement in which he forgave Gurriel and asked people to learn from the incident. Somewhat less forgiving, MLB commissioner Rob Manfred suspended Gurriel for the first five games of the ensuing campaign, saying at the time, "There is no excuse or explanation that makes that type of behavior acceptable," and adding, "Notwithstanding Mr. Gurriel's remorse, there needs to be disciplinary consequences to make clear that Major League Baseball is an institution that will not tolerate behavior of this type."

Although Gurriel remained the Astros' primary starter at first base his remaining time in Houston, he displayed his versatility the next two seasons by also starting several games at second and third, proving to be equally proficient at all three positions. Meanwhile, Gurriel contributed on offense to teams that won two division titles and one AL pennant by hitting 13 homers, knocking in 85 runs, scoring 70 times, and batting .291 in 2018; he reached the seats 31 times, driving in 104 runs, scoring 85 others, and batting .298 the following year.

Despite being a free swinger who rarely walked, the 6-foot, 215-pound Gurriel made consistent contact at the plate, striking out more than 70 times just once his entire career. Different from most other right-handed batters in that he hit righties better than lefties, Gurriel also represented something of an anomaly in that he hit breaking balls extremely well, posting a much higher batting average than most against the slider. And even though Gurriel never became known as a true home-run hitter, he had the ability to reach the seats, surpassing 15 homers on three separate occasions.

Experiencing a decline in offensive production during the pandemic-shortened 2020 campaign, Gurriel hit six homers, knocked in only 22 runs, and batted just .232 in 57 games, before rebounding the following year after losing 15 pounds during the offseason to hit 15 homers, drive in 81 runs, and lead the AL with a .319 batting average, making him the first Cuban-born player since Tony Oliva in 1971 to win a batting title. Excelling in the field as well, Gurriel earned Gold Glove honors by leading all AL first basemen in assists, while also ranking among the top players at his position in putouts and fielding percentage.

Far less successful in 2022, Gurriel hit just eight homers, knocked in only 53 runs, and batted just .242 during the regular season. But he proved to be a huge factor during the Astros' successful postseason run to the world championship, batting .400 against Seattle in the ALDS, .333 against the Yankees in the ALCS, and .316 against the Phillies in the World Series.

Nevertheless, with Gurriel having turned 38 years of age, the Astros showed little interest in bringing him back when he became a free agent at the end of the year, forcing him to sign a minor-league contract with the Miami Marlins on March 10, 2023. Upon hearing the news of Gurriel's signing, Astros manager Dusty Baker said, "He was one of my favorites. I'm glad he got a job . . . We were entertaining him coming back here because he's not through. This is a good spot because, if he makes this team, he's right at home."

Gurriel, who left Houston with career totals of 94 homers, 435 RBIs, 400 runs scored, 866 hits, 206 doubles, five triples, and 23 steals, a .284 batting average, a .328 on-base percentage, and a .448 slugging percentage, ended up earning a spot on the Marlins' big-league roster, after which he went on to hit 4 homers, drive in 28 runs, and bat .247 as their primary starter at first base. It remains to be seen whether Gurriel, now 39 years old, will play again in 2024.

ASTROS CAREER HIGHLIGHTS

Best Season

Although Gurriel led the AL with a .319 batting average in 2021, he posted slightly better overall numbers in 2019, when, in addition to batting .298, he established career-high marks with 31 homers, 104 RBIs, 85 runs scored, 305 total bases, a .541 slugging percentage, and an OPS of .884.

Memorable Moments/Greatest Performances

Gurriel led the Astros to an 11–3 win over the Anaheim Angels on September 21, 2018, by hitting a pair of homers and driving in seven runs, homering once with the bases loaded and once with one man aboard.

Gurriel delivered the decisive blow of a 10–6 victory over the Seattle Mariners on April 12, 2019, when he homered with the bases loaded in the top of the eighth inning.

Gurriel experienced a power surge from July 2 to July 7, 2019, homering in five straight games, with his double, two homers, and four RBIs on July 2 leading the Astros to a 9–8 win over the Colorado Rockies.

Gurriel contributed to a 14–3 rout of the Rockies on August 7, 2019, by knocking in a career-high eight runs with a homer, double, sacrifice fly, and groundout; his eight RBIs tied J. R. Towles for the franchise's single-game record.

Gurriel helped lead the Astros to a six-game victory over Boston in the 2021 ALCS by homering once, driving in six runs, scoring four times, batting .455, and compiling an OPS of 1.156.

Gurriel also performed exceptionally well during the Astros' three-game sweep of Seattle in the 2022 ALDS, batting .400 (6-for-15), with one home run and an OPS of 1.000.

Notable Achievements

- Hit more than 30 home runs once (31 in 2019).
- Knocked in more than 100 runs once (104 in 2019).
- Batted over .300 once (.319 in 2021).
- Surpassed 30 doubles five times, topping 40 two-baggers on three occasions.
- Posted slugging percentage over .500 once (.541 in 2019).
- Led AL with .319 batting average and 12 sacrifice flies in 2021.
- Finished second in AL with .383 on-base percentage in 2021.
- Led AL first basemen in assists twice and fielding percentage twice.
- Ranks among Astros career leaders in doubles (11th) and sacrifice flies (tied for 9th).
- Five-time division champion (2017, 2018, 2019, 2021, and 2022).
- Four-time AL champion (2017, 2019, 2021, and 2022).
- Two-time world champion (2017 and 2022).
- Two-time AL Player of the Week.
- July 2019 AL Player of the Month.
- 2021 Gold Glove Award winner.

33

— KEVIN BASS —

A switch-hitting outfielder who possessed good power at the plate and excellent speed on the basepaths and in the outfield, Kevin Bass spent parts of 10 seasons in Houston, proving to be one of the Astros' best all-around players during his two tours of duty with the club. Surpassing 20 homers once, stealing more than 20 bases three times, and batting over .300 on three separate occasions, Bass earned one All-Star nomination and one top-10 finish in the NL MVP voting. Nevertheless, Bass is perhaps remembered more than anything for making the final out of the 1986 NLCS, thereby ending the Astros' season and sending the New York Mets to the World Series.

Born in Redwood City, California, on May 12, 1959, Kevin Charles Bass grew up in nearby Menlo Park, just off the San Francisco Bay. A cousin of Hall of Fame wide receiver James Lofton and the nephew of former professional baseball player Stan Johnson, Bass got his start in organized ball at the age of nine as a shortstop on a local Little League team coached by his father. Deciding a few years later that he wanted to pursue a career in baseball, Bass recalled, "At the age of 14, I made a conscious decision to become a big-league player."

An outstanding all-around athlete, Bass played basketball and earned All-League honors in football and baseball at Menlo Park High School, with his exceptional play on the diamond prompting the High School Division of the American College of Baseball Coaches to accord him First-Team All-America honors at the end of his senior year. After initially fielding several college scholarship offers for football, Bass chose to focus exclusively on baseball, remembering, "I really loved playing football. I had aspirations to play college football. My junior year [of high school], I decided to just skip the basketball season and focus on lifting to get strong for my senior football. When baseball started, scouts started coming out to watch me play. After being drafted, I was flattered and surprised."

Selected by Milwaukee in the second round of the 1977 MLB Amateur Draft, Bass drew praise at the time from Brewers scout Roland LeBlanc, who said of the 18-year-old outfielder, "He's got a good arm, good speed, and he has an excellent instinct about going after the ball."

Bass subsequently spent nearly five years advancing through Milwaukee's farm system, before finally earning a roster spot with the parent club in 1982. But after Bass appeared in only 18 games with them over the season's first five months, the Brewers sent him and a pair of minor leaguers to the Astros on September 3 to complete a trade for pitcher Don Sutton. Starting seven games in the Houston outfield the rest of the year, Bass collected just one hit in 24 official at-bats, giving him a batting average of .042. Assuming a part-time role in 1983, Bass fared somewhat better, homering twice, driving in 18 runs, scoring 25 times, and compiling a batting average of .236 in 88 games and 206 total plate appearances.

Kevin Bass batted over .300 for the Astros three times.

Seeing much more action in 1984 after beginning the regular season on the disabled list with a severely pulled right thigh muscle, Bass hit two homers, knocked in 29 runs, scored 33 others, and batted .260 in 121 games, while splitting his time between right field and center. Finally becoming a regular member of the Astros starting lineup in 1985 after the team moved in the outfield fences at the Astrodome, Bass had a solid offensive season, hitting 16 homers, knocking in 68 runs, scoring 72 times, batting .269, and stealing 19 bases. Meanwhile, Bass, who spent time at all three outfield positions, threw out 10 runners on the basepaths and committed just one error all year, giving him a fielding percentage of .997 that placed him first among all NL outfielders. Bass followed that with arguably his finest all-around season, helping the Astros capture the NL West title in 1986 by hitting 20 homers, driving in 79 runs, scoring 83 times, stealing 22 bases, finishing fourth in the league with a .311 batting average, and compiling an OPS of .842. Although Bass subsequently batted .292 against the Mets in the NLCS, he came up short when it mattered most, failing to drive in a single run in 28 total plate appearances and striking out with two men out and the tying and winning runs on base in the bottom of the 16th inning of a 7–6 loss to the Mets in the series finale.

Looking back on his lone postseason appearance years later, Bass said, "My adrenaline was so high for the whole series; most of it was like a blur, except for that last at-bat."

The switch-hitting Bass, who stood 6 feet and weighed close to 185 pounds, possessed decent power from both sides of the plate, although he typically posted a significantly higher average as a right-handed batter. More of a line-drive hitter than a true slugger, Bass drove the ball well to the outfield gaps, amassing at least 27 doubles and five triples four times each during his time in Houston. Extremely aggressive at the plate, Bass never walked more than 53 times in a season, allowing him to compile an OPS over .360 just once. On the other hand, Bass did not strike out a great deal, fanning more than 70 times just twice. Meanwhile, Bass made good use of his speed on the basepaths and in the outfield, consistently ranking among the Astros team leaders in stolen bases and the league's top players at his position in putouts.

Claiming that the Astrodome, with its hard surface and large outfield, suited his game perfectly, Bass said, "I played with four other clubs, but Houston was the most productive place for me. The Astrodome fit my game. I really enjoyed playing there. It was a different game back then than it is today. I'm not saying that it was better, but it was different."

Playing right field exclusively in 1987, Bass had another excellent year, concluding the campaign with 19 homers, 85 RBIs, 83 runs scored, 21 stolen bases, a batting average of .284, and an OPS of .793. Remaining in right full-time for one more season, Bass hit 14 homers, knocked in 72 runs, scored 57 times, stole 31 bases, batted .255, and compiled an OPS of .704 in 1988, before missing nearly half of the ensuing campaign with a broken right shinbone he sustained when he fouled off a pitch from Bill Landrum of the Pittsburgh Pirates. Still, Bass performed well in the 87 games in which he appeared, hitting five homers, driving in 44 runs, scoring 42 times, batting an even .300, and posting an OPS of .792.

A free agent at the end of the year, Bass chose to sign with the San Francisco Giants for three years and $5.25 million after they inserted a no-trade clause in the contract that the Astros refused to include in their offer to him, stating during a conference call held shortly thereafter, "That ended up being the key factor. I think the Astros were pretty serious about signing me, but the Giants were more serious."

Looking back on his decision the following spring, Bass said, "It was tough leaving Houston. I had been there for so long, and they treated me pretty good. But the offer came up, and it was a chance to come back home."

Hampered by an injury to his left knee that required surgery following the conclusion of the 1990 campaign, Bass failed to contribute to the Giants as much as he would have liked over the course of the next two-and-a-half seasons, compiling a composite batting average of just .249, hitting only 24 homers, and driving in just 102 runs in 274 games and 924 total plate appearances. Commenting on his inability to live up to the terms of his contract his first two years in San Francisco, Bass said at spring training in March 1992, "I didn't realize how important speed was to me. Man, if you can't run, you can't hit. If you can't run, you can't play defense."

Dealt to the Mets on August 8, 1992, Bass finished out the season in New York, before re-signing with the Astros when he became a free agent again at the end of the year. Assuming a part-time role in Houston the next two seasons, Bass performed well in somewhat limited duty, posting batting averages of .284 and .310, while splitting his time between right field and left.

A free agent again at the end of 1994, Bass signed with the Baltimore Orioles, for whom he appeared in 111 games in 1995, announcing his retirement when the team released him following the conclusion of the campaign. Over parts of 14 big-league seasons, Bass hit 118 homers, knocked in 611 runs, scored 609 times, collected 1,308 hits, 248 doubles, and 40 triples, stole 151 bases, batted .270, compiled an on-base percentage of .323, and posted a slugging percentage of .411. As a member of the Astros, Bass hit 87 homers, knocked in 468 runs, scored 465 times, amassed 990 hits, 194 doubles, and 30 triples, swiped 120 bags, batted .278, compiled a .330 on-base percentage, and posted a .423 slugging percentage.

Since retiring from baseball, Bass has kept himself busy by managing the Texas real-estate business he and his wife, Elaine, originally founded in 1993. He also spends a great deal of time on the golf course.

ASTROS CAREER HIGHLIGHTS

Best Season

Bass had the finest season of his career in 1986, when he earned his lone All-Star nomination and a seventh-place finish in the NL MVP voting by hitting 20 homers, driving in 79 runs, scoring 83 times, collecting 33 doubles, stealing 22 bases, and ranking among the league leaders with 184 hits, a .311 batting average, and a .486 slugging percentage.

Memorable Moments/Greatest Performances

Bass led the Astros to a 4–2 win over the Montreal Expos on July 5, 1985, by hitting a pair of solo homers.

Bass contributed to a 9–3 victory over the Phillies on July 24, 1986, by going a perfect 5-for-5 at the plate, driving in two runs, and scoring twice.

Bass helped lead the Astros to a 6–5 win over the Giants on June 27, 1987, by going 4-for-4, with a homer, triple, two doubles, and four RBIs.

After hitting a solo home run earlier in the game, Bass gave the Astros a 5–3 win over the Giants on August 3, 1987, when he homered with one man aboard in the bottom of the 13th inning.

Bass made history on September 2, 1987, when, during a 10–1 rout of the Cubs in which he went 4-for-4 with two home runs, a double, three RBIs, and four runs scored, he became the first NL player to homer from both sides of the plate in a game twice in one season.

Bass had another big day on September 14, 1987, collecting four hits, homering once, and driving in four runs during an 8–1 win over the Dodgers.

Bass plated all four runs the Astros scored during a 4–1 win over the Padres on July 27, 1988, with a pair of two-run homers off San Diego starter Ed Whitson.

After homering with no one on base earlier in the contest, Bass gave the Astros an 8–4 victory over the Cubs on August 20, 1989, when he hit a grand slam home run off Mitch Williams in the bottom of the ninth inning.

Bass led the Astros to a 15–5 romp over the Cardinals on April 23, 1994, by going 5-for-6, with a homer, double, three RBIs, and four runs scored.

Notable Achievements

- Hit 20 home runs in 1986.
- Batted .300 or better three times.
- Surpassed 30 doubles twice.
- Stole more than 20 bases three times, topping 30 thefts once (31 in 1988).
- Finished fourth in NL with .311 batting average in 1986.
- Led NL outfielders and NL right fielders in fielding percentage once each.
- 1986 division champion.
- Two-time NL Player of the Week.
- June 1986 NL Player of the Month.
- Finished seventh in 1986 NL MVP voting.
- 1986 NL All-Star selection.

34

DALLAS KEUCHEL

One of the American League's better pitchers from 2014 to 2018, Dallas Keuchel spent parts of seven seasons in Houston, proving to be a significant contributor to teams that won two division titles, one pennant, and one World Series. The third Astros pitcher to win the Cy Young Award, Keuchel also earned two All-Star nominations and one top-five finish in the league MVP voting by posting 20 victories once, compiling an ERA under 3.00 three times, recording more than 200 strikeouts once, and throwing more than 200 innings on three separate occasions. An exceptional fielder as well, Keuchel won four of his five Gold Gloves as a member of the Astros, before signing with the Atlanta Braves as a free agent in 2019.

Born in Tulsa, Oklahoma, on January 1, 1988, Dallas Keuchel attended local Bishop Kelley High School, where he starred in multiple sports, excelling as a quarterback on the gridiron and a pitcher on the diamond. Offered an athletic scholarship to the University of Arkansas after leading Bishop Kelley's baseball team to the state championship in his senior year, Keuchel pitched his best ball for the Razorbacks as a junior, helping them advance to the 2009 College World Series by compiling a record of 7-3 and an ERA of 3.92.

Subsequently selected by the Astros in the seventh round of the 2009 MLB Amateur Draft, Keuchel spent the next three seasons pitching for four different minor-league teams, before being summoned to Houston in June 2012. Starting 16 games the rest of the year, Keuchel performed terribly, posting a record of 3-8 and an ERA of 5.27 for an Astros team that ended up winning just 55 games. Unfortunately, neither Keuchel nor the Astros fared any better the following season, with the 25-year-old southpaw going 6-10 with a 5.15 ERA, and Houston posting four fewer victories.

Despite Keuchel's early struggles, Astros GM Jeff Luhnow remained convinced that he had the ability to be a big winner at the major-league level, prompting him to instruct pitching coach Brent Strom to make him his pet project prior to the start of the 2014 campaign, with Strom

Dallas Keuchel earned AL Cy Young honors in 2015.
Courtesy of Keith Allison

recalling, "Jeff said, 'You have to keep an eye on this guy; he's going to be very good,' and Jeff was dead right. Dallas made some changes."

With Strom and bullpen coach Craig Bjornson suggesting to Keuchel that he make better use of the lower half of his body, the 6'2", 205-pound left-hander became more consistent in his release point and gained better overall command of his pitches, allowing him to flourish as never before. While the Astros improved their record somewhat, surpassing 70 victories for the first time in four years, Keuchel developed into the ace of the pitching staff, going 12-9, with a 2.93 ERA, a 1.175 WHIP, and a league-leading five complete games, while also winning his first Gold Glove.

Performing even better in 2015, Keuchel helped the Astros advance to the playoffs as a wild card by leading all AL hurlers with 20 victories (against eight losses), a WHIP of 1.017, two shutouts, and 232 innings pitched, placing second in the league with a 2.48 ERA, and finishing fifth in the circuit with 216 strikeouts, earning Cy Young honors and his first All-Star selection. Also named the winner of the Warren Spahn Award, presented annually to the best left-handed pitcher in the game, Keuchel proved to be particularly effective at home, compiling a perfect 15-0 record at Minute Maid Park. Although the Astros ultimately suffered a five-game defeat at the hands of the Kansas City Royals in the ALDS, Keuchel continued his exceptional pitching in the postseason, winning both his starts and compiling a composite ERA of 2.57. Especially outstanding against the Yankees in the wild card game, Keuchel struck out seven batters and allowed just three hits over the first six innings of a 3–0 Astros win.

Despite his high strikeout total in 2015, Keuchel relied primarily on his excellent control and the location of his pitches to navigate his way through opposing lineups, never fanning more than 153 batters in any other season. Recording most of his outs on groundballs, Keuchel threw an 89-mph sinker and an 89-mph four-seam fastball, both of which dropped as they approached home plate, causing hitters to hit an inordinate number of grounders. Keuchel's repertoire of pitches also included an 86-mph cut fastball, a 79-mph slider, and an 80-mph changeup. Employing a smooth and seemingly effortless over-the-top delivery, Keuchel drew praise for his pitching motion from Hall of Fame hurler and MLB Network analyst John Smoltz, who said, "The guy has mastered his mechanics."

Bothered by pain in his throwing shoulder that limited him to 26 starts in 2016, Keuchel failed to perform at the same elite level, going just 9-12 with a 4.55 ERA and a WHIP of 1.286. Despite missing several starts the following season as well due to neck issues that forced him to serve two stints on the disabled list, Keuchel rebounded in a big way, earning his second All-Star nomination by compiling a record of 14-5, an ERA of 2.90, and a WHIP of 1.119 for an Astros team that went on to win the World Series. Fully healthy in 2018, Keuchel had a solid season, going 12-11 with an ERA of 3.74 and a WHIP of 1.314, while also recording 153 strikeouts in 204⅔ innings pitched and leading all AL hurlers with 34 starts.

A free agent following the conclusion of the 2018 campaign, Keuchel elected to sign with the Atlanta Braves for one year and $13 million, ending his lengthy association with the Astros. Keuchel, who, over parts of seven seasons in Houston, compiled an overall record of 76-63, an ERA of 3.66, and a WHIP of 1.250, threw 12 complete games and four shutouts, and struck out 945 batters in 1,189⅓ innings pitched, ended up starting just 19 games for the Braves in 2019 due to injury, before inking a three-year, $55.5 million deal with the Chicago White Sox at season's end. Performing well for the White Sox during the pandemic-shortened 2020 campaign,

Keuchel went 6-2 with a 1.99 ERA. However, Keuchel has since fallen on hard times. After compiling a record of 9-9 and an ERA of 5.28 in 2021, Keuchel went a combined 2-9 with a 9.20 ERA for the White Sox, Arizona Diamondbacks, and Texas Rangers in 2022, causing him to be released by all three teams.

After sitting out the first half of the 2023 campaign, Keuchel signed a minor-league deal with the Minnesota Twins on June 22. He subsequently spent the next six weeks in the minors, before being promoted to the parent club in early August. Making a total of 10 appearances with the Twins the rest of the year, mostly as a starter, Keuchel went 2-1 with a 5.97 ERA. Whether or not Keuchel ever pitches in the major leagues again remains very much an unanswered question heading into 2024. If he never throws another pitch in the majors, Keuchel will end his big-league career with a record of 103-92, an ERA of 4.02, a WHIP of 1.320, 12 complete games, 4 shutouts, and 1,243 strikeouts in 1,625.2 innings pitched.

ASTROS CAREER HIGHLIGHTS

Best Season

Although Keuchel also performed extremely well in 2017, earning his second All-Star nomination by winning 14 games and compiling an ERA of 2.90, he pitched the best ball of his career in 2015, earning AL Cy Young honors and a fifth-place finish in the league MVP voting by compiling a record of 20-8 and an ERA of 2.48, registering 216 strikeouts, and leading all AL hurlers with 232 innings pitched, two shutouts, and a WHIP of 1.017.

Memorable Moments/Greatest Performances

Keuchel tossed a complete-game four-hitter against Seattle on May 25, 2014, allowing just one unearned run during a 4–1 Astros win.

Although Keuchel didn't figure in the decision, he allowed just two hits and no runs over the first nine innings of an 11-inning, 5–4 win over Oakland on April 24, 2015.

Keuchel shut out the White Sox, 3–0, on May 30, 2015, surrendering just four hits, issuing no walks, and recording 11 strikeouts along the way.

Keuchel threw another shutout on June 25, 2015, this time yielding six hits, issuing one walk, and striking out 12 batters during a 4–0 win over the Yankees.

In addition to recording a career-high 13 strikeouts during a 10–0 blowout of the Texas Rangers on July 19, 2015, Keuchel allowed just two hits in seven innings of work.

Keuchel dominated the Texas lineup again on August 5, 2016, going the distance and yielding just three hits, walking two batters, and striking out seven during a 5–0 Astros win.

Keuchel earned a victory over the Yankees in Game 1 of the 2017 ALCS by recording 10 strikeouts and allowing just four hits over seven scoreless innings of a 2–1 Astros win.

Notable Achievements

- Won 20 games in 2015.
- Posted winning percentage over .700 twice.
- Compiled ERA under 3.00 three times.
- Struck out more than 200 batters once (216 in 2015).
- Threw more than 200 innings three times.
- Led AL in wins, WHIP, shutouts, innings pitched, and complete games once each.
- Finished second in AL in ERA once and shutouts once.
- Two-time division champion (2017 and 2018).
- 2017 AL champion.
- 2017 world champion.
- Two-time AL Player of the Week.
- Four-time AL Pitcher of the Month.
- Four-time Gold Glove Award winner (2014, 2015, 2016, and 2018).
- 2015 *Sporting News* AL Pitcher of the Year.
- 2015 AL Cy Young Award winner.
- Finished fifth in 2015 AL MVP voting.
- Two-time AL All-Star selection (2015 and 2017).

35

DEREK BELL

One of the original "Killer Bs" that also included Jeff Bagwell, Craig Biggio, and third baseman Sean Berry, Derek Bell spent five seasons in Houston serving as the starting right fielder for Astros teams that won three straight NL Central Division titles. A solid hitter and run producer the Astros acquired in the infamous trade that sent Ken Caminiti, Steve Finley, and Andújar Cedeño to San Diego, Bell hit more than 20 homers once, knocked in more than 100 runs twice, and batted over .300 on two separate occasions, before his abrasive personality and narcissistic nature bought him a ticket out of Houston.

Born in Tampa, Florida, on December 11, 1968, Derek Nathaniel Bell got his start in organized baseball with the local Belmont Heights Little League team that won the US championship in both 1980 and 1981, before losing to Taiwan in the world championship game both years. Developing into an outstanding player during his teenage years, Bell excelled on the diamond at Tampa's C. Leon King High School, prompting the Toronto Blue Jays to select him in the second round of the 1987 MLB Amateur Draft, with the 49th overall pick.

Bell subsequently spent most of the next five seasons advancing through Toronto's farm system, winning two batting titles and one league MVP award, before finally joining the parent club during the latter stages of the 1991 campaign. After serving Toronto as a fourth outfielder the following year, Bell headed to San Diego when the Blue Jays traded him to the Padres for veteran outfielder Darrin Jackson in March 1993.

Performing well for the Padres the next two seasons, Bell hit 21 homers, knocked in 72 runs, batted .262, and compiled an OPS of .720 in 1993, before hitting 14 homers, driving in 54 runs, batting .311, and posting an OPS of .808 during the strike-shortened 1994 campaign. But with Bell and a teammate having been arrested in New York City early in 1994 for soliciting an undercover policewoman prior to a game with the Mets, the Padres chose to include him in a 12-player trade they completed with the

Derek Bell helped the Astros win three straight NL Central Division titles.

Astros on December 28, 1994, that sent him, outfielder Phil Plantier, utility infielders Ricky Gutiérrez and Craig Shipley, and pitchers Doug Brocail and Pedro Martínez (not *the* Pedro Martínez) to Houston for a package of six players that included third baseman Ken Caminiti, outfielder Steve Finley, and shortstop Andújar Cedeño.

Despite missing nearly a month of action in 1995 due to injury, Bell had an excellent year for the Astros, earning MVP consideration by finishing fourth in the league with a .334 batting average, hitting eight homers, driving in 86 runs, scoring 63 times, stealing 27 bases, and compiling an OPS of .827. Bell followed that by hitting 17 homers, knocking in 113 runs, scoring 84 times, amassing 40 doubles, stealing 29 bases, batting .263, and posting an OPS of .729 in 1996, while also leading all NL right fielders with 16 assists. After hitting 15 homers, knocking in 71 runs, batting .276, and compiling an OPS of .782 in 1997, Bell helped lead the Astros to their second straight division title the following year by driving in 108 runs, batting .314, and establishing career-high marks with 22 homers, 111 runs scored, 198 hits, 41 doubles, and an OPS of .855.

The right-handed-hitting Bell, who stood 6'2" and weighed 215 pounds, possessed slightly above average power and speed, making him an effective middle-of-the-order hitter, a good baserunner, and a solid defensive outfielder. A free-swinger, Bell tended to expand the strike zone, drawing more than 55 bases on balls just once his entire career, while striking out more than 120 times on five separate occasions. Nevertheless, Bell proved to be a key contributor to the Astros on offense, driving in runs from his cleanup spot in the batting order while also providing protection for Jeff Bagwell, who typically batted immediately in front of him.

Bell spent one more season in Houston, hitting 12 homers, knocking in 66 runs, and batting just .236 in 1999, before his selfish behavior prompted the Astros to deal him elsewhere at the end of the year. With manager Larry Dierker returning to the team in July following a month-long absence after undergoing emergency brain surgery, he chose to drop the slumping Bell down to the number six spot in the batting order. Displaying a total lack of sensitivity toward Dierker's plight, Bell ranted after the game, "It's a slap in the face to be dropped to the sixth spot. I'm to the point now that I feel like I'm not wanted."

With Astros fans reacting harshly to his words, Bell subsequently became persona non grata in Houston, causing management to complete a trade with the Mets on December 23, 1999, that sent him and star pitcher Mike Hampton to New York for outfielder Roger Cedeño, reliever Octavio Dotel, and minor leaguer Kyle Kessel. Exhibiting their desire to rid themselves of Bell during trade negotiations, the Astros let it be known that they would not include Hampton in any deal unless their trade partner was also willing to accept the disgruntled outfielder.

Expressing his happiness to be leaving Houston upon learning of the trade, Bell said, "Christmas came early for me. I'm very happy. I told my agent I'm going to run, I'm so excited."

Bell, who hit 74 homers, knocked in 444 runs, scored 386 times, collected 770 hits, 153 doubles, and 10 triples, stole 102 bases, batted .284, compiled a .341 on-base percentage, and posted a .430 slugging percentage as a member of the Astros, ended up spending just one season with the Mets, hitting 18 homers, driving in 69 runs, scoring 87 times, and batting

.266 for their 2000 NL pennant-winning ballclub, before being allowed to leave via free agency at the end of the year.

Finding few takers, Bell ultimately signed a two-year, $9 million deal with the lowly Pittsburgh Pirates, for whom he batted just .173 in 46 games in 2001. Told by reporters the following spring that they had been informed by team management that he needed to compete for a starting job, Bell responded by saying, "Nobody told me I was in competition. If there is competition, somebody better let me know. If there is competition, they better eliminate me out of the race and go ahead and do what they're going to do with me. I ain't never hit in spring training, and I never will. If it ain't settled with me out there, then they can trade me. I ain't going out there to hurt myself in spring training battling for a job. If it is a competition, then I'm going into 'Operation Shutdown.' Tell them exactly what I said. I haven't competed for a job since 1991."

Leaving the Pirates for his yacht on March 29, Bell was released two days later, prompting Pittsburgh sports columnist Mark Madden to write a column he entitled, "Derek Bell Becomes Pirate: Lives on a Boat and Steals Money." Bell, who never appeared in another major-league game, ended his playing career with 134 homers, 668 RBIs, 642 runs scored, 1,262 hits, 232 doubles, 15 triples, 170 stolen bases, a .276 batting average, a .336 on-base percentage, and a .421 slugging percentage.

After retiring from baseball, Bell returned to Tampa, Florida, where he spent several years serving as an assistant coach at C. Leon High School and Tampa Catholic High School. Unfortunately, Bell has continued to conduct himself inappropriately in retirement, being arrested on three separate occasions on charges of felony cocaine possession and possession of drug paraphernalia, with his most recent arrest coming on November 16, 2022. Having squandered most of the $26 million he made during his playing career, Bell had to auction off the World Series ring he earned with the Blue Jays in 1992.

ASTROS CAREER HIGHLIGHTS

Best Season

Bell performed extremely well for the Astros in both 1995 and 1996, batting a career-high .334 in the first of those campaigns and driving in a career-best 113 runs in the second. But he posted his best overall numbers in 1998, finishing the season with 22 homers, 108 RBIs, 111 runs scored, 198 hits, 41 doubles, a .314 batting average, and an OPS of .855.

Memorable Moments/Greatest Performances

Bell starred in defeat on May 23, 1995, going 5-for-5, with two doubles, two stolen bases, two RBIs, and two runs scored during a 10–5 loss to the Reds.

Bell punctuated an outstanding 4-for-6 performance on June 23, 1995, by delivering an RBI single in the bottom of the 12th inning that gave the Astros a 3–2 win over the Cubs.

Bell led the Astros to an 11–4 victory over the Giants on July 20, 1995, by driving in six runs with a homer, single, and sacrifice fly.

Bell delivered the decisive blow of a 7–5 win over the Reds on April 21, 1996, when he homered in the bottom of the eighth inning with two men out and two men on.

Bell contributed to a lopsided 15–2 victory over the Colorado Rockies on April 3, 1998, by going 3-for-4, with a homer, double, two walks, six RBIs, and three runs scored.

Bell gave the Astros a 6–5 victory in the first game of their doubleheader split with the Mets on September 15, 1998, when he led off the bottom of the 12th inning with a home run off Jeff Tam.

Notable Achievements

- Hit more than 20 home runs once (22 in 1998).
- Knocked in more than 100 runs twice.
- Scored more than 100 runs once (111 in 1998).
- Batted over .300 twice.
- Surpassed 40 doubles twice.
- Stole more than 20 bases twice.
- Led NL with 10 sacrifice flies in 1998.
- Led NL right fielders with 16 assists in 1996.
- Finished fourth in NL with .334 batting average in 1995.
- Three-time division champion (1997, 1998, and 1999).
- Two-time NL Player of the Week.

36

ENOS CABELL

A versatile player who manned multiple positions during his two tours of duty with the Astros, Enos Cabell spent parts of eight seasons in Houston, starting at first base, third base, and both corner outfield positions at various times. The Astros' regular third baseman from 1976 to 1980, Cabell played the best ball of his career during that five-year stretch, scoring more than 100 runs once and stealing more than 30 bases four times, while also leading all NL third sackers in putouts once. A solid line-drive hitter who batted over .280 three times for the Astros, Cabell compiled a lifetime mark of .277 over the course of his 15-year big-league career that also included stints with the Baltimore Orioles, San Francisco Giants, Detroit Tigers, and Los Angeles Dodgers.

Born in Fort Riley, Kansas, on October 8, 1949, Enos Milton Cabell moved with his family to Los Angeles at an early age, recalling, "I grew up in Los Angeles. I went to Gardena High School during integration. I played point guard in basketball, but I was 6-5 and weighed 165 pounds. My father taught me everything I knew. I was an Army baby. I played baseball ever since I was seven years old. I just loved baseball."

A standout on the diamond at Gardena High, Cabell drew the attention of scouts from UCLA and USC. But when neither university offered him an athletic scholarship, Cabell enrolled at Los Angeles Harbor Junior College in Wilmington, California, where he earned All-Conference honors in baseball in each of the next two seasons. Nevertheless, because of Cabell's small-college background, no team selected him in the 1968 MLB Amateur Draft, prompting him to sign with the Baltimore Orioles as an undrafted free agent.

Cabell subsequently spent the next six years advancing through Baltimore's farm system, performing well at every stop. But, with Cabell's primary positions being first base and third, he found his path to a starting job in the big leagues being blocked by Boog Powell and Brooks Robinson. Finally promoted to the majors for good in 1974 after appearing briefly with the parent club in each of the previous two seasons, Cabell assumed the role of a utility player, batting .241, hitting three homers, and driving in 17 runs in 80 games and 174 official at-bats.

Traded to the Astros the following offseason for slugging first baseman Lee May and minor-league outfielder Jay Schlueter, Cabell garnered significantly more playing time his first year in Houston, when, appearing in 117 games and accumulating a total of 348 official at-bats, he homered twice, knocked in 43 runs, scored 43 times, and batted .264, while splitting his time between first, third, and the outfield. Receiving his big break when the Astros traded Doug Rader to the San Diego Padres on December 11, 1975, Cabell laid claim to the starting third base job, after which he went on to hit two homers, drive in 43 runs, score 85 times, steal 35 bases, bat .273, and compile an OPS of .638.

Enos Cabell stole more than 30 bases four times for the Astros.

Firmly ensconced at third by the start of the 1977 campaign, Cabell had arguably his finest season, hitting 16 homers, knocking in 68 runs, batting .282, posting an OPS of .751, and placing in the league's top 10 with 101 runs scored, 176 hits, 36 doubles, and 42 stolen bases, while also leading all NL third sackers in putouts. Cabell followed that with another excellent year, earning team MVP honors in 1978 by hitting seven homers, driving in 71 runs, scoring 92 times, stealing 33 bases, batting .295, compiling an OPS of .720, and finishing third in the league with 195 hits.

An extremely aggressive hitter who swung at anything close to home plate, the right-handed-hitting Cabell rarely walked, drawing as many as 30 bases on balls in a season just once in his career. Long and lean at 6'5" and 180 pounds, Cabell also did not possess a great deal of power, finishing in double digits in homers just once. But Cabell, whose infectious smile and tremendous hustle made him a favorite of the hometown fans, did an excellent job of slapping the ball to all fields and using his speed to turn singles into doubles and doubles into triples, topping 30 two-baggers three times, while also amassing at least seven three-baggers on four separate occasions.

Embracing the philosophy employed by his Astros teammates, Cabell said, "In the Astrodome, you had to hit it all the way up in the stands. They didn't have those short fences like they have these days. We played defense and pitched. We were more comfortable playing a 1–0 or 2–1 game than a 10–8 game."

Cabell had two more solid seasons for the Astros, totaling eight homers, 122 RBIs, 129 runs scored, and 58 stolen bases from 1979 to 1980, while posting batting averages of .272 and .276, before being traded to the San Francisco Giants for pitcher Bob Knepper and outfielder Chris Bourjos at the 1980 winter meetings. Cabell subsequently spent just one season in San Francisco, driving in 36 runs and batting .255 for the Giants during the strike-shortened 1981 campaign, before being dealt to the Detroit Tigers the following offseason. Playing under manager Sparky Anderson the next two years, Cabell performed well for the Tigers, compiling a career-high .311 batting average in 1983. But, when he became a free agent at season's end, Cabell chose to leave Detroit and return to Houston.

Moving across the diamond to first base after signing with the Astros, Cabell had one of his better offensive seasons, batting .310, while also hitting eight homers, driving in 44 runs, and scoring 52 times in 127 games and 436 official at-bats. But when Cabell's batting average slipped to .245 over the first half of the 1985 season, the Astros traded him to the Dodgers for minor-league pitcher Rafael Montalvo and a player to be named later.

After finishing out the year in Los Angeles, Cabell joined six other players in being suspended for the entire 1986 campaign for admitting during the Pittsburgh drug trials that he had been involved in cocaine abuse. However, MLB later reinstated all seven players after they agreed to donate 10 percent of their salary to charity and perform community service.

Cabell ended up assuming the role of a utility player for the Dodgers in 1986, before age and his tarnished reputation made him an unwanted man when he became a free agent at season's end. Forced into retirement, Cabell ended his career with 60 homers, 596 RBIs, 753 runs scored, 1,647 hits, 263 doubles, 56 triples, 238 stolen bases, a .277 batting average, a .308 on-base percentage, and a .370 slugging percentage. As a member of the Astros, Cabell hit 45 homers, knocked in 405 runs, scored 522 times, collected 1,124 hits, 175 doubles, and 45 triples, stole 191 bases, batted .281, compiled an on-base percentage of .313, and posted a slugging percentage of .381.

After retiring from baseball, Cabell returned to Houston, where he opened a car dealership, later saying, "I went into the car business for 14 years. I had 250 employees, and it was kind of tough. I didn't like being the boss of 250 people. I came back to the game."

An analyst on Home Sports Entertainment telecasts of Astros home games from 1991 to 1994, Cabell also hosted the weekly call-in radio show, *Astros Report*, from 1991 to 1996. Cabell served as a member of the Texas Southern University Board of Regents from 1995 to 2001, before accepting a position in the Astros front office as a special assistant to the general manager. In that role, Cabell helps evaluate talent in the organization at both the major- and minor-league levels.

The 74-year-old Cabell, who currently lives with his wife, Ruby, in Missouri City, Texas, says, "I play golf now. Golf is my passion . . . and my grandkids. My boys never played (baseball) because I think the pressure was on them a lot to be like me, or play like me, which I didn't like. They took after their mother. They are real smart."

ASTROS CAREER HIGHLIGHTS

Best Season

In addition to batting .295, compiling an OPS of .720, scoring 92 runs, and stealing 33 bases in 1978, Cabell established career-high marks with 195 hits, eight triples, and 71 RBIs. But he posted slightly better overall numbers the previous season, concluding the 1977 campaign with a career-best 16 homers, 101 runs scored, 36 doubles, and 42 stolen bases, while also driving in 68 runs, collecting 176 hits, batting .282, and compiling an OPS of .751.

Memorable Moments/Greatest Performances

Cabell helped lead the Astros to a 7–6 win over the Padres on June 27, 1977, by going 4-for-5, with two doubles, two RBIs, and two runs scored.

Cabell collected three hits, drove in a run, scored three times, and stole two bases during a 7–5 win over the Giants on August 11, 1977.

Although the Astros lost to the Phillies, 7–3, on August 21, 1977, Cabell homered twice in one game for the only time in his career, hitting a pair of solo homers off Steve Carlton.

Cabell contributed to a 6–0 win over the Braves on May 19, 1978, by going a perfect 4-for-4 at the plate, with three RBIs and one run scored.

Cabell led the Astros to a 9–8 win over the Pirates on April 27, 1979, by going 3-for-5, with a homer, double, two RBIs, and three runs scored.

Notable Achievements

- Batted over .300 once (.310 in 1984).
- Scored more than 100 runs once (101 in 1977).
- Surpassed 30 doubles three times.
- Stole more than 30 bases four times, topping 40 thefts once (42 in 1977).
- Led NL in games played and at-bats once each.
- Led NL third basemen in putouts once.
- Finished third in NL with 195 hits in 1978.
- Ranks among Astros career leaders in hits (11th), triples (8th), and stolen bases (tied for 9th).
- 1980 division champion.
- 1978 Astros team MVP.

37

GERRIT COLE

Although Gerrit Cole spent just two seasons with the Astros, the dominance that he displayed over the course of those two seasons earned him a place in these rankings. Reaching the apex of his career during his time in Houston, Cole won 20 games once, compiled an ERA under 3.00 twice, and recorded more than 200 strikeouts twice, setting the franchise's all-time single-season mark in the last category. A member of Astros teams that won two division titles and one pennant, Cole earned two All-Star selections, one runner-up finish in the AL Cy Young voting, one top-10 finish in the league MVP balloting, and one *Sporting News* AL Pitcher of the Year nomination, before signing with the Yankees as a free agent following the conclusion of the 2019 campaign.

Born in Newport Beach, California, on September 8, 1990, Gerrit Alan Cole grew up some 15 miles north, in the city of Orange. Developing into a star pitcher at Orange Lutheran High School, Cole earned a spot on *USA Today*'s All-USA high school baseball team his senior year by compiling a record of 8-2 and an ERA of 0.47, while also striking out 121 batters in 75 innings of work.

Subsequently selected by the Yankees in the first round of the 2008 MLB Amateur Draft, with the 28th overall pick, Cole chose to delay the beginning of his professional career and instead attend the University of California, Los Angeles (UCLA) on a baseball scholarship. He then spent the next three years at UCLA, pitching his best ball for the Bruins as a sophomore, when he helped lead them to a record of 51-17 and a berth in the 2010 College World Series, going 11-4 with a 3.37 ERA and striking out 153 batters in 123 innings pitched. Electing to turn pro when Pittsburgh selected him with the first overall pick of the 2011 MLB Draft, Cole signed with the Pirates for $8 million, after which he spent a little over one year pitching for three different minor-league teams, before joining the parent club early in 2013.

Gerrit Cole earned *Sporting News* AL Pitcher of the Year honors in 2019, when he set a single-season franchise record by striking out 326 batters.
Courtesy of Ken Lund

Performing well for the Pirates as a rookie, Cole compiled a record of 10-7 and an ERA of 3.22, while also striking out 100 batters in 117⅓ innings of work. After another solid season in 2014, Cole emerged as one of the NL's best pitchers the following year, when he earned All-Star honors and a fourth-place finish in the Cy Young voting, going 19-8 with a 2.60 ERA and recording 202 strikeouts in 208 innings pitched. But with Cole failing to perform at the same elite level the next two seasons, the Pirates traded him to the Astros on January 13, 2018, for a package of four young players that included pitcher Joe Musgrove and infielder Colin Moran.

Urged by team officials following his arrival in Houston to scrap his two-seam fastball and rely more heavily on his four-seamer, which tends to rise as it approaches home plate, Cole reached a level of excellence he never attained in Pittsburgh. With the hard-throwing right-hander targeting the upper portion of the strike zone with a pitch that typically registers close to 100 mph on the radar gun, he became far more difficult to hit, enabling him to earn All-Star honors and a fifth-place finish in the AL Cy Young voting by compiling a record of 15-5 and an ERA of 2.88, while also finishing second in the league with 276 strikeouts. Cole followed that with an even more impressive 2019 campaign, earning a second-place finish in the Cy Young balloting by going 20-5, with a league-leading 2.50 ERA and 326 strikeouts, which established a new single-season franchise record.

A consummate power pitcher, the 6'4", 220-pound Cole enjoys challenging hitters with his high, hard one, which he does not hesitate to throw on any count. And, somewhat surprisingly, Cole loses little, if any, velocity on his fastball during the latter stages of contests, often delivering it to home plate at a speed of 100 mph in the seventh or eighth inning of games. Far from one dimensional, Cole also possesses a wide assortment of offspeed pitches that includes a slider, knuckle curve, and changeup, all of which he throws from a low three-quarters position.

While Cole's physical talent helped make him the dominant pitcher he eventually became, former Astros manager A. J. Hinch claimed that his mental makeup separated him from other similarly gifted hurlers, saying, "His biggest strength is his mind. . . . You can never underestimate the 95 to 100 (velocity), the power that comes with his game, the pure dominance. That's what people think of when they think big, power, physical, ace, starter. He goes to areas of the strike zone whenever he needs to, whenever he wants to, whenever he sees something. That's creative. When we talk about creative, we often talk about guys that don't have elite stuff like this. He can execute virtually any game plan for a reason."

Hinch then added, "Very rarely in the big leagues can you go to the same area at-bat after at-bat after at-bat. He pitches deep enough into games to get to face these guys three, sometimes four times. His mind and his ability to trust his adjustments set him apart."

Extremely popular with his teammates, Cole also drew praise from George Springer, who stated toward the end of the 2019 season, "I feel like he's been here forever. The way he gets along with all of us in the clubhouse, the way he came in and bought into us as a team, how our team likes to play the game. He's extremely fun in the clubhouse. . . . I honestly feel like he's been here for five, six years."

Unfortunately, Cole's time in Houston proved to be all too brief. Offered a nine-year, $324 million contract by the Yankees when he became a free agent at the end of 2019, Cole chose to go to New York, having compiled an overall record of 35-10, an ERA of 2.68 and a WHIP of 0.962

as a member of the Astros, while also registering 602 strikeouts in 412⅔ innings of work.

Continuing to excel on the mound for the Yankees the past four seasons, Cole has earned three All-Star nominations, one Cy Young Award, and two other top-five finishes in the voting by posting an overall mark of 86-33 and an ERA of 2.93 during his time in New York. Cole will enter the 2024 campaign with a career record of 145-75, an ERA of 3.17, a WHIP of 1.087, 8 complete games, 5 shutouts, and 2,152 strikeouts in 1,859 innings pitched.

ASTROS CAREER HIGHLIGHTS

Best Season

After winning 15 games, compiling an ERA of 2.88, posting a WHIP of 1.033, and recording 276 strikeouts the previous year, Cole performed even better in 2019, earning a runner-up finish to teammate Justin Verlander in the AL Cy Young voting by going 20-5 with a WHIP of 0.895, and leading the league with a 2.50 ERA and 326 strikeouts, with his 326 Ks in 212⅓ innings pitched making him the first full-time starting pitcher in MLB history to average more than 1½ strikeouts per inning in a season. At different points during the campaign, Cole also became the second pitcher ever to strike out 14 or more batters in three consecutive games and the first hurler to record at least 10 strikeouts in nine straight outings.

Memorable Moments/Greatest Performances

Cole turned in arguably the most dominant performance of his career on May 4, 2018, when he shut out the Arizona Diamondbacks on just one hit, recording 16 strikeouts and allowing only a fourth-inning walk to left fielder David Peralta and a fifth-inning double to second baseman Chris Owings during an 8–0 Astros win.

Cole pitched the Astros to a 3–1 victory over Cleveland in Game 2 of the 2018 ALDS, surrendering just three hits and one run in seven innings of work, while registering 12 strikeouts.

Cole turned in a similarly impressive performance during a 6–3 win over Detroit on August 22, 2019, striking out 12 batters and yielding just two hits and one walk over seven shutout innings.

Cole dominated the Seattle lineup on September 8, 2019, recording 15 strikeouts, issuing no walks, and allowing just one hit (a fourth-inning homer by second baseman Shed Long) over the first eight innings of a 21–1 Astros win.

Cole again proved to be too much for the Mariners to handle on September 24, 2019, yielding just two hits and striking out 14 batters over the first seven innings of a 3–0 Astros win.

Cole continued his brilliant pitching in the 2019 postseason, allowing four hits and recording 15 strikeouts over 7⅔ shutout innings during a 3–1 victory over Tampa Bay in Game 2 of the ALDS. Returning to the mound for Game 5, Cole struck out 10 batters and surrendered just two hits and one run over the first eight innings of a 6–1 win that clinched the series for the Astros.

Notable Achievements

- Won 20 games in 2019.
- Posted winning percentage of .750 or better twice.
- Compiled ERA under 3.00 twice.
- Posted WHIP under 1.000 once (0.895 in 2019).
- Struck out more than 250 batters twice, topping 300 strikeouts once (326 in 2019).
- Threw more than 200 innings twice.
- Led AL in ERA once, strikeouts once, strikeouts per nine innings pitched twice, and shutouts once.
- Finished second in AL in wins once, winning percentage once, WHIP once, strikeouts once, and strikeouts-to-walks ratio once.
- Holds Astros single-season records for most strikeouts (326 in 2019) and most strikeouts per nine innings pitched (13.818 in 2019).
- Two-time division champion (2018 and 2019).
- 2019 AL champion.
- September 29, 2019, AL Player of the Week.
- Three-time AL Pitcher of the Month.
- 2019 *Sporting News* AL Pitcher of the Year.
- 2019 All-MLB First Team.
- Finished second in 2019 AL Cy Young voting.
- Finished 10th in 2019 AL MVP voting.
- Two-time AL All-Star selection (2018 and 2019).

38

ROGER CLEMENS

One of the most decorated pitchers in baseball history, Roger Clemens earned 11 All-Star nominations, one league MVP trophy, and a record seven Cy Young Awards over the course of a 24-year major-league career that included stints with four different teams. Although Clemens garnered most of those accolades before he joined the Astros in 2004, he experienced considerable success during his three years in Houston, winning 18 games once and compiling an ERA under 3.00 three straight times, en route to earning his final two All-Star selections and the last of his seven Cy Youngs. The winner of 354 games during his illustrious career, Clemens received a No. 53 ranking on the *Sporting News'* 1999 list of Baseball's 100 Greatest Players. Nevertheless, allegations of repeated steroid use have prevented Clemens from gaining induction into the Baseball Hall of Fame.

Born in Dayton, Ohio, on August 4, 1962, William Roger Clemens grew up barely knowing his father, whom his mother left when he was only five months old. Although his mother remarried two years later, young Roger became fatherless again at the age of eight when his stepdad died of a heart attack. Seeking a male role model, Roger turned to his older brother, Randy, recalling, "While I was growing up, Randy was the star as far as I was concerned."

Clemens, who spent most of his youth in Vandalia, Ohio, before moving with his family to Houston, Texas, at the age of 15, starred in baseball, football, and basketball at Spring Woods High School, proving to be especially proficient on the diamond, where he patterned himself after his favorite pitcher, Nolan Ryan. After graduating from high school, Clemens spent one year at San Jacinto College in Pasadena, Texas, before transferring to the University of Texas at Austin. Clemens subsequently earned All-America honors twice while pitching for the Longhorns, leading them to victory in the 1983 College World Series.

Selected by the Red Sox in the first round of the 1983 MLB Amateur Draft, with the 19th overall pick, Clemens advanced quickly through

Roger Clemens won the last of his seven Cy Youngs as a member of the Astros.
Courtesy of Christopher Ebdon

Boston's farm system, spending just one year in the minors before making his big-league debut on May 15, 1984. Acquitting himself fairly well over the course of the next two seasons despite being plagued by shoulder problems that forced him to undergo surgery during the latter stages of the 1984 campaign, Clemens compiled an overall record of 16-9 and a composite ERA of 3.88, before emerging as the finest pitcher in the game in 1986, when he earned AL MVP and Cy Young honors by going 24-4, with 238 strikeouts and a league-leading 2.48 ERA and 0.969 WHIP for the pennant-winning Red Sox.

Clemens followed up his virtuoso performance with six more stellar seasons, winning at least 20 games another two times and leading all AL hurlers in virtually every major statistical category on multiple occasions, en route to earning two more Cy Youngs and another three top-10 finishes in the league MVP balloting.

Recognized as the American League's most overpowering pitcher, the right-handed-throwing Clemens, who stood 6'4" and weighed 220 pounds, intimidated opposing batters with his blazing fastball, willingness to throw inside, and fierce competitive spirit. In discussing the ferocious attitude that he took with him to the mound before each start, Clemens explained, "Everybody kind of perceives me as being angry. It's not anger . . . it's motivation."

A prototypical power pitcher, Clemens relied primarily on a 98-mph fastball and a hard breaking ball early in his career. He also possessed outstanding control and flawless mechanics, which he learned from Tom Seaver, who helped turn him into more of a complete pitcher after he joined the Red Sox during the second half of 1986.

Plagued by injuries and inconsistency from 1993 to 1996, Clemens failed to perform at the same elite level, compiling an overall record of just 40-39 during that time. Believing that the 34-year-old right-hander had already seen his best days, the Red Sox allowed Clemens to sign a four-year, $40 million free agent deal with the Toronto Blue Jays following the conclusion of the 1996 campaign that brought his time in Boston to an end.

Eager to prove his former employers wrong, Clemens recaptured the fire of his youth after he arrived in Toronto, subsequently putting together two of the finest seasons of his career. After earning Cy Young honors in 1997 by leading all AL hurlers with a record of 21-7, a 2.05 ERA, 292 strikeouts, and 264 innings pitched, Clemens gained that distinction again the following year by going 20-6, with a 2.65 ERA and 271 strikeouts.

Dealt to the Yankees for three players prior to the start of the 1999 campaign, Clemens proved to be somewhat less dominant over the course of the next five seasons while pitching for teams that won four pennants and two World Series. Yet, even though Clemens never posted an ERA under 3.51 or struck out more than 213 batters during his time in New York, he compiled an overall record of 77-36 and won his sixth Cy Young Award.

Choosing to announce his retirement at the end of 2003, Clemens seemed content to leave the game with a total of 310 victories to his credit. However, after close friend and former Yankees teammate Andy Pettitte signed as a free agent with the Astros, the 41-year-old Clemens decided to come out of retirement and ink a one-year deal with his adopted hometown team.

Proving that he still had a lot left in the tank, Clemens earned All-Star and Cy Young honors his first year in Houston by compiling a record of

18-4 and an ERA of 2.98, while also registering 218 strikeouts in 214⅓ innings of work. Receiving very little run support the following year (the Astros lost five of his starts by a score of 1–0 and were shut out in nine of his 32 starts), Clemens went just 13-8. But he led all NL hurlers with a career-best 1.87 ERA, struck out 185 batters in 211⅓ innings pitched, and posted a WHIP of 1.008 that represented the second-best mark of his career. After retiring for a second time at the end of 2005, Clemens decided to pitch one more season. Although Clemens ended up making just 19 starts for the Astros after signing with them on May 31, he performed well whenever he took the mound, compiling an ERA of 2.30 and a WHIP of 1.041, despite winning just seven of his 13 decisions.

Evolving into a different kind of pitcher during the latter stages of his career, Clemens, whose once-blazing 98-mph fastball had settled in the 91–94 mph range by the time he arrived in Houston, developed a devastating split-fingered fastball and a slider that registered somewhere in the mid-80s on the radar gun. But even though Clemens altered his approach on the mound somewhat, he never lost his competitive edge, which helped lead the Astros to consecutive playoff appearances in 2004 and 2005 and a trip to the World Series in the second of those campaigns.

Yet, even as Clemens's list of career accomplishments continued to grow, his narcissistic nature became increasingly evident to the general public. In addition to coming out of retirement no fewer than three times and demanding that he be paid an inordinately high sum of money for appearing in fewer and fewer games each year, Clemens insisted that various perks be included in his contract, one of which made it unnecessary for him to accompany his team on road trips during which he was not scheduled to pitch.

Clemens again displayed his self-absorbed and avaricious ways on May 6, 2007, when, after retiring for a third time, he unexpectedly appeared in the owner's box at Yankee Stadium during the seventh inning stretch of a game against the Seattle Mariners and announced to the crowd in attendance, "Thank y'all. Well, they came and got me out of Texas, and I can tell you it's a privilege to be back. I'll be talkin' to y'all soon." The Yankees simultaneously announced that they had signed Clemens to a pro-rated one-year deal worth slightly more than $28 million. Clemens ended up making $18.7 million over the length of the contract, or just over $1 million per start. For their investment, the Yankees received from Clemens a 6-6 record and a 4.18 ERA.

No longer able to hold up teams for ransom, Clemens retired for good at the end of the year with a career record of 354-184, an ERA of 3.12, a

WHIP of 1.173, 118 complete games, 46 shutouts, and 4,672 strikeouts in 4,917 innings of work, with his 4,672 strikeouts placing him third all-time, behind only Nolan Ryan and Randy Johnson. Clemens also ranks among MLB's all-time leaders in wins (9th) and starts (7th). As a member of the Astros, Clemens compiled a record of 38-18, an ERA of 2.40, and a WHIP of 1.074, threw one complete game, and struck out 505 batters in 539 innings pitched.

Since retiring as an active player, Clemens has remained in Houston, where he and his wife, Debbie, continue their work to benefit children through the Roger Clemens Foundation they established during his playing days. Clemens also serves as a special assistant to the Astros general manager.

Unfortunately, most of the things Clemens accomplished after he left Boston later came into question when the Mitchell Report alleged that he used anabolic steroids during the second half of his career. Although Clemens has consistently refuted such charges by stating that his extensive workout regimen enabled him to continue to perform at such a high level into his late 30s and early 40s, his former trainer Brian McNamee suggested otherwise, claiming that he injected Clemens with Winstrol on at least three separate occasions between 1998 and 2001. Clemens denied all these allegations under oath before Congress, leading congressional leaders to refer his case to the Justice Department on suspicions of perjury. Although various legal machinations eventually enabled Clemens to be cleared of all charges, he remains guilty in the court of public opinion, causing his career numbers to be tainted in the minds of most people and preventing him from being voted into the Hall of Fame during his 10-year period of eligibility. If Clemens is ever going to gain admission to Cooperstown, he will have to do so through the Contemporary Baseball Era Committee.

ASTROS CAREER HIGHLIGHTS

Best Season

Clemens performed exceptionally well in 2004, when he earned Cy Young honors for the seventh time by going 18-4, with a 2.98 ERA, 218 strikeouts, and a WHIP of 1.157. But even though poor run support limited him to just 13 victories the following year, Clemens proved to be a bit more dominant in 2005, leading all NL hurlers with an ERA of 1.87 and finishing second in the league with a WHIP of 1.008.

Memorable Moments/Greatest Performances

Clemens performed brilliantly in his first start for the Astros, allowing just one hit, issuing three walks, and recording nine strikeouts in seven innings of work during a 10–1 win over the Giants on April 7, 2004.

Clemens surrendered just three hits and one run over the first seven innings of a 6–1 win over the Florida Marlins on May 11, 2004, while also walking one batter and striking out nine.

Clemens turned in perhaps his most dominant performance as a member of the Astros on September 19, 2004, when he earned a 1–0 victory over the Milwaukee Brewers by yielding just two hits and recording 10 strikeouts in eight innings of work.

Although Clemens didn't figure in the decision, he dominated the Milwaukee lineup again in his next start, allowing five hits and registering 12 strikeouts over the first 7⅓ innings of a 1–0 Astros win on September 24, 2004.

Even though the Astros ultimately lost to the Mets in 11 innings by a score of 1–0 on April 13, 2005, Clemens turned in another superb effort, yielding just two hits and striking out nine batters over the first seven innings.

After entering Game 4 of the 2005 NLDS as a pinch-hitter in the 15th inning, Clemens made his first relief appearance since 1984, throwing three scoreless innings of one-hit ball, earning a 7–6 victory over the Braves that clinched the series for the Astros.

Notable Achievements

- Won 18 games in 2004.
- Posted winning percentage over .800 once (.818 in 2004).
- Compiled ERA under 3.00 three times, posting mark below 2.00 once (1.87 in 2005).
- Struck out more than 200 batters once (218 in 2004).
- Threw more than 200 innings twice.
- Led NL in winning percentage once and ERA once.
- Finished second in NL in wins once and WHIP once.
- Ranks among Astros career leaders in ERA (2nd), winning percentage (2nd), and WHIP (3rd).
- 2005 NL champion.
- April 2004 NL Pitcher of the Month.
- 2004 NL Cy Young Award winner.

- Finished third in 2005 NL Cy Young voting.
- Two-time NL All-Star selection (2004 and 2005).
- Number 53 on the *Sporting News'* 1999 list of Baseball's 100 Greatest Players.

39

KEN CAMINITI

A hard-hitting, slick-fielding third baseman who spent parts of 10 seasons in Houston, Ken Caminiti started for the Astros at the hot corner from 1989 to 1994—a period during which he established himself as one of the league's better all-around players at his position. En route to earning one All-Star nomination, Caminiti knocked in at least 75 runs three times, batted over .280 twice, and led all NL third sackers in fielding percentage once. Experiencing even greater success after he left Houston, Caminiti earned one NL MVP award, two All-Star selections, and three Gold Gloves as a member of the San Diego Padres, before rejoining the Astros during the latter stages of his career. But by the time Caminiti returned to Houston, he had immersed himself in a web of deception and a world of artificial stimulants that led to his ultimate demise, making him very much a tragic figure.

Born in the San Joaquin Valley city of Hanford, California, on April 21, 1963, Kenneth Gene Caminiti grew up some 180 miles northwest, in the city of San Jose, where he starred in football and baseball at Lehigh Valley High School. Caminiti, who learned how to play baseball from his father, Lee, a former semipro player, spent one year further honing his skills at San Jose City College, before accepting an athletic scholarship to nearby San Jose State University, where he gained All-America recognition from the *Sporting News* his senior year.

Selected by the Astros in the third round of the 1984 MLB Amateur Draft, Caminiti subsequently began his pro career with the Class A Osceola Astros in the Florida State League, for whom he hit four homers, knocked in 73 runs, stole 14 bases, and batted .284 in his first full season the following year. Impressed with the powerfully built 22-year-old switch-hitting third baseman, Osceola manager Dave Cripe said, "He has one of the better arms I've seen when he's healthy. He has good hands and good reactions defensively. As for his hitting, he's still learning to switch. He doesn't have what you'd call a home run swing, but he has the power to hit the ball to the gaps."

Ken Caminiti served as the regular starting third baseman for the Astros from 1989 to 1994.

Meanwhile, Caminiti, a natural right-handed batter who began switch-hitting in college, expressed the belief that he had the ability to develop into a home-run hitter, stating, "I always took batting practice left-handed, so I just kept practicing. I have just as much power from either side. . . . I think I could be a power hitter."

After another year-and-a-half in the minors, Caminiti joined the Astros midway through the 1987 campaign. Appearing in 63 games and garnering 218 total plate appearances over the next three months, Caminiti hit three homers, knocked in 23 runs, and batted .246, before being returned to the minors for more seasoning at the end of the year. After making a brief appearance with the Astros during the latter stages of the 1988 campaign, Caminiti arrived in the majors to stay the following year, when, after being named the team's starting third baseman, he hit 10 homers, knocked in 72 runs, scored 71 times, batted .255, and compiled an OPS of .685.

Caminiti subsequently suffered through a disappointing 1990 season in which he hit just four homers, knocked in only 51 runs, and batted just .242. But he rebounded the following year to begin a four-year stretch during which he averaged 14 homers and 73 RBIs, while also consistently ranking among the top players at his position in putouts, assists, and double plays turned. Particularly effective in 1992 and 1994, Caminiti homered 13 times, knocked in 62 runs, batted .294, and compiled an OPS of .790 in the first of those campaigns, before hitting 18 homers, driving in 75 runs, batting .283, and posting an OPS of .847 in the second.

Although the 6-foot, 200-pound Caminiti never developed into a true home-run threat during his time in Houston, he displayed an ability to drive the ball with authority to the outfield gaps, collecting at least 30 doubles on four separate occasions. And despite being a natural right-handed hitter, Caminiti proved to be more effective from the left side of the plate, exhibiting more power and hitting for a significantly higher batting average.

Meanwhile, Caminiti demonstrated outstanding athleticism and a very strong throwing arm at third base, where his acrobatic stops helped make him a fan favorite. Caminiti further endeared himself to the hometown fans with his regular attendance at celebrity golf tournaments and offseason banquets. Extremely popular with his teammates as well, Caminiti worked hard to improve himself offensively and defensively, often played hurt, and served as one of the clubhouse leaders.

Nevertheless, with the Astros seeking to cut payroll, they completed a trade with the Padres on December 28, 1994, that sent Caminiti, outfielder Steve Finley, and four other players to San Diego for a package of six players that included outfielder Derek Bell and pitcher Doug Brocail.

Finding San Diego very much to his liking, Caminiti played the best ball of his career over the course of the next four seasons, averaging 30 homers and 99 RBIs, while also batting over .300 twice, despite having to contend with numerous injuries. Performing especially well in 1995 and 1996, Caminiti hit 26 homers, knocked in 94 runs, batted .302, and compiled an OPS of .894 in the first of those campaigns, before earning NL MVP honors the following year by ranking among the league leaders with 40 homers, 130 RBIs, a .326 batting average, and an OPS of 1.028.

Praising Caminiti for his exceptional play and tremendous determination, Padres manager Bruce Bochy described him as "the guts of the team" and added, "He played with maniacal zeal that left those in his wake astounded."

Bringing a new level of toughness and intensity to the Padres, Caminiti battled through several injuries, the most serious of which proved to be a torn rotator cuff he suffered during the early stages of his MVP campaign. However, to do so, Caminiti resorted to taking steroids, which also helped dramatically improve his on-field performance. Still, Caminiti later said, "The thing is, I didn't do it to make me a better player. I did it because my body broke down."

Increasing his steroid intake prior to the start of the 1998 season, Caminiti recalled, "I showed up at spring training as big as an ox." Subsequently plagued by many of the health issues that typically surface in steroid users, Caminiti spent the year being hampered by frequent hamstring and quadriceps strains, various ruptured tendons and ligaments, and torn muscles that continued to limit his playing time for the rest of his career.

Allowed to leave San Diego via free agency at the end of the year, Caminiti signed with the Astros, saying at the time, "I think happiness is being with my family, my kids, and my wife," all of whom had remained in Texas while he played for the Padres.

Although Caminiti performed well upon his return to Houston, posting batting averages of .286 and .303 in 1999 and 2000, he found himself being sidelined for much of each season, enabling him to total just 28 home runs and 101 RBIs. And despite being surrounded by his loved ones, Caminiti fell into old habits and fed new addictions. After undergoing alcohol rehabilitation a few years earlier, Caminiti resumed drinking. He also became addicted to pain medication, expanded his use of steroids, and began using cocaine.

After appearing in only 59 games with the Astros in 2000, Caminiti signed with the Texas Rangers as a free agent. He subsequently split the 2001 campaign between the Rangers and Atlanta Braves, before announcing his retirement at the end of the year with career totals of 239 homers, 983 RBIs, 894 runs scored, 1,710 hits, 348 doubles, 17 triples, and 88 stolen bases, a .272 batting average, a .347 on-base percentage, and a .447 slugging percentage. During his time in Houston, Caminiti hit 103 homers, knocked in 546 runs, scored 496 times, collected 1,037 hits, 204 doubles, and 14 triples, stole 48 bases, batted .264, compiled a .330 on-base percentage, and posted a .402 slugging percentage.

Falling into an even deeper abyss following his playing days, Caminiti drew the ire of many when, during a 2002 interview with *Sports Illustrated* in which he admitted to using steroids during and after his MVP season of 1996, he also stated that he believed that approximately 50 percent of major-league players used some form of performance-enhancing drug.

Having already become persona non grata in baseball circles after making his declaration, Caminiti later divorced his wife and tested positive for cocaine possession on three separate occasions, forcing him to undergo regular drug tests, enter a Texas criminal drug-treatment program, and spend 180 days in jail. Released from prison on October 5, 2004, Caminiti died five days later in a seedy Bronx apartment after he suffered a heart attack from a drug overdose.

Upon learning of the 41-year-old Caminiti's passing, San Diego Padres general manager Kevin Towers said, "I'm still in shock. He was one of my favorite all-time players."

Towers then added, "The best way to describe him is that he was a warrior in every sense of the word. I can't tell you how many times I remember him hobbling into the manager's office, barely able to walk, and saying, 'Put me in the lineup.'"

Former Astros and Padres teammate Steve Finley also expressed his sense of loss, stating, "Man, that's just a tough one. I played with him for eight years. He was a great player, but he got mixed up in the wrong things—taking drugs. It's a sad reminder of how bad drugs are and what they can do to your body. It's a loss all of us will feel."

ASTROS CAREER HIGHLIGHTS

Best Season

Although Caminiti had most of his finest seasons for the San Diego Padres after he left Houston, he played his best ball for the Astros in 1994, when he earned his first All-Star selection by hitting 18 homers, driving in 75 runs, scoring 63 times, batting .283, and posting an OPS of .847.

Memorable Moments/Greatest Performances

Caminiti made his big-league debut a memorable one, going 2-for-3, with a homer, triple, walk, and two runs scored during a 2–1 victory over the Phillies on July 16, 1987.

Caminiti helped lead the Astros to an 8–4 win over the Cardinals on May 30, 1989, by driving in five runs with a homer, double, and single.

Caminiti contributed to a 12–6 victory over the Cubs on July 3, 1994, by hitting a pair of homers and knocking in four runs.

Caminiti again homered twice during a convincing 8–1 win over the Montreal Expos on September 3, 1999, this time driving in six runs.

Although the Astros lost to the Milwaukee Brewers, 6–5, in 16 innings on May 16, 2000, Caminiti had the only five-hit game of his career, going 5-for-7, with a pair of doubles.

Notable Achievements

- Batted over .300 once (.303 in 2000).
- Surpassed 30 doubles four times.
- Compiled on-base percentage over .400 once (.419 in 2000).
- Posted slugging percentage over .500 once (.582 in 2000).
- Posted OPS over 1.000 once (1.001 in 2000).
- Led NL third basemen in fielding percentage once.
- Ranks among Astros career leaders in RBIs (11th), doubles (12th), and intentional bases on balls (tied for 8th).
- 1999 division champion.
- Three-time NL Player of the Week.
- 1994 NL All-Star selection.

40

BRAD AUSMUS

Once called by *Sports Illustrated* "among the finest ever to have played the catcher position," Brad Ausmus used his exceptional defensive ability to carve out a lengthy 18-year career in the majors that saw him excel behind the plate for four different teams. Known for his strong arm, quick release, nimble footwork, deft framing of pitches, and superior handling of pitchers, Ausmus established himself as arguably the finest defensive receiver of his era, leading all players at his position in assists twice, caught stealing percentage once, and putouts and fielding percentage four times each. The Astros regular starting catcher for 10 seasons during his two tours of duty with the club, Ausmus proved to be a huge contributor to teams that captured three division titles and one NL pennant, winning three Gold Gloves during his time in Houston. Although not nearly as proficient as a hitter, Ausmus also contributed to the Astros on offense, delivering several clutch hits, including one that led to a huge victory over the Braves in the 2005 NLDS.

Born in New Haven, Connecticut, on April 14, 1969, Bradley David Ausmus first revealed his goals to his parents at the age of five, when he told his father that, when he grew up, he wanted to go to Dartmouth and play baseball. The son of a Protestant father and a Jewish mother, Ausmus did not feel a particularly strong connection to either religion during his childhood, although he later came to embrace his Jewish heritage, telling the *Jewish Journal* a few years back, "I wasn't raised with the Jewish religion, so, in that sense, I don't really have much feeling toward it. But, in the last 10 years or so, I have had quite a few young Jewish boys who will tell me that I am their favorite player, or they love watching me play, or they feel like baseball is a good fit for them because it worked for me. It has been a sense of pride. If you can have a positive impact on a kid, I'm all for it."

Developing into a star athlete at Cheshire High School in Cheshire, Connecticut, Ausmus excelled in both basketball and baseball, proving to be particularly outstanding in the latter. After moving from shortstop to catcher prior to the start of his junior year, Ausmus compiled batting averages of .436 and .411 the next two seasons, earning a pair of All-State selections and Cheshire Area High School Player of the Year honors as a senior.

Meanwhile, Ausmus's leadership skills left a lasting impression on everyone with whom he came into contact, with Cheshire teammate Nick Carparelli Jr. recalling, "Looking back now, we all realized how confident Brad was, and how intelligent he was. And if any of us forgot, he wasn't bashful about reminding us."

Nick Carparelli Sr., Cheshire High's head baseball coach, also spoke of the confidence Ausmus displayed, saying, "He was always the type of kid in control of things—in control of the game, of a pitcher."

Recruited to play baseball by Dartmouth, Harvard, and Princeton as graduation neared, Ausmus had a difficult decision to make when the Yankees selected him in the 48th round of the 1987 MLB Amateur Draft. But after initially refusing to sign with the Yankees, Ausmus relented when they

Brad Ausmus won three Gold Gloves for his exceptional defensive work behind home plate.
Courtesy of Adam Baker

agreed to allow him to attend classes at Dartmouth and play in the minors during the offseason.

Ausmus subsequently spent five long years in the Yankees farm system, before being selected by the Colorado Rockies in the 1992 expansion draft. Looking back on his lengthy stint in the minors years later, Ausmus said, "I was naïve. In my mind, I was going to make it eventually, and I just kept slogging away. My first year, I think I got paid $700 a month. I didn't know any better. I just assumed the best and that eventually I would make it. I didn't realize how stacked the odds were against me."

After spending the first half of the 1993 campaign in the minor leagues, Ausmus headed to San Diego when the Rockies traded him to the Padres on July 26. Starting behind the plate for the Padres the rest of the year, Ausmus hit five homers, knocked in 12 runs, and batted .256 in 49 games. Remaining San Diego's primary receiver for the next two-and-a-half seasons, Ausmus posted batting averages of .251, .293, and .181, before being dealt to the Detroit Tigers on June 18, 1996. After finishing out the season in Detroit, Ausmus joined the Astros when they acquired him and four other players from the Tigers on December 10, 1996, for a package of four players that included outfielder Brian Hunter and pitchers Doug Brocail and Todd Jones.

Named the Astros starting catcher upon his arrival in Houston, Ausmus retained that role for the next two seasons, compiling batting averages of .266 and .269, while also helping to further develop the pitching skills of Mike Hampton, Darryl Kile, and Shane Reynolds, with each of the last two hurlers having the finest season of their respective careers throwing to Ausmus. Nevertheless, the Astros traded Ausmus back to the Tigers in January 1999, after which he went on to have two of his most productive offensive seasons, earning his lone All-Star selection in 1999 by hitting nine homers, driving in 54 runs, scoring 62 times, and batting .275, before hitting seven homers, knocking in 51 runs, scoring 75 others, and batting .266 the following year.

Dealt back to the Astros on December 11, 2000, as part of a six-player trade that sent him, Doug Brocail, and pitcher Nelson Cruz to Houston for outfielder Roger Cedeño, pitcher Chris Holt, and catcher Mitch Meluskey, Ausmus subsequently began an eight-year stint as their first-string catcher—a period during which he proved to be an invaluable member of teams that made three playoff appearances and earned one trip to the World Series.

Although the right-handed-swinging Ausmus never developed into anything more than a marginal hitter, failing to hit more than six homers, drive in more than 50 runs, or bat any higher than .269 as a member of the Astros, he did a superb job for them behind the plate. The winner of three Gold Gloves, Ausmus, who stood 5'11" and weighed just under 200 pounds, exhibited superior range, tremendous quickness, and an innate ability to guide his pitchers through games by identifying their strengths and weaknesses.

Also praised by scouts for his ability to recognize the weaknesses of opposing hitters, Ausmus became to many another manager on the field, once saying, "I'm thinking, 'What's the score, what inning are we in, how many outs, what's this hitter's weakness, what's this pitcher's strengths, who's on deck, who could pinch-hit, who is up after the hitter on deck?' and you kind of go through all of these things in an instant. And then you make a decision and put down the next signal."

Astros pitchers also became accustomed to Ausmus preparing graphs for them before each series that showed the strengths and weaknesses of every player on the opposing team.

Praising Ausmus for the many contributions he made to the Astros during their successful run to the pennant in 2005, team president Tal Smith stated, "He deserves an awful lot of credit for our success. It was like having another manager on the field. He was very active with the pitching staff. He was so knowledgeable, so savvy. I thought he was instrumental with our success."

Ausmus also delivered arguably the biggest hit of the season in Game 4 of the NLDS, when he hit a game-tying home run against the Braves in the bottom of the ninth inning of a contest the Astros went on to win in extra innings.

After sharing playing time with J. R. Towles and Humberto Quintero in 2008, the 39-year-old Ausmus stated toward the end of the season that he did not expect to return to Houston, saying at the time, "Large chunks of time away from home is not in the best interest of my family."

Released by the Astros at the end of the year, Ausmus initially contemplated retirement, before signing with the Dodgers as a free agent. He spent the next two seasons in Los Angeles assuming a backup role, before officially announcing his retirement at the end of the 2010 season after undergoing surgery earlier in the year to repair a herniated disc in his lower back. Over the course of 18 big-league seasons, Ausmus hit 80 homers, knocked in 607 runs, scored 718 times, collected 1,579 hits, 270 doubles, and 34 triples, stole 102 bases, batted .251, compiled a .325 on-base percentage, and posted a .344 slugging percentage; he ended his career with the third-most putouts (12,839) and the seventh-most games caught (1,938) by a catcher in major-league history. During his time in Houston, Ausmus hit 41 homers, knocked in 386 runs, scored 415 times, amassed 970 hits, 162 doubles, and 19 triples, swiped 51 bags, batted .246, compiled an on-base percentage of .318, and posted a slugging percentage of .327.

Following his playing days, Ausmus spent three years working in the San Diego Padres front office, before becoming manager of the Detroit Tigers in 2014. After leading the Tigers to a record of 314-332 over the course of the next three seasons, Ausmus spent two years in Los Angeles, first serving the Angels as their general manager, before taking over their vacant managerial position in 2019. Dismissed by ownership at the end of the year after leading the team to a record of 72-90, Ausmus remained away from the game until 2022, when he became bench coach of the Oakland Athletics.

ASTROS CAREER HIGHLIGHTS

Best Season

Known primarily for his defensive prowess, Ausmus never posted particularly impressive offensive numbers in any single season. However, he performed reasonably well at the plate in two or three years, one of those being 1998, when he hit six homers, knocked in 45 runs, scored 62 times, batted .269, and compiled an OPS of .713.

Memorable Moments/Greatest Performances

Ausmus had a huge hand in a 9–7, 15-inning win over the Cubs on July 14, 1997, driving in five runs with a homer and single.

Ausmus had another big day against Cubs pitching on August 23, 1998, going 4-for-4, with a homer, five RBIs, and three runs scored during a 13–3 Astros win.

Ausmus contributed to a 16–3 mauling of the Mets on July 30, 2002, by going 4-for-6, with a homer, three RBIs, and three runs scored.

Ausmus hit two home runs in one game for the only time in his career on April 4, 2003, when, after homering with the bases loaded earlier in the contest, he led off the top of the 12th inning with a solo blast that provided the margin of victory in a 6–5 win over the Cardinals.

Ausmus delivered what longtime Houston executive Tal Smith called "one of the greatest hits in Astros history" in the bottom of the ninth inning of Game 4 of the 2005 NLDS, when his two-out solo homer off Braves reliever Kyle Farnsworth tied the score at 6–6, sending the contest into extra innings. Nine innings later, the Astros emerged victorious when Chris Burke hit a game-winning walk-off homer off Joey Devine.

Notable Achievements

- Led NL catchers in putouts twice, fielding percentage three times, and caught stealing percentage once.
- Ranks 10th in franchise history in games played.
- Ranks fourth all-time among MLB catchers with 12,839 putouts.
- Three-time division champion (1997, 1998, and 2001).
- 2005 NL champion.
- Three-time Gold Glove Award winner (2001, 2002, and 2006).

41

DENIS MENKE

Once hailed as "the greatest prospect to come out of the Iowa cornfields since Bob Feller," Denis Menke never quite lived up to his advanced billing. Nevertheless, the versatile infielder proved to be a tremendous asset to three different teams over the course of a lengthy major-league career that spanned 13 seasons. Starting at all four infield positions at one time or another, Menke performed well at each post for the Braves, Astros, and Reds, playing some of his best ball for the Astros from 1968 to 1971. A two-time NL All-Star, Menke knocked in at least 90 runs twice and batted over .300 once during his time in Houston, helping the Astros reach a level of respectability they had not attained before he arrived. Returning to Houston in 1974 after spending the previous two seasons playing for Cincinnati teams that won consecutive division titles and one NL pennant, Menke remained with the Astros until midseason, when he chose to announce his retirement.

Born in Bancroft, Iowa, on July 21, 1940, Denis John Menke grew up on his family's 480-acre farm, some 15 miles from Minnesota's southern border. Developing into a standout athlete during his teenage years, Menke starred in both baseball and basketball at St. John's High School, performing well enough on the court to be named one of the starting forwards on the North Central Iowa Catholic basketball team his sophomore year. Even more proficient on the diamond, Menke excelled as both a shortstop and pitcher, leading St. John's to the 1957 spring baseball championship and the 1958 fall baseball title.

With word of Menke's talents spreading, almost every team in the majors sent scouts to evaluate him as graduation neared, with the Braves, Orioles, and White Sox being his most ardent suitors. Ultimately choosing to sign with the Braves as an amateur free agent for an estimated $125,000 on May 27, 1958, Menke began his pro career shortly thereafter, spending the next five seasons advancing through Milwaukee's farm system.

Succeeding at every level, Menke made a strong impression on Bob Coleman at the Florida Winter Instructional League after the 1958 season, with the Braves instructor saying, "He's a natural . . . worth every cent of the bonus." Menke drew further praise for his fielding ability the following spring, with the local newspapers applauding him for making "a succession of Pie Traynor plays at third base."

Yet, despite Menke's outstanding play in the minors, Milwaukee's talent at the major-league level prevented him from joining the parent club until 1962. Assuming a backup role with the Braves his first year in the league, Menke appeared in a total of 50 games, compiling a batting average of just .192. Nevertheless, departing Braves manager Birdie Tebbetts commented at season's end, "Menke has the talent, and when he puts it all together, he's going to be great."

Denis Menke played all four infield positions for the Astros at one time or another.

Establishing himself as a full-time starter the following year, Menke spent the next five seasons playing all over the infield, although he saw more action at shortstop than anywhere else. Having his two finest seasons for the Braves in 1964 and 1966, Menke hit 20 homers, knocked in 65 runs, scored 79 times, batted .283, and compiled an OPS of .847 in the first of those campaigns, before reaching the seats 15 times, driving in 60 runs, scoring 55 others, batting .251, and posting an OPS of .767 in the second. But suffering from an ailing knee, Menke slumped to just seven homers, 39 RBIs, and a .227 batting average in 1967, prompting the Braves to trade him and left-handed starting pitcher Denny Lemaster to the Astros for shortstop Sonny Jackson and first baseman Chuck Harrison at the end of the year.

Although Menke arrived in Houston with team management expecting him to assume the role of a utility player, he proved himself worthy of a starting job during spring training. Expressing the belief prior to the start of the regular season that he considered himself best suited to play third base, Menke stated, "My knee is better, but I don't have the range I used to have at short. I think I have the quick reflexes and the arm for third."

However, a season-ending injury to Joe Morgan forced Menke to move across the diamond to second base, where he ended up spending the vast majority of his time. Performing exceptionally well in the 115 games he started at that post, Menke committed only 10 errors, giving him a fielding percentage of .982 that ranked as the second highest among all NL second sackers. Contributing on offense as well in what became known as "The Year of the Pitcher," Menke hit six homers, knocked in 56 runs, scored 56 times, batted .249, and compiled an on-base percentage of .334, with his solid all-around play prompting the Houston baseball writers to name him the Most Valuable Astros Player at the end of the year.

With Morgan returning to action in 1969, Menke moved back to his more familiar position of shortstop, where his somewhat limited range made him less effective than he had been at second. Nevertheless, after getting off to a slow start, Menke had an excellent year at the plate. Advised by Astros manager Harry Walker to "Just try to hit the ball to right field. Forget everything else, and just concentrate on that," Menke went on to hit 10 homers, drive in 90 runs, bat .269, and compile an OPS of .756, earning his first All-Star selection. Menke followed that up with another outstanding season, earning All-Star honors again in 1970 by hitting 13 homers and establishing career highs with 92 RBIs, 82 runs scored, 171 hits, a .304 batting average, and a .392 on-base percentage.

Extremely impressed with Menke's development into the NL's best-hitting shortstop, Reds manager Sparky Anderson, who played with him in the minor leagues several years earlier, said, "There is one of the finest men ever to play this game. I'll never forget him, the way he impressed me back in '62, when we were in Toronto. Here's a guy who drew down a bunch at signing, but he wasn't one of those guys who let a big bonus ruin him. He was out there early every day. He wanted to learn. He was always trying to find ways to improve himself. He talked to everybody, and he was learning all the time. Denis used to try to be a home run hitter, but he found out that wasn't his strongest point. And let me tell you, he worked hard at changing his style. I don't think I have to tell you that it has paid off big for him. I think the game needs more Denis Menkes."

A solid line-drive hitter, the right-handed-swinging Menke, who stood 6 feet and weighed 185 pounds, possessed decent power to all fields. Although Menke occasionally exhibited home-run power, he did a better job of driving the ball to the outfield gaps, collecting at least five triples and 25 doubles in three of his four full seasons with the Astros. A good hitter with men on base, Menke inspired confidence in his ability to deliver in the clutch from Houston manager Harry Walker, who typically placed him either fifth or sixth in the batting order.

But, as Menke grew older, he became increasingly aware of his limited mobility in the field, stating during the latter stages of the 1970 campaign, "Lots of balls, two or three years ago, that I would have cut off out there, I haven't done this year . . . but I think I'll still be in the infield somewhere."

With the Astros acquiring slick-fielding shortstop Roger Metzger from the Chicago Cubs the following offseason, Menke moved to first base, although he also saw some action at third and short. Transitioning seamlessly to his new position, Menke drew praise from Astros announcer Gene Elston, who commented, "Seeing Menke play first points up what Bill Mazeroski said: 'It is the feet that makes the difference.' Well, Menke has great hands, and he moves around first base like a ballet dancer. He's so smooth, he makes everything look easy."

Somewhat less successful at the plate, Menke hit just one homer, knocked in only 43 runs, and batted just .246, prompting the Astros to include him in a massive eight-player trade they completed with the Reds at the end of the year that, among others, sent him and Joe Morgan to Cincinnati for Lee May and Tommy Helms. Inserted at third base upon his arrival in Cincinnati, Menke spent two seasons starting at that post for the Reds, performing well with the glove but continuing to struggle at the bat. With Menke reduced to a part-time role in 1973, he requested a return to Houston at the end of the year to be close to his family and business ventures. Traded back to the Astros for pitcher Pat Darcy and cash on February 18, 1974, Menke batted just .103 in 30 games, before announcing his retirement on July 10, saying at the time, "I've slowed down a little. If I felt like I was helping the ballclub, I might have stayed on. I don't want to back up to the pay window. . . . I'm not made that way. . . . I want to leave with a good taste in my mouth."

Menke, who ended his playing career with 101 home runs, 606 RBIs, 605 runs scored, 1,270 hits, 225 doubles, 40 triples, 34 stolen bases, a .250 batting average, a .343 on-base percentage, and a .370 slugging percentage, hit 30 homers, knocked in 282 runs, scored 269 times, collected 575 hits, 101 doubles, and 20 triples, batted .266, compiled a .355 on-base percentage, and posted a .373 slugging percentage as a member of the Astros.

After briefly doing color commentary on Astros' radio and television broadcasts following his retirement as an active player, Menke began a lengthy coaching career that saw him serve on the staffs of the Toronto Blue Jays, Astros, Phillies, and Reds. Choosing to leave the game altogether after serving as bench coach in Cincinnati from 1997 to 2000, Menke retired to Florida, where he spent the next 20 years fishing and golfing. Menke lived until December 1, 2020, when he died at his home in Tarpon Springs at the age of 80.

Looking back on his life some years earlier, Menke told MLB.com, "I wouldn't have changed anything. Grew up on a farm; entered baseball when I was 17 years old, and 40 years later I decided it was finally time to get out. I really did get out on my own terms. After the 2000 season in Cincinnati, I knew it was time to get out. It was a little harder for me to be around some of the high-priced players and the so-called superstars. And I decided it was time to get out. The scout who signed me said if you ever get tired to the point that you're not enjoying the game, it's time to get out. And that's what I did."

ASTROS CAREER HIGHLIGHTS

Best Season

Menke had a solid year for the Astros in 1969, earning All-Star honors for the first of two straight times by hitting 10 homers, scoring 72 runs, batting .269, compiling an OPS of .756, and leading all NL shortstops with 90 RBIs. But he posted better overall numbers the following season, concluding the 1970 campaign with 13 homers, 92 RBIs, an OPS of .833, and a career-high 82 runs scored, 171 hits, .304 batting average, and .392 on-base percentage.

Memorable Moments/Greatest Performances

Menke helped lead the Astros to a 9–6 win over the Pirates on May 30, 1969, by going 4-for-5 at the plate, with a double and three RBIs.

Menke and teammate Jim Wynn accomplished the rare feat of both homering with the bases loaded in the same inning during a 16–3 rout of the Mets on July 30, 1969, with their dual grand slams highlighting an 11-run rally in the top of the ninth.

Menke contributed to an 8–3 victory over the Dodgers on May 12, 1970, by going 4-for-5, with a homer and four RBIs.

En route to collecting a career-high five RBIs, Menke delivered the big blow of a 9–5 win over the Dodgers on July 9, 1970, when he homered with the bases loaded in the first inning.

Menke homered twice in one game for the only time as a member of the Astros during a 9–5 win over the Mets on August 30, 1970.

Notable Achievements

- Batted over .300 once (.304 in 1970).
- Finished second in NL with nine sacrifice flies in 1970.
- Two-time NL All-Star selection (1969 and 1970).

42

RUSTY STAUB

The only player to accumulate at least 500 hits for four different teams, Rusty Staub amassed a total of 2,716 safeties over the course of a 23-year major-league career that began in Houston in 1963. A member of the Colt .45s/Astros for parts of six seasons, Staub collected almost 800 hits during his time in Texas, earning two NL All-Star selections. Continuing his solid hitting after leaving Houston, Staub earned All-Star honors another four times by hitting more than 20 home runs and batting over .300 four times each, while dividing the remainder of his career primarily among the Montreal Expos, New York Mets, and Detroit Tigers.

Born in New Orleans, Louisiana, on April 1, 1944, Daniel Joseph Staub acquired the nickname Rusty before he even left the hospital, with his mother, Alma, recalling, "I wanted to name him Daniel so I could call him Danny for short. But one of the nurses nicknamed him Rusty for the red fuzz he had all over his head, and it stuck."

Although Rusty and his older brother, Chuck, acquired their love of baseball from their father, Ray, a schoolteacher and former minor-league catcher, Chuck remembered in the book, *Rusty Staub of the Expos*, "He [Ray] didn't push us into sports. It was just there, and we loved it. But I'm sure if Rusty or myself wanted to play the violin, Dad would have bust a gut swinging a deal for the best violin money could buy."

After combining with his brother to help lead Jesuit High School to the 1960 American Legion national championship and the 1961 Louisiana State AAA championship, Rusty received several college scholarship offers for both baseball and basketball, before ultimately deciding to sign with the newly minted Houston Colt .45s of the National League for $100,000 in September 1961. Beginning his pro career in the Arizona Fall League, the 17-year-old Staub batted .299, earning him a promotion to the Durham Bulls of the Class B Carolina League, for whom he hit 23 homers, knocked in 93 runs, and batted .293 in 1962.

Rusty Staub earned his first two All-Star selections as a member of the Astros.

Given a chance to earn a spot on the big-league roster at the beginning of the ensuing campaign, Staub made an extremely favorable impression on team management during spring training, with GM Paul Richards stating, "Staub, right now, is the best hitter on our ballclub. I realize that may not sound so good at the end of the first 30 days if we decide he'd be better off playing in San Antonio. But I repeat, right now he's the best hitter we have."

Though barely 19 years old by the time the regular season got under-way, Staub found himself starting in right field and batting cleanup on Opening Day. Proving that he had been rushed somewhat by the organiza-tion, Staub ended up hitting just six homers, driving in only 45 runs, and batting just .224 in 150 games, while splitting his time between first base and right field. Nevertheless, Staub retained a positive outlook heading into

1964, saying during spring training, "Everybody asks if being overpublicized hurt me. Not that much. It was a great year for me. . . . I made a lot of lousy, stupid plays, but the mistakes stick with you. When you make a mistake up here, you remember it and don't do it again if you can help it."

However, after struggling terribly at the plate the first half of the season, Staub spent the next two-and-a-half months at Triple-A Oklahoma City in the Pacific Coast League, rediscovering his swing, before returning to Houston in mid-September. Appearing in a total of 89 games with the big club in 1964, Staub hit eight homers, knocked in 35 runs, and batted .216.

Far more confident in his abilities by the start of the 1965 season, the now 21-year-old Staub laid claim to the starting right field job, after which he went on to hit 14 homers, drive in 63 runs, and bat .256 for the newly named Astros. Improving upon those numbers the following year, Staub hit 13 homers, led the team with 81 RBIs, and batted .280, before emerging as a star in 1967, when, after altering his approach at the plate somewhat, he homered 10 times, knocked in 74 runs, finished fifth in the league with a .333 batting average, and topped the circuit with 44 doubles.

In discussing how he changed his mindset in the batter's box, Staub stated at season's end, "I stopped trying to go for the long ball. I thought I was a home run hitter when I signed, but now I don't go for the pump (long ball), especially since we play 81 games in the Astrodome."

Certainly, the dimensions and cold air at Houston's home ballpark negatively impacted Staub's home run production. But the lefty-swinging outfielder/first baseman, who stood 6'2" and weighed 190 pounds his first few years in the league before ballooning up to well over 200 pounds by the latter stages of his career, was more of a line-drive hitter at heart than a true home-run threat. Extremely consistent at the plate, Staub generally made solid contact with the ball, striking out more than 61 times just once his entire career. Blessed with a keen batting eye and outstanding patience as well, Staub typically walked far more often than he struck out, drawing more than 100 bases on balls on two separate occasions.

Expressing his admiration for Staub as a hitter, Joe Torre, who played both with and against him at different times, stated, "He was a good hitter. He was a very studious hitter. When he was young and had a lean body, he was scary."

Meanwhile, although Staub lacked foot speed, he proved to be a capable outfielder, catching virtually everything within his reach and using his strong throwing arm to collect at least 10 outfield assists for the Astros three straight times.

After holding out for more money prior to the start of the 1968 season, Staub moved back to first base, where he ended up starting 146 of the 161 games in which he appeared. But even though Staub again posted solid numbers, concluding the campaign with six homers, 72 RBIs, 37 doubles, and a .291 batting average, he experienced differences with new Astros manager, Harry "The Hat" Walker, the team's former batting coach, who objected to the fact that he frequently experimented with batting stances and grips on his own.

With the two men often clashing and MLB expanding to four new cities in 1969, the time seemed perfect for a change in scenery for Staub, who headed to Montreal when the Astros traded him to the expansion Expos for veteran first baseman Donn Clendenon and 26-year-old outfielder Jesús Alou on January 22, 1969. Commenting on the deal years later, Jonah Keri wrote in his history of the Expos, "Seizing on an opportunity to bail on a player he didn't like, Walker huddled with [Astros GM Spec] Richardson on trade possibilities that could whisk Staub out of town, preferably for proven talent. The Expos, by their own design, would prove to be the perfect fit. . . . They'd collected multiple flappable veterans to dangle in trade for just such an opportunity."

Although the Expos later had to send pitcher Jack Billingham and $100,000 to the Astros to complete the trade when Clendenon refused to report to Houston since he considered the Mississippi-born Walker to be a racist, Staub ultimately arrived in Montreal, where he became the organization's first true star and an incredibly popular figure. Staub, who left Houston with career totals of 57 homers, 370 RBIs, 297 runs scored, 792 hits, 156 doubles, and 12 triples, a .273 batting average, a .346 on-base percentage, and a .393 slugging percentage, developed an immediate connection with the fans of Montreal, who appreciated his willingness to learn the French language and his many contributions to their team on the playing field. Nicknamed *Le Grand Orange* for the color of his hair, Staub had arguably the three most productive seasons of his career at Parc Jarry, whose inviting dimensions allowed him to become more of a home-run hitter and run producer. An All-Star in each of his three seasons with the Expos, Staub averaged 26 homers, 90 RBIs, and 94 runs scored for them from 1969 to 1971, while also compiling batting averages of .302, .274, and .311, and posting a career-high OPS of .952 in the first of those campaigns.

Nevertheless, the Expos traded Staub to the New York Mets for three promising young players just prior to the start of the 1972 regular season, sadly bringing to an end his love affair with the city of Montreal. Staub subsequently spent the next four seasons with the Mets, driving in 105 runs for them in 1975, after helping them capture the NL pennant two years earlier. Dealt to the Tigers for Mickey Lolich at the end of 1975, Staub spent three-and-a-half extremely productive years in Detroit, surpassing 20 homers and 100 RBIs twice each while serving the Tigers almost exclusively as a designated hitter. Traded back to the Expos during the latter stages of the 1979 campaign, Staub finished out the season in Montreal, before spending one year with the Texas Rangers. A free agent at the end of 1980, Staub signed with the Mets, for whom he assumed the role of a part-time player and pinch-hitter the next five seasons, before announcing his retirement following the conclusion of the 1985 campaign with career totals of 292 home runs, 1,466 RBIs, 1,189 runs scored, 2,716 hits, 499 doubles, 47 triples, and 47 stolen bases, a .279 batting average, a .362 on-base percentage, and a .431 slugging percentage.

In summarizing Staub's playing career some years later, former player and longtime announcer Tim McCarver said, "Rusty was just a good all-around player for four different teams. He was a very good offensive player when he was older and a very good defensive player when he was younger."

Lee Mazzilli also spoke of his former Mets teammate, saying, "He was a situational-type hitter that knew what to look for, when to look for it, how to look for it in situations. When I played with Rusty, and then when I played against him, I always felt that he was going to hit the ball hard somewhere—like hard contact and be a tough out. . . . And if you needed a home run to beat you, he could do that too."

After retiring from baseball, Staub, a lifelong bachelor and gourmet cook who opened the first of his two self-named restaurants in 1977, remained in the New York area for many years, continuing to operate his eateries well into the 1990s, while also providing radio and television color commentary for Mets home games from 1986 to 1995. Staub also spent decades giving back to the community, raising millions of dollars to fight hunger and founding the New York Police and Fire Widows' and Children's Benefit Fund, which raised money and provided additional support to families of first responders killed in the line of duty.

After surviving a heart attack that he suffered almost three years earlier, Staub passed away in a West Palm Beach, Florida, hospital on March 29, 2018, just three days before his 74th birthday, succumbing to organ failure following a month-long battle with pneumonia.

COLT .45S/ASTROS CAREER HIGHLIGHTS

Best Season

Although Staub hit three more homers and knocked in a few more runs the previous year, he posted his best overall numbers as a member of the Astros in 1967, when he earned his first All-Star nomination by hitting 10 homers, driving in 74 runs, scoring 71 times, leading the NL with 44 doubles, and ranking among the league leaders with 182 hits, a .333 batting average, a .398 on-base percentage, and an OPS of .871.

Memorable Moments/Greatest Performances

Staub proved to be the difference in a 2–1 win over the Dodgers on June 3, 1963, hitting his first big-league homer off Don Drysdale with one man aboard in the bottom of the fourth inning.

Staub led the Colt .45s to a 5–2 win in the first game of their doubleheader sweep of the Braves on June 21, 1964, by going 4-for-4, with two home runs and three RBIs, with one of his homers coming off Hall of Famer Warren Spahn.

Staub gave the Astros their first-ever win in the Astrodome on April 23, 1965, when he drove home Al Spangler from second base with an RBI single with two men out in the bottom of the 12th inning of a 4–3 victory over the Pirates.

Staub contributed to an 11–5 win over the Cubs on May 9, 1965, by going 3-for-5, with a homer, double, five RBIs, and two runs scored.

Staub provided most of the offensive firepower when the Astros defeated the Cardinals, 6–5, on July 10, 1966, homering twice and knocking in four runs, with his two-run blast off starter Al Jackson in the top of the eighth inning highlighting a three-run rally that provided the winning margin.

Staub helped lead the Astros to a lopsided 10–2 victory over the Giants on May 6, 1968, by going 4-for-4, with a career-high six RBIs.

Notable Achievements

- Batted over .300 once (.333 in 1967).
- Surpassed 30 doubles twice.
- Led NL with 44 doubles in 1967.
- Finished fourth in NL in on-base percentage twice and doubles once.
- Two-time NL All-Star selection (1967 and 1968).

43

MIKE HAMPTON

cquired from the Seattle Mariners after the 1993 season in one of the
best trades the Astros ever made, Mike Hampton spent the next six
years in Houston serving as a key member of three division-winning
ballclubs. Having most of his finest seasons for the Astros, Hampton posted
double-digit win totals four straight times, with his 22 victories in 1999
setting a single-season franchise record that still stands. Dealt to the Mets
at the end of 1999, Hampton ended up winning at least 14 games another
three times, before rejoining the Astros for one more season during the
latter stages of his career.

Born in Brooksville, Florida, on September 9, 1972, Michael William
Hampton grew up some 25 miles northwest, in the city of Homosassa,
where he starred in multiple sports while attending Crystal River High
School. Recruited to play college football as a defensive back at Notre
Dame, Florida State, and the University of Miami, Hampton instead chose
to sign with the Seattle Mariners after they selected him in the sixth round
of the 1990 MLB Amateur Draft.

Hampton subsequently spent the next three years advancing through
Seattle's farm system, before being promoted to the parent club during
the early stages of the 1993 campaign after he compiled a record of 13-8
and an ERA of 3.12 with High-A San Bernadino in the California League
the previous season. Overmatched at the big-league level, the 20-year-old
Hampton won just one of his four decisions and posted an ERA of 9.53 in
13 games and 17 total innings of work.

Dealt to the Astros at the end of the year for veteran outfielder Eric
Anthony, Hampton acquitted himself much better in his first season in
Houston, when, working exclusively out of the bullpen, he went 2-1, with
a 3.70 ERA and 24 strikeouts in 41⅓ innings pitched. Inserted into the
starting rotation the following year, Hampton compiled a record of 9-8 and
an ERA of 3.35 for an Astros team that finished second in the NL Central
Division, nine games off the pace, with a record of 76-68. Posting similar

numbers in 1996, Hampton went 10-10 with a 3.59 ERA, before helping the Astros capture the first of their three consecutive division titles the following year by going 15-10, with a 3.83 ERA, seven complete games, two shutouts, and 139 strikeouts in 223 innings of work.

Despite completing just one of his 32 starts in 1997, Hampton had another solid season, compiling a record of 11-7 and an ERA of 3.36, while also striking out 137 batters in 211⅔ innings pitched. Hampton reached the apex of his career the following year, when he earned his first All-Star selection, *Sporting News* NL Pitcher of the Year honors, and a runner-up finish to Randy Johnson in the NL Cy Young voting by compiling a record of 22-4 and an ERA of 2.90, tossing a pair of shutouts, and registering 177 strikeouts in 239 innings of work.

More of a finesse pitcher than a power pitcher, the left-handed-throwing Hampton, who stood just 5'10" and weighed 185 pounds, depended primarily on changing speeds and the location and movement of his pitches to retire opposing batters. In addition to a sinking fastball that he used as his

Mike Hampton's 22 victories in 1999 remain the highest single-season total in franchise history

"out" pitch, Hampton threw a curveball and changeup that made his favorite offering look that much faster. Quick as a cat on the mound, Hampton also fielded his position extremely well, consistently ranking among the league's top pitchers in assists. An exceptional all-around athlete, Hampton also proved to be one of the game's best-hitting pitchers, homering 16 times, driving in 79 runs, and compiling a batting average of .246 in 845 total plate appearances over the course of his career, en route to winning five Silver Sluggers.

An excellent teammate as well, Hampton possessed an "old school" mentality, once saying, "When I go out there, I'm doing whatever it takes to help my team win. If that means taking one off the face, or jumping in front of a ball, or hitting, or getting hit with a pitch, I'll do it. That goes back to the way I was raised to win at all costs."

Yet, despite Hampton's many contributions to the team, his impending free agency and a desire to part ways with churlish outfielder Derek Bell prompted the Astros to complete a trade with the Mets on December 3, 1999, that sent Hampton and Bell to New York for outfielder Roger Cedeño, reliever Octavio Dotel, and minor-league pitcher Kyle Kessel.

Expressing his surprise upon learning of the deal, Hampton said, "It's a little bit overwhelming, a little bit shocking. It seems like it all happened rather quickly."

Meanwhile, Mets GM Steve Phillips told reporters, "We've waited for this opportunity for a long time, to secure a starter of Mike Hampton's ilk. We had to step up and do this."

Performing well for the Mets in 2000, Hampton helped them earn a spot in the playoffs and a trip to the World Series by going 15-10 with a 3.14 ERA during the regular season, before winning another two games in the NLCS. In his first start against his former team, Hampton made an extremely favorable impression on longtime teammate Jeff Bagwell, who said afterwards, "That's one thing that was interesting about facing Hampy. I always knew he was a real good pitcher, obviously, but until I faced him as an opposing player, I don't think I ever fully appreciated how good he is. When you see it from my angle, from 60 feet, 6 inches, you say, 'You know what, that fool's got an idea out there.'"

A free agent at the end of the year, Hampton signed a blockbuster eight-year, $121 million contract with the Colorado Rockies that made him the highest paid player in the game. But, unable to overcome the horrible pitching conditions at Coors Field, Hampton struggled terribly over the course of the next two seasons, going a combined 21-28 with a composite ERA of 6.44. Traded to the Braves prior to the start of the 2003 season,

Hampton ended up spending six injury-marred years in Atlanta, missing two seasons entirely after undergoing elbow surgery, before returning to Houston when he became a free agent again at the end of 2008. Forced to undergo surgery on both knees and his left shoulder after he compiled a record of 7-10 and an ERA of 5.30 for the Astros in 2009, Hampton threw a total of 4⅓ innings for the Arizona Diamondbacks the following year, before announcing his retirement prior to the start of the ensuing campaign.

Over parts of 16 big-league seasons, Hampton compiled a record of 148-115, an ERA of 4.06, and a WHIP of 1.442, threw 21 complete games and nine shutouts, and struck out 1,387 batters in 2,268⅓ total innings of work. As a member of the Astros, Hampton went 76-50, with a 3.59 ERA, a WHIP of 1.370, 13 complete games, six shutouts, and 767 strikeouts in 1,138 innings pitched.

After retiring as an active player, Hampton spent one year coaching in the minor leagues and another two seasons serving as the bullpen coach for the Seattle Mariners, before handing in his resignation on July 9, 2017.

ASTROS CAREER HIGHLIGHTS

Best Season

Was there ever any doubt? Hampton had easily the finest season of his career in 1999, when he earned a runner-up finish in the Cy Young voting, a spot on the NL All-Star team, and *Sporting News* NL Pitcher of the Year honors by compiling a record of 22-4, an ERA of 2.90, and a WHIP of 1.285, registering 177 strikeouts, and throwing 239 innings, with his 22 victories and .846 winning percentage both placing him first in the league rankings.

Memorable Moments/Greatest Performances

Hampton tossed a three-hit shutout on May 1, 1996, also issuing two walks and striking out five batters during a 3–0 win over the Braves.

Hampton threw another three-hit shutout on August 2, 1997, walking three batters and striking out seven during a 6–0 win over the Mets.

Hampton earned a 3–2 victory over the Braves on August 25, 1998, by allowing six hits and two runs in eight innings of work, while also recording a career-high 12 strikeouts.

Hampton shut out the Pirates on just five hits on May 10, 1999, issuing no walks and striking out seven batters during a 6–0 Astros win.

Hampton tossed a four-hit shutout on July 18, 1999, issuing two walks and recording eight strikeouts during a 2–0 win over Cleveland.

Notable Achievements

- Led NL with 22 wins and .846 winning percentage in 1999.
- Compiled ERA under 3.00 once (2.90 in 1999).
- Threw more than 200 innings three times.
- Ranks 10th in franchise history with .603 career winning percentage.
- Holds single-season franchise records for most wins (22) and highest winning percentage (.846).
- Three-time division champion (1997, 1998, and 1999).
- 1999 Silver Slugger Award winner.
- Finished second in 1999 NL Cy Young voting.
- 1999 *Sporting News* NL Pitcher of the Year.
- 1999 *Sporting News* NL All-Star selection.
- 1999 NL All-Star selection.

44

KEN FORSCH

A key member of the Astros' pitching staff for more than a decade, Ken Forsch spent parts of 11 seasons in Houston, making significant contributions to the team as both a starter and a reliever. Doing whatever was asked of him, Forsch assumed a regular spot in the starting rotation for five years and worked primarily out of the bullpen in five others, in helping the Astros reach a level of respectability they had not attained prior to his arrival. Known for his consistency, poise, and versatility, Forsch compiled an ERA under 3.00 five times, threw more than 200 innings twice and 10 complete games once, and finished in double digits in saves twice, once placing second in the NL in the last category. A two-time All-Star, Forsch earned that honor once with the Astros and again with the California Angels, with whom he spent his final few years in the big leagues.

Born in Sacramento, California, on September 8, 1946, Kenneth Roth Forsch grew up with his younger brother, Bob, on the family's chicken farm. The son of Herbert Forsch, who, in addition to running his farm, owned Forsch Electric Motors and played semipro ball on several teams in the Sacramento area, Ken seemed destined for a career in baseball at birth, recalling, "I had a baseball uniform and bat and mitt in my crib when I was brought home from the hospital."

Despite his love for the game, Herbert Forsch never forced either of his sons into baseball (Bob also became a major-league pitcher). Nevertheless, he and his wife, Freda, gave the boys everything they needed to succeed, including building a baseball diamond on the acreage behind their house. Ken's dad also played pepper with him and his brother for half an hour when he returned home from work each evening, with his mother often assuming the role of catcher.

Diminutive throughout his formative years, Ken, who never played any position other than pitcher, often found it difficult to reach home plate from the mound while competing in Little League Baseball. Still small when he entered Hiram Johnson High School, Forsch failed to make the

Ken Forsch excelled for the Astros as both a starter and a reliever.

varsity squad until he experienced a six-inch growth spurt prior to his senior year. With his newfound height also making him far more proficient on the basketball court, Forsch ended up being named both Most Valuable Player in baseball and the school's Most Valuable Athlete in his final year at Hiram Johnson High.

Asked years later if any pro teams scouted him in high school, Forsch recalled, "I was not very strong then. . . . I was still growing; had sore arm problems. . . . I think the Pittsburgh Pirates were going to draft me, but my father told (Pirates scout) Ronnie King, 'I don't think you should sign him because he's been battling a sore arm.' So, the Pirates backed off."

Ultimately enrolling at Sacramento City College, the sore-armed Forsch spent his freshman year playing only for the school's basketball team, remembering, "My arm hurt so bad, I couldn't throw for over a year.

I couldn't even go out for the SCC baseball team." But, after receiving therapy for his injury, Forsch made a full recovery, allowing him to resume his baseball career in his sophomore year.

Drafted by the California Angels in the ninth round of the 1966 MLB Amateur Draft, Forsch chose instead to return to SCC. However, he changed his plans when he received an offer to attend Oregon State University on a baseball scholarship. Excelling on the mound for the Beavers the next two seasons, Forsch proved to be particularly dominant his senior year, when he earned Second-Team All–Pac 8 honors by setting a single-season school record for strikeouts (121). Impressed with Forsch's exceptional pitching, the Astros selected him in the 18th round of the 1968 MLB Amateur Draft, after which they immediately signed him to a contract.

Forsch subsequently spent the next two-and-a-half years working his way up the organizational ladder, performing well at five different stops despite suffering minor injuries in an automobile accident in 1969 and being sidelined for a month later that year with a bulging muscle in his back. Promoted to the parent club during the latter stages of the 1970 campaign after posting 17 victories at the Triple-A level, Forsch failed to make much of an impression, going 1-2 with a 5.63 ERA in his four starts.

Despite the difficulties he experienced in his first stint in the majors, Forsch found himself competing for a regular spot in the Astros' starting rotation the following spring. Continuing to show his support of the 24-year-old rookie right-hander after he struggled somewhat in a few exhibition outings, Astros manager Harry Walker said, "More important than his size is his desire. . . . What attracted our attention was the way he always battled back the next time out. He didn't get discouraged and quit. He kept punching. He showed us a lot of courage under pressure. And he improved steadily. . . . Poise—that describes him best, I suppose. Nothing ruffles him."

Echoing those sentiments, Astros pitching coach Jim Owens stated, "The first time I saw him, he was further along than most pitchers four or five years older. He must have been born with poise."

Meanwhile, in discussing his ability to bounce back from a poor performance, Forsch said, "What really happens, I think is that I just get mad at myself and want to prove something. I can't wait for another chance after I've flubbed up."

Although Forsch also spent some time working out of the bullpen in 1971, he ended up starting 23 games for the Astros, compiling a record of 8-8, finishing fourth in the league with an ERA of 2.53, posting a WHIP of 1.142, throwing seven complete games and two shutouts, and striking out 131 batters over 188⅓ innings. Primarily a starter the following year as well, Forsch went 6-8, with a 3.91 ERA and 113 strikeouts in 156⅓ innings of work.

Essentially a two-pitch pitcher early in his career, Forsch depended almost entirely on his fastball and slider, saying in 1972, "I try to get ahead of the hitter right away. When you get behind, the hitter knows you've got to come in to him and is looking for heat somewhere in the strike zone. If you get ahead, you can work on him a little, try for the corners, or try to make him chase a slider."

Forsch remained a starter for the first half of the 1973 campaign, before moving to the bullpen later in the year. Somewhat less effective than he had been in each of the previous two seasons, Forsch finished the year with a record of 9-12, an ERA of 4.20, five complete games, four saves, and 149 strikeouts in 201⅓ innings pitched.

When asked about his new role, Forsch admitted, "I've always wanted to be a starter. Doesn't every pitcher? I still think I can be."

Adding that he employed basically the same philosophy as a reliever, Forsch said, "I just go in and throw as hard as I can. . . . There's not much new out there. Trouble is still trouble, no matter how you look at it. I've pitched out of enough jams in my life as a starter, so I know what it's like when I'm out there in relief. I just go to my power pitches—my fastball and my slider. I give them my best."

Working almost exclusively out of the bullpen the next five years, Forsch established himself as one of the NL's better relievers, compiling an ERA under 3.00 four times and twice saving more than 10 games. Particularly outstanding in 1976, Forsch earned All-Star honors by going 4-3, with a 2.15 ERA and 19 saves.

Aided by Astros pitching coach Roger Craig, the 6'4", 210-pound Forsch altered his mindset somewhat as he continued to adapt to his relief role, saying, "Roger has made me think more aggressively, and he's brought a change in my attitude. He's built my confidence up. I go at the hitters more and pitch quicker to them. This keeps the defense on their toes, and I think it's a reason I've had so many good plays made behind me."

Craig also helped Forsch add to his repertoire of pitches, saying of his protégé in 1975, "As a reliever, he was using his fastball all the time. Now he's developed his overhand curve and changeup."

Meanwhile, Forsch, who later developed a forkball as well, explained, "In the past, I gripped the ball across the seams and my fastball would rise. Roger suggested I try gripping it with the seams. Now the ball is sinking instead of rising, and they're hitting it on the ground instead of in the air, and I'm getting 'em out."

Despite the success he experienced as a reliever, Forsch returned to the Astros' starting rotation in 1979, going 11-6, with a 3.04 ERA, 10 complete games, and a league-leading 1.069 WHIP. Forsch followed that with another solid season, compiling a record of 12-13 and an ERA of 3.20, tossing three shutouts, and throwing six complete games and 222⅓ innings in 1980. But when new Astros GM Al Rosen signed free agent pitcher Don Sutton and traded for left-hander Bob Knepper the following offseason, Forsch appeared to be headed for a return to the bullpen. Unhappy over the prospect, Forsch requested a trade to a contending team, saying at the time, "If that's the way they reward loyalty, then I don't want to pitch for this club."

Subsequently dealt to the California Angels for shortstop Dickie Thon on April 1, 1981, Forsch left Houston with a career record of 78-81, an ERA of 3.18, a WHIP of 1.250, 36 complete games, nine shutouts, 50 saves, and 815 strikeouts in 1,493⅔ innings pitched.

Forsch ended up spending three full seasons with the Angels, earning AL All-Star honors in 1981 by going 11-7, with a 2.88 ERA, 10 complete games, and a league-leading four shutouts, before suffering a career-ending injury to his right shoulder early in 1984 when he dove to first base after fielding a slowly hit groundball. Following two unsuccessful comeback attempts, Forsch announced his retirement in August 1986, ending his career with a record of 114-113, a 3.37 ERA, a 1.249 WHIP, 70 complete games, 18 shutouts, 51 saves, and 1,047 strikeouts in 2,127⅓ total innings of work.

Choosing to remain in California following his playing days, Forsch spent several years working in commercial real estate for two different companies, before going out on his own once he obtained his broker's license. Eventually returning to baseball, Forsch became the Angels director of player development in 1994. Promoted to assistant general manager in 1998, Forsch spent 13 years in that post, before retiring to private life following his dismissal in 2011. Now 77 years old, Forsch spends much of his time golfing and fly fishing.

ASTROS CAREER HIGHLIGHTS

Best Season

Forsch performed well as a starter in 1979, going 11-6 with a 3.04 ERA, tossing 10 complete games, and leading all NL hurlers with a WHIP of

1.069. But Forsch made a greater overall impact in 1976, when, working exclusively out of the bullpen, he went 4-3 with a 2.15 ERA, posted a WHIP of 1.109, and finished second in the league with 19 saves, earning his only All-Star nomination as a member of the Astros.

Memorable Moments/Greatest Performances

Forsch tossed a complete-game three-hitter against the Reds on May 29, 1971, also issuing two walks and recording seven strikeouts during a 2–1 Astros win.

Forsch shut out the Dodgers on just four hits on August 4, 1971, issuing three walks and registering nine strikeouts during a 2–0 Astros win.

Forsch displayed his mettle on September 24, 1971, surrendering just six hits and one run to the San Diego Padres over the first 13 innings of a game the Astros went on to win, 2–1, in 21 innings.

Forsch threw a two-hit shutout against the Dodgers on September 8, 1978, allowing just one walk, a third-inning single by catcher Joe Ferguson, and a sixth-inning single by second baseman Davey Lopes during a 5–0 Astros win.

Forsch no-hit the Braves on April 7, 1979, yielding just two walks and striking out three batters during a 6–0 Astros win.

Forsch tossed a three-hit shutout on April 29, 1980, also issuing three walks during a 3–0 win over the Reds.

Notable Achievements

- Compiled ERA below 3.00 five times, posting mark under 2.50 once (2.15 in 1976).
- Threw more than 200 innings twice.
- Threw no-hitter vs. Atlanta on April 7, 1979.
- Led NL pitchers with WHIP of 1.069 in 1979.
- Finished second in NL with 19 saves in 1976.
- Ranks among Astros career leaders in wins (11th), ERA (10th), saves (11th), shutouts (tied for 9th), complete games (10th), innings pitched (10th), and pitching appearances (3rd).
- 1980 division champion.
- April 8, 1979, NL Player of the Week.
- April 1979 NL Pitcher of the Month.
- 1976 NL All-Star selection.

45

DICKIE THON

The victim of a terrible beaning that left him with permanent partial blindness, Dickie Thon never attained the level of greatness others predicted for him when he first entered the major leagues in 1979. Nevertheless, after joining the Astros prior to the start of the 1981 campaign, Thon gave us a brief glimpse into what might have been in his two full seasons as the team's starting shortstop. Establishing himself as arguably the NL's finest all-around player at his position, Thon hit 20 homers once, stole more than 30 bases twice, and led all league shortstops in assists once, earning one All-Star selection and one top-10 finish in the NL MVP voting. Struck in the head with a pitch early in 1984, Thon never again performed at an elite level. But, through faith and hard work, he persevered through 15 big-league seasons, seven of which he spent in Houston.

Born in South Bend, Indiana, on June 20, 1958, Richard William Thon moved with his family to Puerto Rico at an early age when his father, Frederick Thon Jr., decided to return to his homeland after he obtained his undergraduate degree in business from Notre Dame. Growing up in the Rio Piedras section of San Juan, where his grandfather, a former pitcher in the Puerto Rican Winter League, had settled after migrating from Germany, Thon naturally gravitated toward baseball, recalling, "From the time I was little, I saw how important baseball was to the people of Puerto Rico. My grandfather told me stories about his days with San Juan in the 1940s and early 1950s. He talked about Monte Irvin, Joshua Gibson, and others who came down here."

Developing into an outstanding all-around athlete during his formative years, Thon excelled in several sports, with his father remembering, "At first, Dickie didn't think about a career in baseball because he was so good at other sports. He was an excellent sprinter, volleyball player, and basketball guard. He was the type of kid who walked around and dressed like an adult, and, when he was young, his technical knowledge of baseball was as good as that of any college player."

After graduating from high school, Thon helped lead Puerto Rico's Puerto Nuevo team to a third-place finish in the 1975 American Legion world championships, setting off a recruiting frenzy among big-league scouts. Ultimately signing with the California Angels as an amateur free agent for $20,000, Thon recalled, "I was ready to play for anything, but when the Brewers and Pirates offered me bonuses of only $5,000, my father made me hold out for more."

Thon subsequently spent most of the next four seasons advancing through California's farm system, with his outstanding play at each level prompting then-Angels' director of minor-league operations, Tom Sommers, to call him "the best natural-looking infielder I've ever seen."

Meanwhile, Dick Miller of the *Sporting News* wrote in 1977, "The best prospect in the Angels' farm system is a 19-year-old shortstop named Dickie Thon."

A serious beaning prevented Dickie Thon from realizing his enormous potential.

After making a brief appearance with the parent club the previous season, Thon arrived in the majors to stay in 1980. Appearing in 80 games with the Angels, Thon batted .255, knocked in 15 runs, and scored 32 times in 285 total plate appearances. But with California's roster littered with veteran middle infielders such as Bobby Grich, Bert Campaneris, Rick Burleson, and Freddie Patek, the Angels completed a trade with the Astros on April 1, 1981, that sent Thon to Houston for pitcher Ken Forsch.

Assuming the role of a utility infielder his first year in Houston, Thon appeared in 49 games, batting .274 in 95 official at-bats, while seeing action at second, short, and third. Displacing veteran Craig Reynolds as the team's starting shortstop the following year, Thon performed well in his first season as a full-time starter, hitting three homers, driving in 36 runs, scoring 73 times, stealing 37 bases, batting .276, and leading the league with 10 triples, while also ranking among the top players at his position in fielding percentage and double plays turned. Emerging as the league's best shortstop in 1983, Thon earned All-Star honors and a seventh-place finish in the NL MVP voting by hitting 20 homers, driving in 79 runs, scoring 81 times, stealing 34 bases, batting .286, compiling an OPS of .798, ranking among the league leaders with nine triples and 283 total bases, and leading all players at his position with 533 assists.

Commenting on Thon's exceptional season, then-Astros GM Al Rosen said, "When I see Dickie Thon, I see a future Hall of Famer."

Equally impressed, Astros second baseman Bill Doran stated, "I'd be afraid to think how great Dickie can become."

Meanwhile, Cincinnati Reds pitcher Rich Gale described Thon as "the best all-around shortstop in the National League."

The right-handed-hitting Thon, who stood 5'11" and weighed 170 pounds, had surprising power for a man his size, with his 16 homers away from the Astrodome in 1983 serving as a true indication of his ability to reach the seats. Primarily a pull hitter, Thon employed a short, quick swing that enabled him to make consistently hard contact with the ball. Thon also possessed good speed, outstanding range, and soft hands in the field, with Ozzie Smith saying of his fellow shortstop, "I first saw Dickie Thon in A ball in 1977. I could tell he'd be a fine addition to any club. The first thing I look for in a shortstop is soft hands. The next thing is quick feet. Then you go to the arm. He had all those qualities."

Praising Thon for the way he delivered the ball to him at second base, Bill Doran stated, "I always know I'm going to get a good throw from him on the double play, and it'll be accurate and have something on it—a rare combination."

Thon began the 1984 campaign in fine fashion, batting .375 in the season's first four contests. But his career, and his life, changed forever on April 8, when, in his second at-bat against pitcher Mike Torrez in a home game against the New York Mets, the big right-hander struck him with a pitch just above the left eye.

Recalling the unfortunate incident, Torrez said, "He [Thon] has a tendency to crowd the plate and lunge for balls, so I thought I'd jam him. It was a strategy decision, nothing more. But my ball was sailing that day."

Torrez shouted out a warning after he released the ball, but Thon failed to hear him, remembering, "When I saw where the ball was, it was too late to get out of the way."

After the ball glanced off Thon's ear flap and struck him above the left eye, he lay prone on the field for several minutes as team physician William Bryan checked on his condition, with Bryan later saying, "I heard a bone break. I heard the ball hitting the bone, like a dull thud."

Meanwhile, Thon recalled, "I kept thinking, 'I want to live. I want to see my family again.' I didn't know how bad it was. I was scared. I said, 'Is this really happening?'"

Subsequently diagnosed with a fracture of the orbital rim (the bone above the left eye), Thon underwent surgery three days later, after which he spent the rest of the year on the disabled list as he continued to deal with headaches, blurred vision, and nausea. Yet even though Thon found himself unable to either read or drive for several months, he remained convinced that he would return to the playing field at some point, saying, "The doctors say I can adjust to seeing a blurry ball in time. If it's a matter of work, I'll do it. I'm not down, and I'm not giving up."

After rejoining the Astros in the spring of 1985, Thon stated, "My timing is bad. I'm rushing everything. I don't do anything smoothly. Hopefully it's getting better. I'm seeing the ball better and better. Sometimes it's hard to overcome the fear of being hurt. I'm trying to concentrate on seeing the ball and getting out of the way. I know I can do it. It's something I am working on. I have a lot of faith in God. If He wants me to play again, I will."

Meanwhile, Al Rosen told reporters, "If he does come back to his old form, we're a contender. People talk about whether he's as good as [Cal] Ripken or [Robin] Yount, but I think he's a better player than either one of them."

Thon ended up appearing in 84 games, somehow managing to hit six homers, drive in 29 runs, and compile a batting average of .251, even though the ball appeared somewhat blurry to him as it approached home plate. But when Thon continued to experience problems with his vision the next two seasons, he grew increasingly frustrated, causing him to leave the team on multiple occasions. After batting just .212 in 32 games with the Astros in 1987, Thon left the team on July 3, saying at the time, "I feel sad because I wish I could have done more for the team. I feel a lot for this team. I feel I'll always be one of them."

Following an unsatisfactory meeting with new Astros GM Dick Wagner, Thon was placed on the disqualified list, prompting him to say, "The way Wagner has been dealing with my situation, I won't be around here anymore. It's difficult to walk away from a game I'd do anything to play."

Eventually released by the Astros, Thon left Houston having hit 33 homers, driven in 172 runs, scored 226 times, collected 492 hits, 85 doubles, and 22 triples, stolen 94 bases, batted .270, compiled an on-base percentage of .329, and posted a slugging percentage of .395 as a member of the team.

Signed by the Padres as a free agent the following offseason, Thon assumed a part-time role in San Diego in 1988, batting .264 in 95 games, before being dealt to the Phillies at the end of the year. Experiencing something of a rebirth in Philadelphia after changing his batting stance to allow his right eye to compensate for his left, Thon batted .271, hit 15 homers, and knocked in 60 runs as the Phillies' starting shortstop in 1989. Retaining that role for the next two seasons, Thon posted decent numbers, before spending his final two seasons serving the Texas Rangers and Milwaukee Brewers as a part-time player. Announcing his retirement in March 1994 after complaining of not seeing the ball well in the field, Thon ended his playing career with 71 homers, 435 RBIs, 496 runs scored, 1,176 hits, 193 doubles, 42 triples, 167 stolen bases, a .264 batting average, a .317 on-base percentage, and a .374 slugging percentage.

Recalling his former teammate years later, Enos Cabell said, "Dickie was probably going to be a Hall of Fame player. He knew how to play. Dickie became a really good ballplayer even after the head injury."

Meanwhile, Bill Doran said wistfully, "He could hit, he had the quickness, he had the range, he had the arm strength, he could steal bases. Dickie was about to set a different standard for shortstops, and he was just getting started."

Following his playing days, Thon briefly served as the Astros' minor-league baserunning and infield instructor, before returning to Puerto Rico, where he remains involved with the winter league and youth baseball.

Admitting during a 2015 interview with Greg Hanlon of vicesports. com that he spent the last nine years of his career playing with vision in one eye described as "looking through a sheet of wax paper," Thon revealed that he became good at guessing the answers during eye tests, saying, "I was afraid they wouldn't give me a chance to play."

Stating that he still had a difficult time reading and driving, Thon added, "I didn't enjoy the game the same way. It was more work for me. Before, it was fun. After that, it was, 'I gotta do this to work for my family, to work for my future.'"

Thon also stated that he harbored no ill feelings toward Mike Torrez, who called him in the hospital to apologize after the incident, saying, "I don't really think he threw at me to hurt me. I don't blame him. He was trying to throw inside, and the ball slipped, and I should have gotten out of the way. I have no hard feelings. It was part of the game."

A devout Catholic, Thon said that his life has had "many blessings," and that he sees his injury as a stroke of bad luck in a life otherwise defined by good luck, adding, "One thing I've learned is that you should always believe in yourself and accomplish everything you want in life, with hard work and determination. Don't listen to negative stuff. Always concentrate on believing that you can accomplish anything if you are willing to work hard."

ASTROS CAREER HIGHLIGHTS

Best Season

Thon played his best ball for the Astros in 1983, when he earned his lone All-Star nomination, Silver Slugger, and top-10 finish in the NL MVP voting by establishing career-high marks in nine different offensive categories, including homers (20), RBIs (79), runs scored (81), hits (177), batting average (.286), and slugging percentage (.457), while also leading all NL shortstops in assists.

Memorable Moments/Greatest Performances

Thon contributed to a 7–3 win over the Reds on August 15, 1982, by going 4-for-5 at the plate, with three doubles, three runs scored, and a stolen base.

Thon helped lead the Astros to a 7–6 win over the Montreal Expos on April 15, 1983, by going 3-for-5, with a homer and four RBIs.

Thon homered twice in one game for the first time in his career during a 4–1 win over the San Diego Padres on June 17, 1983.

Thon gave the Astros a 4–3 victory over the Padres on August 10, 1983, when he homered with two men out and no one on base in the bottom of the 14th inning.

Thon helped the Astros even the 1986 NLCS at two games apiece when he hit a solo home run off left-hander Sid Fernandez in the top of the fifth inning of a 3–1 win over the Mets.

Notable Achievements

- Hit 20 home runs in 1983.
- Stole more than 30 bases twice.
- Surpassed 30 doubles once (31 in 1982).
- Led NL with 10 triples in 1982.
- Led NL shortstops in assists once.
- 1986 division champion.
- Finished seventh in 1983 NL MVP voting.
- 1983 Silver Slugger Award winner.
- 1983 NL All-Star selection.

46

SHANE REYNOLDS

A mainstay of the Astros pitching staff for much of the 1990s, Shane Reynolds spent parts of 11 seasons in Houston, contributing significantly to teams that won four division titles. A control pitcher who relied primarily on his split-fingered fastball and sharp-breaking curve to navigate his way through opposing lineups, Reynolds won at least 16 games and threw more than 200 innings three times each, en route to establishing himself as one of the franchise's all-time leaders in both categories. Houston's Opening Day starter for five straight seasons, Reynolds earned one All-Star nomination, before being further honored following the conclusion of his playing career by being inducted into the Astros Hall of Fame.

Born in Bastrop, Louisiana, on March 26, 1968, Richard Shane Reynolds learned the value of hard work from his father at an early age, recalling, "My parents, especially my dad, instilled a work ethic in me. He worked hard in his job his whole life. He was my Little League coach from eight years old until 18. He was very instrumental in my preparation and how I worked."

Developing into a star in multiple sports at Ouachita Christian High School in Monroe, Louisiana, Reynolds excelled in baseball and basketball, with his high school coach often stating that his skills on the court surpassed his abilities on the diamond. Nevertheless, Reynolds earned three All-State selections as a pitcher and outfielder, performing especially well in his senior year, when he set a then single-season school record by hitting 11 home runs in just 22 games. Following his graduation from OCHS, Reynolds spent two years at Faulkner University, a private Christian school located in Montgomery, Alabama, before transferring to the University of Texas at Austin, where he earned consecutive Southwest Conference First-Team nominations.

Selected by the Astros in the third round of the 1989 MLB Amateur Draft, Reynolds subsequently spent three years advancing through Houston's farm system, during which time roving minor-league pitching coach Brent Strom helped turn him into the pitcher he eventually became.

Crediting Strom for much of the success he experienced in the majors, the right-handed-throwing Reynolds, who stood 6'3" and weighed 210 pounds, said, "He completely changed me. My mechanics were like a power pitcher, but I only threw about 90. You're not really a power pitcher throwing 90 miles per hour. I had a so-so curveball and not a really good changeup."

Revealing that Strom helped him develop a more upright delivery, add movement to his fastball, gain better control of his curve, and add a split-fingered fastball to his repertoire of pitches, Reynolds stated, "I think that made my career and helped me get to the big leagues and stay there. Brent Strom—yeah, I owe pretty much everything to him."

Recalling his star pupil, Strom said, "He always had that little chip on his shoulder and worked extremely hard. . . . He was my favorite pitcher I ever worked with. I've never had a pitcher who took the information that I gave—take the information and work as hard."

Promoted to the majors midway through the 1992 campaign, Reynolds ended up appearing in a total of 13 games with the parent club over the

Shane Reynolds helped the Astros win four division titles.

course of the next two seasons, compiling an overall record of 1-3, while splitting his time between the Astros and their Triple-A affiliate. Arriving in Houston to stay in 1994, the 26-year-old Reynolds became part of an up-and-coming team that featured young stars Jeff Bagwell and Craig Biggio. Seeing extensive action as both a starter and a reliever in his first full season, Reynolds went 8-5, with an ERA of 3.05 and 110 strikeouts in 124 innings pitched.

Looking back on the strike-shortened 1994 campaign years later, Reynolds said, "The nucleus of those guys was just kind of getting there. What I remember most about 1994 is when Terry Collins was the manager, and he gave me the ability to start the season and make the team out of the 'pen, which was great. It wasn't until '97 when we won our division, but it took three or four years with the young nucleus we had. Mike Hampton was coming into the mix, and a lot of young kids were getting their feet wet with Biggio and Bagwell."

Joining the starting rotation full-time the following year, Reynolds went 10-11, with a 3.47 ERA, two shutouts, and 175 strikeouts in 189⅓ innings of work, before establishing himself as the ace of Houston's pitching staff in 1996, when he finished 16-10, compiled an ERA of 3.65 ERA, and ranked among the league leaders with 204 strikeouts, 239 innings pitched, and a WHIP of 1.134. Plagued by injuries in 1997, Reynolds finished just 9-10, with a 4.23 ERA and 152 strikeouts in 181 innings of work. But he returned to top form in 1998, posting a record of 19-8 and an ERA of 3.51, striking out 209 batters, and throwing 233⅓ innings. Reynolds had another solid year in 1999, going 16-14, with a 3.85 ERA, 197 strikeouts, and 231⅔ innings pitched, while also leading all NL pitchers in starts (35) for the second straight season.

A true workhorse from 1995 to 1999, Reynolds consistently ranked among the league leaders in starts, innings pitched, and complete games. Crediting the right-hander's durability to his grueling workout regimen, Astros strength and conditioning coach Gene Coleman said, "There have been very few people who put in the work like Shane. There's Nolan Ryan, Roger Clemens, and Shane that worked that hard. . . . He was almost obsessive-compulsive about working out. If we did 10 rotations with a (medicine) ball to the right and only nine to the left, he'd let me know about it. We'd have to do it again."

After missing only a handful of starts the previous five seasons, Reynolds took the mound just 22 times in 2000 due to an assortment of injuries that sidelined him for the final two months of the campaign. Yet even though Reynolds finished the year with a record of 7-8 and an ERA of 5.22, he received his only All-Star nomination.

Rebounding somewhat in 2001, Reynolds went 14-11 with a 4.34 ERA. But lacking the same velocity and bite on his split-fingered fastball, he struck out just 102 batters in 182⅔ innings of work. Plagued by a pinched nerve in his back the following year, Reynolds made just 13 starts, going 3-6 with a 4.86 ERA, before having to undergo season-ending surgery.

Subsequently released by the Astros in the spring of 2003, Reynolds later expressed the shock he felt at the time, saying, "I was taking my time and making sure I was healthy and going to be 100 percent, and the next thing you know, they released me. That was tough. I definitely wanted to stay and had been there my whole career. . . . I had been there for so long and didn't want to go anywhere, but they made their decision."

In explaining the release of Reynolds, Astros GM Gerry Hunsicker stated, "This was a very difficult decision. But from what we saw this spring, with the options that we had, the goal is to take the best team to Houston with the best chance to win. I just felt that we had better options."

Reynolds, who left Houston with a career record of 103-86, an ERA of 3.95, a WHIP of 1.292, 20 complete games, seven shutouts, and 1,309 strikeouts in 1,622⅓ innings pitched, ended up spending the 2003 campaign with the Atlanta Braves, going 11-9 with a 5.43 ERA, before announcing his retirement after he made just one start for the Arizona Diamondbacks in 2004. Following his playing days, Reynolds returned to the Monroe/Bastrop region of Louisiana, where be became an assistant coach for his alma mater, Ouachita Christian High School.

Looking back on how the arduous exercise program he employed during his playing career may have affected his longevity, Reynolds says, "I may have shortened my career because I worked myself so hard to be prepared, but I don't have any regrets. Working so hard, my pitching days were the easiest days. But the wear and tear—five knee surgeries, shoulder surgery, back surgery—yeah, that stuff will slow you down big-time."

ASTROS CAREER HIGHLIGHTS

Best Season

Although Reynolds had an excellent year for the Astros in 1996, he performed slightly better two years later, concluding the 1998 campaign with a record of 19-8, an ERA of 3.51, a WHIP of 1.329, a career-high 209 strikeouts, and 233⅓ innings pitched, with his 19 victories placing him second in the league rankings.

Memorable Moments/Greatest Performances

Reynolds shut out the Pirates on just four hits on July 23, 1994, issuing no walks and recording 11 strikeouts during an 11–0 win.

In addition to limiting the Reds to six hits and three runs over the first seven innings of a 9–4 Astros win on April 11, 1996, Reynolds went 2-for-4 at the plate and hit the first of his five career home runs.

Reynolds dominated the Padres lineup on April 27, 1996, allowing just four hits, issuing three walks, and striking out four batters during a 6–0 complete-game win.

Reynolds proved to be equally dominant on August 3, 1996, yielding just three hits, walking two batters, and recording eight strikeouts during a 4–1 complete-game victory over the Giants.

Although Reynolds lost to the Pirates, 2–0, on August 15, 1999, he went the distance, allowing five hits and a pair of solo homers, while recording a career-high 14 strikeouts.

Notable Achievements

- Won at least 16 games three times.
- Posted winning percentage over .700 once.
- Struck out more than 200 batters twice.
- Threw more than 200 innings three times.
- Led NL pitchers in strikeouts-to-walks ratio once, fewest walks allowed per nine innings pitched once, double plays turned once, and starts twice.
- Finished second in NL in wins once, shutouts once, and strikeouts-to-walks ratio twice.
- Ranks among Astros career leaders in wins (8th), strikeouts (6th), innings pitched (8th), starts (7th), and strikeouts-to-walks ratio (2nd).
- Four-time division champion (1997, 1998, 1999, and 2001).
- 2000 NL All-Star selection.
- Inducted into Astros Hall of Fame in 2019.

47

HUNTER PENCE

An old-school player whose exceptional work ethic and all-out style of play made him a favorite of the hometown fans, Hunter Pence spent parts of five seasons in Houston, proving to be one of the few bright spots on mostly losing teams. A solid offensive performer, Pence hit more than 20 homers three times, knocked in more than 90 runs once, and batted over .300 twice, while also posting an OPS over .800 on three separate occasions. An excellent defender as well, Pence led all NL right fielders in assists three times and putouts once, with his strong all-around play earning him team MVP honors once and a pair of trips to the All-Star Game. Continuing to perform well after he left Houston during the latter stages of the 2011 campaign, Pence served as a key contributor to San Francisco Giants teams that won two World Series.

Born in Fort Worth, Texas, on April 13, 1983, Hunter Andrew Pence grew up some 15 miles east, in the city of Arlington, where he starred in baseball while attending Arlington High School. An outfielder at Arlington High, Pence assumed the role of designated hitter at Texarkana College, before returning to his preferred position after he transferred to the University of Texas at Arlington (UTA) following his freshman year. Excelling on the diamond at UTA, Pence earned First-Team All–Southland Conference honors as a sophomore by batting .347, before being named Conference Player of the Year the following season after he led the league with a .395 batting average.

Selected by the Astros in the second round of the 2004 MLB Amateur Draft, the 64th overall pick, Pence began his professional career with the Class A Tri-City ValleyCats in Troy, New York, where he helped lead the 'Cats to a 50-win season in the New York–Penn League. Advancing rapidly through Houston's farm system the next two seasons, Pence earned a spot on the *Baseball America* Minor League All-Star Team in 2006 by hitting 28 homers, driving in 95 runs, and batting .283 for Double-A Corpus Christi, prompting the Astros to promote him to the majors the following year.

Despite missing more than a month of action in 2007 with a small fracture in his right wrist, Pence performed exceptionally well in his first big-league season, earning a third-place finish in the NL Rookie of the Year voting by hitting 17 homers, knocking in 69 runs, scoring 57 times, ranking among the league leaders with nine triples, batting .322, and compiling an OPS of .899. Pence followed that with another productive year, hitting 25 homers, driving in 83 runs, scoring 78 times, batting .269, and posting an OPS of .783, while also leading all NL right fielders with 340 putouts and 16 assists. Pence subsequently earned All-Star honors for the first time in 2009 by hitting 25 homers, knocking in 72 runs, scoring 76 times, batting .282, compiling an OPS of .818, and once again leading all players at his position with 16 assists, before posting equally impressive numbers the following year, when he reached the seats 25 times, knocked in 91 runs, scored 93 others, batted .282, and compiled an OPS of .786.

Displaying good power at the plate and speed on the basepaths, the right-handed-hitting Pence, who stood 6'4" and weighed close to 220

Hunter Pence hit more than 20 home runs three times for the Astros.

pounds, drove the ball to the outfield gaps with authority and ran the bases well, allowing him to surpass five triples and 30 doubles twice each during his time in Houston. Though not particularly selective at the plate (he never drew more than 58 bases on balls in a season), Pence proved to be an extremely productive hitter, topping 20 homers seven times and driving in more than 90 runs four times over the course of his career.

All arms and legs, Pence appeared awkward when he ran the bases or patrolled the outfield. Nevertheless, he got the job done, stealing as many as 22 bases one season, while also throwing out 16 runners on three separate occasions. And even though Pence suffered from Scheuermann's disease, a spinal disorder that develops in adolescence, he played the game with reckless abandon, with his aggressive and unconventional style of play endearing him to the fans of Houston.

In discussing the qualities that made Pence a favorite of the hometown fans, former Astros teammate Wesley Wright said, "I first met Hunter in 2008 when I made the team, and he was always the type of guy that was easy to get along with and made everyone feel welcome. He was one of the hardest-working people that I had seen in baseball at that time. He was all about winning, and whatever it took to win, that's what he would do. . . . The Astros fans embraced him because of the way he played the game. He would play hard, and his style was kind of unorthodox, but he would get the job done. I think the fans loved the way he went about his business."

An incredibly hard worker, Pence took it upon himself to spend extra time in the batting cage and the weight room, recalling, "They would only let you have a little bit of time in the cage and a little bit of time in the weight room. I remember I would go get my own weight room member-ships because I was like, 'That's not enough!' I just wanted it so bad."

A student of the game, Pence also asked questions of those more experi-enced than himself, remembering, "I had a notebook. I wanted to interview them. I wanted to go to breakfast. I wanted to learn all their secrets. What was cool is that I would even talk to people from other teams and stuff. And what I would find is that, a lot of times, I would try and do something someone else's way, and I would actually get worse."

Eventually coming to embrace himself and his unique style, Pence added, "You have to know yourself. You have to find out what works for you. By being the scientist and going out and trying to learn from everyone, I just took a little bit from each one and saw which ones worked for me."

Pence remained in Houston until the end of July 2011, when, after he hit 11 homers, knocked in 62 runs, batted .308, and compiled an OPS of .828 during the first four months of the season, a pending change in ownership and a desire to lower the team's payroll prompted the Astros to trade him to the Phillies for four minor-league prospects.

Upon completing the deal, Phillies general manager Ruben Amaro Jr. stated, "He's a guy that I think our fans will take to very well."

Meanwhile, Phillies manager Charlie Manuel said of his new right fielder, "He's a .300 hitter. He's got some power. He's a good player. I like him. Yes, I like him quite a bit."

During his time in Houston, Pence hit 103 homers, knocked in 377 runs, scored 353 times, collected 768 hits, 145 doubles, and 24 triples, stole 61 bases, batted .290, compiled a .339 on-base percentage, and posted a .479 slugging percentage. He ended up spending almost one year in Philadelphia, before the Phillies sent him to the Giants for three players just prior to the July 31, 2012, trade deadline. After signing a lengthy contract extension with the Giants at the end of the year, Pence spent the next six seasons in San Francisco, playing his best ball during that time in 2013 and 2014. After hitting 27 homers, driving in 99 runs, batting .283, and scoring 91 runs in the first of those campaigns, Pence earned his third All-Star nomination the following year by hitting 20 homers, knocking in 74 runs, scoring 106 times, and batting .277 for the eventual world champions. Pence subsequently split the next two seasons between the Giants and Texas Rangers, before announcing his retirement following the conclusion of the 2020 campaign with career totals of 244 homers, 942 RBIs, 891 runs scored, 1,791 hits, 324 doubles, 55 triples, and 120 stolen bases, a batting average of .279, an on-base percentage of .334, and a slugging percentage of .461.

After retiring as an active player, Pence spent one season doing color commentary for Giants telecasts on NBC Sports Bay Area, before joining MLB Network as an analyst in 2022. Pence, who currently lives with his wife in San Francisco, also remains active in several charitable causes and continues to make appearances at the Hunter Pence Baseball Academy that he founded during his time in Houston.

ASTROS CAREER HIGHLIGHTS

Best Season

Pence posted his best overall numbers as a member of the Astros in 2010, when he hit 25 homers, knocked in 91 runs, scored 93 times, collected 173 hits, stole 18 bases, batted .282, and compiled an OPS of .786.

Memorable Moments/Greatest Performances

Pence helped lead the Astros to a 12–9 win over the Texas Rangers on June 24, 2007, by going 4-for-6 at the plate, with a homer, double, and four runs scored.

Pence gave the Astros a dramatic 5–4 victory over the Phillies on July 3, 2007, when he led off the bottom of the 13th inning with a homer off relief ace Jose Mesa.

Pence hit two home runs in one game for the first time in his career on August 31, 2007, homering once with two men on base and once with one man aboard during a 6–1 win over the Cubs.

Pence gave the Astros an 8–6 win over the Milwaukee Brewers on May 4, 2008, when he hit a two-run homer in the bottom of the 12th inning.

Pence drove in all the runs the Astros scored during a 4–2 win over the Cubs on May 20, 2008, when he homered off Chicago starter Ryan Dempster with the bases loaded in the bottom of the fourth inning.

Pence had his only five-hit game as a member of the Astros on May 27, 2008, going 5-for-5, with a double and two RBIs during an 8–2 win over the Cardinals.

Pence led the Astros to a 6–4 win over the Colorado Rockies on June 3, 2009, by going 4-for-5, with a homer, triple, three RBIs, and two runs scored.

Pence contributed to a 14–6 victory over the Florida Marlins on August 12, 2009, by hitting a pair of three-run homers.

Pence's three-run homer and solo blast off Johan Santana on August 17, 2010, gave the Astros all the runs they needed to defeat the Mets by a score of 4–3.

Pence hit safely in 23 consecutive games from May 19 to June 13, 2011, going a combined 39-for-96 (.406), with four homers, one triple, seven doubles, 19 RBIs, and 19 runs scored.

Notable Achievements

- Hit more than 20 home runs three times.
- Batted over .300 twice.
- Surpassed 30 doubles twice.
- Posted slugging percentage over .500 once (.539 in 2007).
- Led NL outfielders in assists twice.
- Led NL right fielders in assists three times and putouts once.

- Ranks among Astros career leaders in batting average (10th) and slugging percentage (tied for 11th).
- May 2007 NL Rookie of the Month.
- Two-time NL Player of the Week.
- 2010 Astros team MVP.
- Two-time NL All-Star selection (2009 and 2011).

48

BOB ASPROMONTE

An original member of the Houston Colt .45s, Bob Aspromonte holds a special place in franchise history. The first expansion-draft selection to take the field for the team, Aspromonte later became the first player in team annals to step to the plate, hit safely, score a run, and homer at the newly opened Astrodome. A solid player who spent all seven of his seasons in Houston starting at third base for the Colt .45s/Astros, Aspromonte batted over .280 twice and performed exceptionally well at the hot corner, leading all NL third sackers in fielding percentage twice. A onetime team MVP, Aspromonte later received the additional honor of being inducted into the Astros Hall of Fame.

Born in Brooklyn, New York, on June 19, 1938, Robert Thomas Aspromonte grew up with his two older brothers in the borough's Benson-hurst section, which became known for its large constituency of Italian and Jewish residents. Raised in a baseball-oriented family, Aspromonte and his brothers received a tremendous amount of support from their father when it came to their athletic pursuits, with Bob remembering his dad telling him, "I work. I want you guys to play baseball because you have the talent."

After getting his start in organized sports in the Brooklyn Grasshopper Little League, Aspromonte went on to earn All-Star honors in the Coney Island and Kiwanis Leagues as a teenager, while also excelling in both baseball and basketball at Lafayette High School. Invited to try out with five different teams following his graduation, Aspromonte made an extremely favorable impression on Dodger scout Al Campanis, who assessed him as follows in his report to general manager Buzzie Bavasi: "What first attracted my attention was his batting form. He does things naturally up there. He's smart and always seems to know what he's doing. He's got an old head on a pair of young shoulders. And he not only can hit the long ball occasionally, but he seldom strikes out—usually gets a piece of the ball . . . that's an important asset."

Bob Aspromonte led all NL third basemen in fielding
percentage twice.

Although Aspromonte originally aspired to obtain a bachelor's degree
in physical education from Long Island University, he ultimately chose to
sign with the Dodgers on July 20, 1956, with his oldest brother, Charles,
a former minor-league player in the Philadelphia Athletics farm system,
acting as his agent and legal guardian during the signing process. Sent to
the team's Class A affiliate in Macon, Georgia, Aspromonte appeared in 13
games, before joining the parent club for one game in late September.

Aspromonte subsequently spent the next three years advancing through
the Dodgers farm system, while also serving in the Army Reserves. Summoned to Los Angeles for a brief stay in 1961, Aspromonte batted just .182
in 21 games, before arriving in the majors for good the following season.
However, even though Aspromonte remained with the Dodgers the entire
year, he appeared in only 47 games, compiling a batting average of .241 in
his 62 trips to the plate.

Finally receiving his big break when the National League expanded to 10 teams in 1962, Aspromonte headed to Houston when the Colt .45s selected him as the third overall pick of that year's expansion draft. Immediately establishing himself as the team's starting third baseman, Aspromonte performed well in his first full big-league season, hitting 11 homers, driving in 59 runs, scoring 59 others, batting .266, posting an OPS of .708, and finishing second among all NL third sackers with a .967 fielding percentage.

Plagued by a bad back in 1963 that at times made it difficult for him to field groundballs, Aspromonte batted just .214, hit only eight homers, and knocked in just 49 runs. But following an offseason of rest and exercises that helped strengthen the frayed lumbar disc in his lower back, Aspromonte rebounded in 1964 to hit 12 homers, drive in 69 runs, bat .280, compile an OPS of .721, and lead all players at his position with a .973 fielding percentage, prompting the Houston Chapter of the Baseball Writers Association of America to name him the team's Most Valuable Player.

With the Astros moving into the Astrodome in 1965, the right-handed-swinging Aspromonte, who stood 6'2" and weighed close to 195 pounds, failed to hit more than eight home runs in any of the next three seasons. Nevertheless, he remained one of the better hitters on an Astros team that finished near the bottom of the NL standings all three years, performing especially well in 1967, when, in addition to hitting six homers and driving in 58 runs, he posted career-high marks in batting average (.294) and OPS (.755).

With young third baseman Doug Rader being groomed as his replacement at the hot corner, Aspromonte saw some action in left field in 1968. And after he hit just one homer, knocked in only 46 runs, and batted just .225, Aspromonte found himself no longer a member of the team he had been with since its inception when the Astros completed a trade with the Braves on December 4, 1968, sending him to Atlanta for utility infielder Marty Martínez.

Looking back on the deal years later, Aspromonte said, "Everyone was kind of shocked when I got traded because I had such a great 1967. I had a great start in '68, but they put Rader in, and I realized what they were doing. I was about 30 years old, and change was taking place. But they did it too often (with the trades), and they made some amazing mistakes."

Aspromonte, who left Houston having hit 51 homers, driven in 385 runs, scored 336 times, collected 925 hits, 111 doubles, and 24 triples, batted .258, and compiled an OPS of .658 during his time there, spent two seasons in Atlanta serving the Braves as a part-time player, before ending his career in his hometown of New York as a member of the Mets in 1971.

Over parts of 13 big-league seasons, Aspromonte hit 60 homers, knocked in 457 runs, scored 386 others, amassed 1,103 hits, 135 doubles, and 26 triples, batted .252, and compiled an OPS of .644.

Following his playing days, Aspromonte returned to Houston, where he formed a partnership with his brothers to obtain a Coors distributorship that they named Aspromonte-Coors Distributing Company. With Bob managing the business for the next 25 years, Aspromonte-Coors proved to be extremely profitable, allowing the youngest of the Aspromonte brothers to retire a wealthy man when he sold his majority interest in 2000. Remaining active in the Houston community, Aspromonte lent his name to the YMCA, the Lions Eye Bank Foundation, and Houston Eye Associates. Known for his kindness and generosity to others, Aspromonte also became involved in several other worthy causes, making him even more popular in Houston than he had been during his playing days.

An inaugural member of the Astros Hall of Fame that first opened in 2019, Aspromonte, who is 85 years old as of this writing, received the following words of praise from former teammate Larry Dierker upon his induction: "In all my years of baseball, I have never known a player with more class than Bob Aspromonte."

COLT .45S/ASTROS CAREER HIGHLIGHTS

Best Season

Although Aspromonte compiled a slightly higher batting average (.294) and OPS (.755) in 1967, he had his finest all-around season in 1964, when he earned team MVP honors by establishing career-high marks with 12 homers, 69 RBIs, and 155 hits, while also batting .280, posting an OPS of .721, and leading all NL third basemen with a .973 fielding percentage.

Memorable Moments/Greatest Performances

Aspromonte experienced arguably the most memorable moment of his career on May 7, 1962, when, after being asked earlier in the day by a sick child in the hospital to hit a home run for him, he delivered a three-run blast in the bottom of the seventh inning that provided the margin of victory in a 9–6 win over the Dodgers.

Aspromonte starred during a 12-inning, 5–4 win over the Mets on September 20, 1962, going 5-for-6, with an RBI and two runs scored.

Aspromonte gave the Colt .45s a 2–1 win over the Cubs on May 12, 1963, when he led off the bottom of the 10th inning with a home run off right-hander Bob Buhl.

Aspromonte continued to be a thorn in the side of the Cubs on June 11, 1963, hitting a grand slam home run off Lindy McDaniel in the bottom of the 10th inning that gave the Colt .45s a 6–2 victory.

Aspromonte delivered the big blow of a 5–3 win over the Reds on June 11, 1964, when he homered with the bases loaded in the bottom of the fifth inning.

Aspromonte feasted on Cincinnati pitching again on August 15, 1964, going 4-for-5 with four RBIs during a 7–4 win.

Aspromonte gave the Astros a 7–4 victory over the Cubs on August 26, 1966, when he homered with the bases loaded in the bottom of the ninth inning.

Aspromonte contributed to a 17–1 rout of the Cardinals on June 7, 1967, by going 5-for-6 at the plate, with three RBIs and two runs scored.

Notable Achievements

- Led NL third basemen in fielding percentage twice.
- Finished second among NL third basemen in putouts twice and fielding percentage three times.
- 1964 Colt .45s MVP.
- Inducted into Astros Hall of Fame in 2019.

49

KYLE TUCKER

One of the American League's better all-around players, Kyle Tucker has excelled for the Astros both at the bat and in the field since laying claim to their starting right field job three seasons ago. A member of teams that have won five division titles, three pennants, and one World Series, Tucker has hit 30 homers twice, knocked in more than 100 runs twice, and compiled an OPS over .900 once, while also leading all players at his position in putouts twice and fielding percentage once. A good baserunner as well, Tucker has stolen more than 20 bases twice, with his strong all-around play earning him two All-Star selections and three All-MLB Second-Team nominations.

Born in Tampa, Florida, on January 17, 1997, Kyle Daniel Tucker starred in baseball at Henry B. Plant High School, drawing comparisons to the legendary Ted Williams with his long, lean frame and smooth left-handed swing. A four-year starter for the Panthers, Tucker began to make a name for himself as a sophomore, when he hit nine homers, knocked in 26 runs, and batted .556. Tucker followed that up by hitting another nine homers, driving in 35 runs, and batting .415 his junior year, before reaching the seats 10 times, knocking in 27 runs, and compiling a batting average of .484 as a senior, with his exceptional hitting earning him Florida Gatorade Player of the Year honors.

Describing the exalted status that Tucker reached during his time at Plant High, head baseball coach Dennis Braun told Jim Halley of *USA Today*, "When he was a sophomore, they called him Ted Williams. Boy, there's nowhere to go but down from that. They throw out so many names, I can't keep track of them. All I know is Kyle can hit. You can't teach putting the barrel on the ball, and that's the quality everybody is looking for."

Selected by the Astros in the first round of the June 2015 MLB Amateur Draft, the fifth overall pick, Tucker chose to put his college education on hold and begin his pro career with the Greeneville Astros of the Rookie-level Appalachian League. Tucker subsequently spent the next two-and-a-half seasons in the minors, playing for six different teams in Houston's farm system, before a .306 performance in 80 games with the Triple-A Pacific Coast League Fresno Grizzlies in 2018 earned him a promotion to the parent club in early July. Failing to make much of an impression over the season's final three months, Tucker batted just .141 with no homers and four RBIs in 72 total plate appearances, prompting the Astros to return him to the minors prior to the start of the ensuing campaign.

Rejoining the Astros in September 2019 after hitting 34 homers, driving in 97 runs, stealing 30 bases, batting .266, and compiling an OPS of .905 with the Triple-A Round Rock Express, Tucker gave a much better account of himself in his second tour of duty with the club, hitting four homers, knocking in 11 runs, scoring 15 times, and batting .269, in 22 games and 72 plate appearances.

Commenting on his young teammate at season's end, Alex Bregman said, "Don't let the fact that he still looks like a teenager and chews gum like

Kyle Tucker has hit 30 home runs for the Astros twice.
Courtesy of Ken Lund

an elementary schooler who's just discovered the stuff fool you. Kyle Tucker is an impact bat. At any level."

A regular member of the Astros' starting lineup the following year, Tucker spent most of the pandemic-shortened 2020 campaign playing left field, although he also saw some action in right. Acquitting himself extremely well, Tucker hit nine homers, knocked in 42 runs, scored 33 times, led the league with six triples, batted .268, and compiled an OPS of .837 in 58 games and just over 200 official at-bats for an Astros team that ended up losing to the Tampa Bay Rays in the ALCS.

Named the Astros starting right fielder prior to the start of the 2021 season, Tucker established himself as one of the AL's best young players by hitting 30 homers, driving in 92 runs, scoring 83 times, stealing 14 bases, batting .294, and ranking among the league leaders with 37 doubles and an OPS of .917, while also leading all players at his position with a .992 fielding percentage.

Extremely impressed with his teammate's performance at the plate, Carlos Correa stated during the latter stages of the campaign, "I think Kyle Tucker was the best hitter in our lineup this year. He is one of the best hitters in the game."

After getting off to a slow start in 2022, Tucker posted excellent numbers once again, earning his first All-Star nomination by hitting 30 homers, finishing third in the league with 107 RBIs, scoring 71 times, stealing 25 bases, batting .257, and compiling an OPS of .808. Also accorded Gold Glove honors for the first time in his career, Tucker led all AL right fielders with 287 putouts.

A dead-pull hitter, Tucker, whose slender 6'4", 200-pound frame belies the outstanding power he possesses at the plate, has exceptional bat speed and superior hand-eye coordination that enable him to bring the bat through the hitter's zone quickly. Also blessed with excellent plate discipline and outstanding pitch recognition, Tucker is a patient and selective hitter who rarely swings at bad pitches. Meanwhile, Tucker's good speed, quick first step, ability to track the flight of the ball off the bat, and strong throwing arm make him a well-above average fielder who is capable of manning any of the three outfield positions.

Tucker had another excellent year in 2023, earning All-Star honors for the second straight time and a fifth-place finish in the AL MVP voting by hitting 29 homers, leading the league with 112 RBIs, scoring 97 times, stealing 30 bases, batting .284, and compiling an OPS of .886. Tucker will enter the 2024 campaign with career totals of 102 homers, 368 RBIs, 309 runs scored, 535 hits, 122 doubles, 16 triples, and 83 stolen bases, a .272 batting average, a .345 on-base percentage, and a .507 slugging percentage—numbers he figures to add to significantly in the years ahead.

CAREER HIGHLIGHTS

Best Season

Tucker performed well for the Astros in both 2021 and 2022, totaling 60 homers and 199 RBIs over the course of those two campaigns. But he had his finest all-around season to date in 2023, when, in addition to hitting 29 home runs, batting .284, and posting an OPS of .886, he established career-high marks in RBIs (112), runs scored (97), hits (163), doubles (37), total bases (297), stolen bases (30), bases on balls (80), and on-base percentage (.369).

Memorable Moments/Greatest Performances

Tucker contributed to a 13–6 rout of Colorado on August 19, 2020, by going 4-for-5, with a homer, two triples, four RBIs, and three runs scored.

Tucker knocked in four runs and homered twice in one game for the first time in his career during a 13–6 pasting of the Angels on April 8, 2022.

Tucker helped lead the Astros to a lopsided 13–4 victory over the Red Sox on May 17, 2022, by driving in six runs with a pair of homers, one of which came with the bases loaded.

Tucker delivered the decisive blow of a 7–5 win over Oakland on August 12, 2022, when he homered off reliever Sam Moll in the bottom of the fifth inning with the bases loaded.

Although the Astros lost Game 1 of the 2022 World Series by a score of 6–5, Tucker collected three hits, knocked in four runs, and homered twice off Phillies starter Aaron Nola.

After singling and doubling earlier in the contest, Tucker hit a two-run homer off reliever Matt Brash in the top of the ninth inning that provided the winning margin in a 6–4 victory over the Seattle Mariners on May 5, 2023.

Tucker gave the Astros a 7–6 victory over the Chicago Cubs on May 17, 2023, by driving in the tying and winning runs with a one-out bases loaded single in the bottom of the ninth inning.

Tucker led the Astros to a 12-11 win over the Texas Rangers on July 3, 2023, by going 4-for-4 at the plate, with a homer, double, four RBIs, and three runs scored.

Tucker proved to be a one-man wrecking crew during a 6-4 victory over Oakland on July 21, 2023, driving in four runs with three homers, two of which came off starter JP Sears.

Tucker delivered the decisive blow of a 7-6 win over the Baltimore Orioles on August 8, 2023, when he homered with the bases loaded in the top of the ninth inning.

Notable Achievements

- Has hit at least 30 home runs twice.
- Has knocked in more than 100 runs twice.
- Has surpassed 30 doubles twice.
- Has stolen more than 20 bases twice.
- Has posted slugging percentage over .500 four times.
- Has posted OPS over .900 once.
- Has led AL in RBIs and triples once each.
- Has finished third in AL in RBIs, slugging percentage, and OPS once each.
- Has led AL right fielders in putouts twice and fielding percentage once.
- Ranks among Astros career leaders with .507 slugging percentage (5th) and .852 OPS (tied for 7th).
- Five-time division champion (2018, 2019, 2021, 2022, and 2023).
- Three-time AL champion (2019, 2021, and 2022).
- 2022 world champion.
- September 2021 AL Player of the Month.
- Finished fifth in 2023 AL MVP voting.
- 2022 Gold Glove winner.
- 2023 Silver Slugger winner.
- Two-time AL All-Star selection (2022 and 2023).
- 2021 *Sporting News* AL All-Star selection.
- Three-time All-MLB Second-Team selection (2021, 2022, and 2023).

50

FRAMBER VALDEZ

A member of Astros teams that have won five division titles, three pennants, and one World Series, Framber Valdez has emerged as one of the AL's top starters the past few seasons after struggling during the early stages of his career while working primarily out of the bullpen. A two-time AL All-Star who has posted double-digit win totals in each of the last three seasons, Valdez has also compiled an ERA under 3.00 twice and thrown more than 200 innings once, with his superb pitching in the 2022 playoffs and World Series helping the Astros capture their second world championship.

Born in Sabana Grande de Palenque, San Cristóbal Province, Dominican Republic, on November 19, 1993, Framber Valdez grew up some 58 miles northeast, in the small town of Guayacanes, where he began pitching while in high school. Signed by the Astros as an international free agent at the rather advanced age of 21 for a bonus of $10,000 following a tryout at the organization's Dominican academy, Valdez addressed his unusually late signing during a 2017 interview with the *Houston Chronicle*, saying through an interpreter, "I wasn't ready when I was younger. I think as I got older, I became more established, I understood what it took, and I had the opportunity with some managers and guys around me who pushed me and got me in the right mentality and got me to prepare for what was to come."

Recalling Valdez's signing, which took place in March 2015, Astros general manager Jeff Luhnow stated, "It was just a really tremendous job of scouting and beating the bushes. It goes to show you that, even in this day of information and everything else, that good scouts can find these players that other scouts haven't identified."

Valdez subsequently spent most of the next four seasons in the minor leagues, compiling an overall record of 21-19 for eight different teams at seven levels of Houston's farm system, before earning a brief callup to the parent club during the latter stages of the 2018 campaign. Faring well in his eight appearances with the Astros, Valdez won four of his five decisions and compiled an ERA of 2.19, while recording 34 strikeouts and walking 24 batters in 37 innings pitched.

Impressed with the 24-year-old southpaw's performance, Jeff Luhnow told reporters, "There's a lot we like about him. He's had success in our system. He flew through a lot of our system last year. . . . He's got a repertoire of pitches that allows him to be a starter from the left side. He's opened [manager] AJ's [Hinch's] eyes."

Returned to the minors prior to the start of the 2019 campaign, Valdez ended up splitting the season between the Astros and their Triple-A affiliate in Round Rock, Texas, compiling a record of 5-2 and an ERA of 3.25 with the Express, but going just 4-7, posting an ERA of 5.86, and issuing 44 bases on balls in just over 70 innings pitched while working as a middle-inning reliever and spot starter with the Astros.

With Valdez displaying a lack of command of his pitches and a tendency to implode at the first sign of trouble, Astros director of Latin-American operations, Caridad Cabrera, suggested that he work with the team's psychologist, Dr. Andy Nunez, the following offseason. Although Valdez

Framber Valdez finished second in the AL with 17 wins in 2022.

initially opposed the idea, believing at the time that psychologists dealt only with mental health issues, he later came to feel differently, saying, "I eventually learned that's not the case. They're there to help your mindset, to help you focus, to help you stay in the right frame of mind."

Taught by Nunez how to meditate and control his breathing in stressful situations, Valdez began the 2020 season with a new mindset. Although it took several months for the lessons he learned to translate to success on the playing field, Valdez became more adept at distancing himself from things over which he had no control, such as when softly hit balls turned into base hits. Better able to control his anger and focus on the task at hand, Valdez concluded the pandemic-shortened 2020 campaign with a record of 5-3, an ERA of 3.57, 76 strikeouts, and only 16 walks in 70⅔ innings pitched after being inserted into the starting rotation early in the year. Making further strides in 2021, Valdez went 11-6, with a 3.14 ERA and 125 strikeouts in 134⅔ innings of work, before earning All-Star honors and a fifth-place finish in the AL Cy Young voting the following year by ranking among the league leaders with 17 victories (against six losses), a 2.82 ERA, and 194 strikeouts, while topping the circuit with 201⅓ innings pitched and three complete games.

Asked to explain the transformation in his game at one point during the 2022 campaign, Valdez said through an interpreter: "Simply, the consistency, the discipline on and off the field. Knowing how to get along with your teammates, knowing how to act during the game. To know how to handle your discipline with your body and mind. How you work, how you think about the games. At home, how you think about maintaining yourself, and that's what I do. I think about things before doing them. I work before I get on the field. And I concentrate to the max to give the best I've got."

Meanwhile, Astros teammate Alex Bregman stated, "It's his focus and his self-confidence. He's confident in himself, he attacks, and he knows that he's got good stuff."

In addition to throwing a cut fastball that typically registers somewhere between 90 and 94 mph on the radar gun, the 5'11", 235-pound Valdez attacks the strike zone with a low-90s sinker, a changeup, and a curveball that routinely registers in the 76 to 80 mph range. A groundball pitcher who, unlike most current hurlers, prefers to pitch to contact, Valdez drew praise from Astros pitching coach, Josh Miller, who said, "Not many guys throw quality sinkers and curveballs as a part of an arsenal. If a guy's got a sinker, it's usually a slider to go with it. If the guy's got a four-seamer, it's usually a curveball. So, it's kind of a unique look. He's differentiated himself from the rest of baseball, in my opinion."

Although somewhat less effective in 2023, Valdez had another solid season, earning his second straight All-Star nomination by going 12-11 with an ERA of 3.45 and a WHIP of 1.126, while also striking out 200 batters in 198 innings of work and leading all AL hurlers with two shutouts. Valdez will enter the 2024 campaign with a career record of 53-34, an ERA of 3.40, a WHIP of 1.217, 6 complete games, 3 shutouts, and 697 strike-outs in 712.1 innings pitched.

CAREER HIGHLIGHTS

Best Season

Valdez had his finest season to date in 2022, when he earned All-MLB First-Team honors by leading all AL hurlers with 201.1 innings pitched and three complete games, while also ranking among the league leaders with 17 wins, a .739 winning percentage, a 2.82 ERA, and 194 strikeouts.

Memorable Moments/Greatest Performances

Valdez became the first relief pitcher in six years to throw five scoreless innings in a playoff game when he yielded just two hits and no runs over the final five frames of a 4–1 win over Minnesota in Game 1 of the 2020 AL Wild Card Series.

Valdez earned a 9–1 victory over Boston in Game 5 of the 2021 ALCS by limiting the Red Sox to just one run and three hits over eight strong innings.

Valdez helped the Astros begin the 2022 campaign on a positive note by surrendering just two hits and no runs in 6⅔ innings of work during a 3–1 win over the Angels on Opening Day.

Valdez earned the first complete-game victory of his career when he allowed just two hits and three walks during a 5–1 win over Oakland on May 30, 2022.

Although Valdez didn't figure in the decision, he recorded a career-high 13 strikeouts and yielded just four hits and two runs over the first six innings of a 4–2 win over the Angels on July 3, 2022, with 12 of his strikeouts coming in succession.

Valdez tossed his first career shutout on September 12, 2022, when he struck out eight batters and allowed six hits and one walk during a 7–0 blanking of the Detroit Tigers.

Valdez defeated the Yankees in Game 2 of the 2022 ALCS, registering nine strikeouts and yielding just four hits and two unearned runs over the first seven innings of a 3–2 Astros win.

Valdez performed brilliantly during the 2022 postseason, compiling an overall record of 4-0 and an ERA of 1.61. Particularly outstanding against Philadelphia in the World Series, Valdez won both his starts, including the Game 6 clincher. After striking out nine batters and allowing just four hits and one run over the first 6⅓ innings of a 5–2 victory in Game 2, Valdez recorded another nine strikeouts and surrendered just two hits and one run over the first six innings of a 4–1 win in Game 6. He finished the Series with a record of 2-0, an ERA of 1.46, and 18 strikeouts in 12⅓ innings of work.

Valdez earned a 3–1 win over the Los Angeles Angels on May 9, 2023, by recording 12 strikeouts and yielding just three hits and one run in eight strong innings of work.

Valdez shut out the Oakland Athletics on just four hits on May 21, 2023, striking out seven batters and issuing no walks during a 2–0 Astros win.

Valdez no-hit Cleveland on August 1, 2023, yielding just one walk and recording seven strikeouts during a 2–0 Astros win.

Notable Achievements

- Won 17 games in 2022.
- Has posted winning percentage over .700 twice.
- Has compiled ERA under 3.00 twice.
- Has struck out 200 batters once.
- Has thrown more than 200 innings once.
- Has led AL in complete games once, shutouts twice, and innings pitched once.
- Finished second in AL with 17 wins in 2022.
- Ranks among Astros career leaders with .609 winning percentage (tied for 6th).
- Five-time division champion (2018, 2019, 2021, 2022, and 2023).
- Three-time AL champion (2019, 2021, and 2022).
- 2022 world champion.
- Finished fifth in AL Cy Young voting in 2022.
- Two-time AL All-Star selection (2022 and 2023).
- 2022 All-MLB First-Team selection.

SUMMARY

aving identified the 50 greatest players in Houston Astros history, the time has come to select the best of the best. Based on the rankings contained in this book, the members of the Astros all-time team are listed below. Our squad includes the top player at each position, along with a pitching staff that features a five-man starting rotation, a setup man, and a closer. Our starting lineup also includes a designated hitter.

STARTING LINEUP		PITCHING STAFF	
PLAYER	POSITION	PLAYER	POSITION
César Cedeñ	CF	Roy Oswalt	SP
Craig Biggio	C	Joe Niekro	SP
José Altuve	2B	Mike Scott	SP
Jeff Bagwell	1B	J. R. Richard	SP
Lance Berkman	DH	Larry Dierker	SP
Jim Wynn	RF	Dave Smith	SU
José Cruz	LF	Billy Wagner	CL
Alex Bregman	3B		
Carlos Correa	SS		

GLOSSARY

ABBREVIATIONS AND STATISTICAL TERMS

1B. First baseman.

2B. Second baseman.

3B. Third baseman.

AVG. Batting average. The number of hits, divided by the number of at-bats.

C. Catcher.

CF. Center fielder.

CG. Complete games pitched.

CL. Closer.

ERA. Earned run average. The number of earned runs a pitcher gives up, per nine innings. This does not include runs that scored as a result of errors made in the field and is calculated by dividing the number of runs given up by the number of innings pitched and multiplying the result by 9.

DH. Designated hitter.

HITS. Base hits. Awarded when a runner safely reaches at least first base upon a batted ball, if no error is recorded.

HR. Home runs. Fair ball hit over the fence, or one hit to a spot that allows the batter to circle the bases before the ball is returned to home plate.

IP. Innings pitched.

LF. Left fielder.

OBP. On-base percentage. Hits plus walks plus hit-by-pitches, divided by plate appearances.

OPS. Offensive production statistic, the sum of a player's slugging percentage and on-base percentage.

RBI. Runs batted in. Awarded to the batter when a runner scores on a safely batted ball, a sacrifice, or a walk.

RF. Right fielder.

RUNS. Runs scored by a player.

SB. Stolen bases.

SHO. Shutouts.

SLG. Slugging percentage. The number of total bases earned by all singles, doubles, triples, and home runs, divided by the total number of at-bats.

SO. Strikeouts.

SP. Starting pitcher.

SS. Shortstop.

SU. Setup man.

WHIP. The sum of a pitcher's walks and hits divided by the number of innings pitched.

W-L. Win-loss record in a season for a pitcher.

WINNING PERCENTAGE. A pitcher's number of wins, divided by his number of total decisions (i.e., wins plus losses).

BIBLIOGRAPHY

BOOKS

James, Bill, and Rob Neyer. *The Neyer/James Guide to Pitchers: An Historical Compendium of Pitching, Pitchers, and Pitches*. New York: Simon & Schuster, 2004.

Keri, Jonah. *Up, Up, and Away: The Kid, the Hawk, Rock, Vladi, Pedro, le Grand Orange, Youppi!, the Crazy Business of Baseball, and the Ill-fated but Unforgettable Montreal Expos*. Toronto, Canada: Penguin Random House, 2014.

McTaggart, Brian. *100 Things Astros Fans Should Know & Do Before They Die*. Chicago: Triumph Books, 2016.

Posnanski, Joe. *The Baseball 100*. New York: Simon & Schuster, 2021.

Robertson, John. *Rusty Staub of the Expos*. Toronto, Canada: Prentice Hall, 1971.

Sandalow, Brian. *José Altuve: Baseball Superstar*. Minneapolis: Abdo Publishing, 2020.

Schlossberg, Dan. *Making Airwaves: 60+ Years at Milo's Microphone*. New York: Sports Publishing, 2006.

Shalin, Mike, and Neil Shalin. *Out by a Step: The 100 Best Players Not in the Baseball Hall of Fame*. Lanham, MD: Diamond Communications, Inc., 2002.

Sowell, Mike. *One Pitch Away: The Players' Stories of the 1986 LCS and World Series*. New York: Macmillan, 1995.

Thorn, John, and Pete Palmer, eds., with Michael Gershman. *Total Baseball*. New York: HarperCollins, 1993.

Wynn, Jimmy, with Bill McCurdy. *Toy Cannon: The Autobiography of Baseball's Jimmy Wynn*. Jefferson, NC: McFarland, 2010.

WEBSITES

The Ballplayers, BaseballLibrary.com
(www.baseballlibrary.com/baseballlibrary/ballplayers)

Bio Project, SABR.org
(www.sabr.org/bioproj/person)

Historical Stats, MLB.com
(www.mlb.com/stats.historical/individual stats player)

The Players, Baseball-Almanac.com
(www.baseball-almanac.com/players).

The Players, Baseball-Reference.com
(www.baseball-reference.com/players)

The Teams, Baseball-Reference.com
(www.baseball-reference.com/teams)